Development
and the
Landowner

Development and the Landowner

An analysis of the British experience

Robin Goodchild
Gerald Eve & Co., Chartered Surveyors, London
and
Richard Munton
Department of Geography, University College London

London
GEORGE ALLEN & UNWIN
Boston   Sydney

George Allen & Unwin (Publishers) Ltd,
40 Museum Street, London WC1A 1LU, UK

George Allen & Unwin (Publishers) Ltd,
Park Lane, Hemel Hempstead, Herts HP2 4TE, UK

Allen & Unwin Inc.,
Fifty Cross Street, Winchester, Mass. 01890, USA

George Allen & Unwin Australia Pty Ltd,
8 Napier Street, North Sydney, NSW 2060, Australia

First published in 1985

British Library Cataloguing in Publication Data

Goodchild, Robin
    Development and the landowner: an analysis
of the British experience.
1. Real estate development – Great Britain
I. Title   II. Munton, Richard
333.3′8   HD598
ISBN 0-04-333021-5

Library of Congress Cataloging in Publication Data

Goodchild, R. N. (Robin N.)
    Development and the landowner.
Bibliography: p.
Includes index.
1. Land use – Great Britain – Planning – Citizen participation.
2. Real estate development – Great Britain – Planning – Citizen
participation.   I. Munton, R. J. C.   II. Title.
HD596.G66   1985   333.73′15′0941   84-28278
ISBN 0-04-333021-5 (alk. paper)

Set in 10 on 11 point Bembo by Computape (Pickering) Ltd, N. Yorkshire
and printed in Great Britain by Butler & Tanner Ltd, Frome and London

Preface

Little attention has been paid to the role of landowners in the development and re-development of land in Britain. Lack of attention may be ascribed partly to the difficulties of acquiring information about owners and partly to the view that it is the developer and the planner that dominate the development process.

Changing attitudes within government which favour the private sector make this an especially opportune time to re-assess the part the landowner plays. The private sector currently has a more favourable policy environment within which to operate than during most of the post-war period. Planners in local authorities are less able to dictate, as opposed to supervise and monitor, the pattern of development than at any time over the past 40 years; home ownership is being strongly encouraged by central government and local authorities have to consult the construction industry in establishing the amount of land to be made available for private residential development; private and institutional investors are being persuaded to invest in the inner city; detailed negotiations between applicants and local development control officers over planning applications are commonplace; and the Local Government, Land and Planning Act 1980 has re-created a free market in development land with the repeal of the Community Land Scheme.

All these changes, directly or indirectly, strengthen the hand of the landowner in influencing the timing, scale and pattern of development, and in this book we review these changes and what they mean for the development process. In the first part of the book we review the context (policy, land market and process) in which development takes place and what this context implies for the behaviour of those landowners seeking to maximise their financial return from their investment in land. In the second, we present findings from detailed case studies conducted in different policy contexts which allow us to draw certain conclusions for policy and which are then discussed in the final chapter.

Our views have evolved significantly since the original surveys were conducted in the late 1970s when we first met. They are our personal views and do not necessarily reflect the views of our colleagues at Gerald Eve & Co. and elsewhere. Throughout the preparation of this book, Murray Stewart has provided considerable encouragement and is also largely responsible for the project starting in the first place. We are grateful, too, to the numerous people who have kindly commented on parts of the text or have helped with the collection of data, and particularly to Peter Humphreys, Basil King and Ann Markwick. More especially we owe a considerable debt to Barry Pearce and Chris Bryant for their detailed criticism and invaluable advice. On the technical side we must thank Claudette John, Susanjane Burley and Jane Gibson, for typing several versions of the manuscript, and Anne Mason and Richard Davidson of the Cartography Unit, Department of Geography, University College London, for preparing the illustrations.

The authors and publishers would like to thank Pavilion Books Limited for their kind permission to reproduce Figure 1.1, and the Copyright Controller,

Ordnance Survey, for permission to reproduce part of Figure 8.1 (Crown Copyright reserved).

Lastly, no book of this length is completed without sacrifices by those who have little choice in the matter, so to our respective wives, Lies and Judy, we are especially grateful.

May 1984   ROBIN GOODCHILD
                                                      RICHARD MUNTON

Contents

List of tables

Abbreviations

BICP	Birmingham Inner City Partnership
BS	British Shipbuilders
CBD	central business district
CGT	capital gains tax
CLA	Community Land Act
CLS	community land scheme
CPO	compulsory purchase order
CRDV	chargeable realised development value
CTT	capital transfer tax
DGT	development gains tax
DLG	derelict land grant
DLT	development land tax
DOE	Department of the Environment
FT	*Financial Times*
GLC	Greater London Council
GNLA	Guidance Notes for Local Authorities
HBF	House Builders' Federation
HLRC	Housing Land Requirements Committee
HMSO	Her Majesty's Stationery Office
JPL	*Journal of Planning and Environment Law*
JURUE	Joint Unit for Research on the Urban Environment
LAW	Land Authority for Wales
LBTH	London Borough of Tower Hamlets
LDDC	London Docklands Development Corporation
LPA	local planning authority
MAFF	Ministry of Agriculture, Fisheries and Food
MCC	Metropolitan County Council
MGB	Metropolitan Green Belt
MHLG	Ministry of Housing and Local Government
ODP	office development permit
OECD	Organisation for Economic Co-operation and Development
OPP	outline planning permission
PAG	Property Advisory Group
PLA	Port of London Authority
PP	planning permission
PSA	Property Services Agency
PTA	Port of Tyne Authority
RHA	regional health authority
RICS	Royal Institution of Chartered Surveyors
RTPI	Royal Town Planning Institute
SCLSERP	Standing Conference on London and South East Regional Planning
SEJPT	South East Joint Planning Team

SI	Statutory Instrument
SOS	Secretary of State
TCPA	Town and Country Planning Act
UDG	urban development grant

1 Land ownership and development

This book examines the role of the landowner in the development process, largely within the confines of England and Wales. This is not a perspective on the development process to have received much attention. Rather more attention has been given to the developer and planner, and recently research has been directed more towards the institutional and ideological context within which development takes place. The importance to the development process of these other participants and the wider economic and political circumstances within which the development and re-development of land occurs cannot be denied, and they are reviewed from the point of view of the landowner in the first half of the book; but it is timely to examine, more thoroughly than hitherto, the motives, aspirations and actions of the landowner. Little enough is known about them.

The current ideological outlook of central government favours a much fuller involvement of private capital and a more restricted role for local planning authorities in development than was anticipated by those who drew up the Town and Country Planning Act 1947 (Hall 1983). In specific terms, current ideology could be said to be embodied in the contents of the Local Government, Planning and Land Act 1980 (DOE 1980a), and the government circulars that arose from them (DOE 1980b, 1980c, 1981a), and in general terms from a climate of governmental opinion that favours reduced public expenditure, home ownership and 'market' solutions to strategic planning.

This outlook has most obviously favoured developers and sources of private and institutional capital but it has also directly and indirectly benefitted the private landowner. For example, continuing attempts by government to stimulate increased home ownership, such as through increased tax relief on mortgages, have contributed to the continuing rise since 1979 of residential development land prices; and, having lowered the rate of Development Land Tax from 80% to 60% in 1979 (see p. 32), the government has not seen fit to increase it in spite of rising land prices. At the same time, these higher prices have discouraged developers from purchasing speculatively the freehold to potential development land, effectively increasing the financial and practical involvement of the owner in the development process. And, more generally, the increasing acceptance as normal of bargaining between applicant and planning authority over planning applications has extended the role and influence of owners in the development of their land.

Nevertheless, in spite of the government's wish to encourage private capital into development and to restrict the scope of planning,[1] few in Britain would today question the need for a land-use planning system of some kind, and some would even argue for its extension to bring certain farming and forestry operations under planning control. What is being questioned, however, is how the planning system should be put into effect, whether it is achieving its aims and, indeed, what these aims should be. Broadly, government wants a flexible planning system primarily aimed at providing a ready supply of residential, industrial and commercial development land where developers and consumers want it, a system that continues to protect the interests of neighbouring property owners when changes of use are proposed and, finally, a system that accords a degree of priority to its own initiatives – such as Urban Development Grants (see Ch. 8) – irrespective of local views (McAuslan 1981). The attempts by local authorities to incorporate within their structure plans social and economic policies relating, for example, to housing, health care and educational policies, that do not accord with the central government's view of things, have often been struck out as being beyond the scope of the planning system and unduly impinging upon the remits of other areas of local and central government policy (Jowell & Noble 1981). But whatever view is held of the role of the planning system, one of its major functions remains the orderly development and use of land, whether on a greenfield site in the urban fringe or on vacant land in the inner city. Unless the public sector is going to carry out all development, the success of the planning system depends on how the private sector responds to planning policy initiatives; and it follows that the behaviour of those whose land is 'planned' is crucial to the success of planning policy initiatives.

One of the potential conflicts within the operation of the planning system arises as a consequence of the legal rights accorded to the landowner. Planners seek to plan in the public interest, as the planning legislation requires them to do, although in no sense can the public interest be conceived as unitary. Land policies, on the other hand, frequently reflect a compromise with property law, an area of law that has evolved through the courts in such a way as largely to protect the interests of the landowner (Boynton 1979, McAuslan 1981). Thus, the attempt to plan by combining a private market in development land in which owners are required to bring land forward with the largely reactive and regulatory powers of the planning system over changes in use, is regularly frustrated by the inherent contradictions contained within it (see Pearce 1981). There is no reason to presume, for example, that the planners' definition of what constitutes appropriate development in the public interest should match the objectives of the private owner or developer, a point that Denman has frequently sought to put across (Denman 1978). We are left with a situation in which the main participants in the development process – landowner, developer, planner, financial institution, and 'public' – all believe that the other participants have too much power whilst they have too little.

On paper and in the urban environment especially, the planner has substantial powers. Landowners and developers must obtain planning permission from the planner in order to change the use of their land, severely restricting, as they see it, their freedom of action. But planners are only able to propose, they cannot insist on their plans being implemented as the political will to employ their compulsory powers to any great extent is missing. This means that development cannot take place until the land is in the hands of a person or body willing and able to carry it out. It follows that how owners behave affects the supply of development land, especially in the short term, and to a degree they can affect its price as well (see Ch. 3). In spite of this, there is little information on who owns land, or how owners respond to the vagaries of the development land market, or what roles they seek to play in the development process.

These and other questions are examined in the course of this book and we draw upon many disparate sources of information in an attempt to relate the actions of landowners to movements in property prices, changes in local planning policies and the characteristics of their properties. Included are detailed empirical findings drawn from three contrasting policy situations, that of an expanding city (Leicester), that of severe restraint (the London green belt), and that of land re-development in the inner city. There are many other books which treat the development process from a technical (Cadman & Austin-Crowe 1983), political (Blowers 1980) or financial standpoint (Moor 1983). No attempt is made here to review in detail the history of land or planning policy, there are a number of excellent and comprehensive accounts elsewhere in the literature each with its own particular emphasis (see, for example, Hall *et al.* 1973, Cullingworth 1982, McKay & Cox 1979, Lichfield & Darin-Drabkin 1980), and we confine ourselves to a brief and general outline in Chapter 2.

Why study landowners?

We begin with the assertion that the roles which landowners adopt in the development process are important and somewhat unpredictable, an assertion that will be substantiated by the empirical material presented later in this book. A study of landowners should, therefore, contribute to an improved understanding of the development process, should help planners realise their plans and should provide policy makers with a better basis upon which to decide whether the development process operates in an efficient and equitable manner.

The first problem facing any enquiry in this field is the general lack of data on land ownership. We know very little about the pattern of land ownership at the level of the individual owner in Britain, despite the existence of the Register of Sasines in Scotland (see McEwen 1981). Figure 1.1 shows one group's idea of who owns Britain. It should not be taken too seriously, but, despite that, it is a remarkably subtle representation. The major builders, like Barratt Homes and Wimpey, do own a significant amount of land on the edge of London while the Forestry Commission is probably the largest landowner in the country (Harrison *et al.* 1977). Yet, for any given area in England and Wales we are often ignorant as to who the owners are, what ownership rights they have or over what areas their rights extend. We are often obliged to draw hazy and generalised deductions about their reasons for owning land, derived either from first principles taken from the economic, social and ideological roles we attribute to land ownership, or from what can be gleaned about their behaviour in the property markets and from the ways in which they manage and maintain their properties. Our deductions may not only be inaccurate in individual cases but may also be misleading in general. Who, for example, prior to the mid-1970s, had identified local authorities rather than private speculators as the owners of most of the vacant land in our inner cities?

It is not that nothing is known about land ownership in England and Wales but that the published information is scattered among numerous data sources which are seemingly designed to make comparison and analysis difficult (see Massey & Catalano 1978). Global estimates are available but only in some areas of property. Take the best documented case, that of agricultural land. It is generally agreed that just over 90% of farmland is privately owned (Northfield

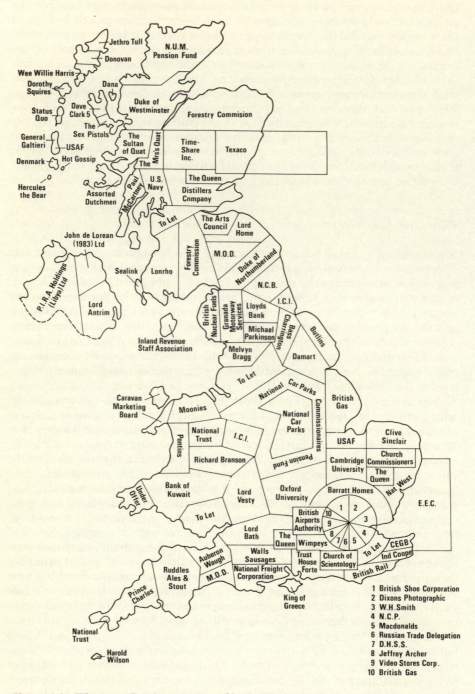

Figure 1.1 Who owns Britain: one view of landownership in Great Britain. (*Source: Not the General Election*. London: Pavilion Books, 1983.)

Committee Report 1979), although even establishing this figure created difficulties for the committee. Some public bodies were not sure exactly how much farmland they owned, or precisely why they owned it. It was ignorance of this kind that helped to persuade central government to establish a system of land registers, one for each local authority in England and Wales, in which publicly owned land surplus to current operational needs is recorded. There are other policy reasons for the compilation and publication of these registers, including the hope that they will increase the supply of development land, and these reasons are discussed further in Chapter 8. Suffice to say here that the 365 registers, which on 1 July 1984 contained details on over 11 000 separate sites covering more than 43 000 hectares, represent a limited but important departure in the publication of information on land ownership.

Generally, however, we live in a society in which the confidentiality of information on private property is widely upheld. It is frequently argued that information on private rights to property need not be made public while society is persuaded that most owners behave in a public-spirited manner. A full land register would indeed be expensive to draw up and to maintain. But some owners do not behave in such a manner and society has of late become increasingly concerned about the ownership of property. Attention has been focused by the effects on asset values of inflation and the indisputable fact that rises in land and property prices in real terms during the 1970s transferred wealth from non-owners to owners. Public consciousness was stirred by the property boom, and its subsequent collapse between 1973 and 1974, and the threat these events posed to sectors of the banking system (Plender 1982). More fundamentally, perhaps, an awareness of property rights has also been promoted by the continued spread of private home ownership and increased public participation in the planning process.

The case for disclosure is strongest in situations of land-use conflict and change, and where society already accepts a significant degree of intervention in market forces through the planning system and its associated land policies. The urban fringe and the inner city are two such situations but we are no better informed about ownership patterns there than elsewhere. Indeed, who are the owners of urban fringe land and why do they own it? How much is held by private individuals, public utilities, local authorities or public companies? Did they inherit the land, buy it with the express purpose of developing it or acquire it incidentally as an asset of an industrial company or public utility? And what are their plans for it?

Our inability to answer questions such as these leads inevitably into considerations of equity and effectiveness in the development process as they affect the landowner. It is not so much a matter of who holds the rights to land but how landowners choose to exercise them. Acceptance of the landowner's role depends as much on their behaviour as it does on the extent of their individual ownerships. Society's views on ownership are thus formed with regard to the following:

(a) The degree to which owners can derive and exploit power and influence from their ownership of a scarce resource and, by implication, the extent to which they can recognise, accept and act upon their obligations to others as a result of their ownership rights

(b) The level of financial advantage (revenue and/or capital) enjoyed by owners over non-owners
(c) The extent to which owners seek to frustrate public policy initiatives, not only over their willingness or reluctance to relinquish their property rights but by the manner in which they maintain their properties.

These matters are related. The first two concern the principle of equity, an issue that has been sharpened by the increasingly widespread inheritance of property, while the latter is more directly associated with the effectiveness of public policy. Planning controls, for example, undoubtedly create a very substantial rise in land values (betterment) for those landowners who obtain planning permission for the development of their land. From the point of view of equity, the main questions that follow from this are what proportion of that rise, if any, should the landowner retain? Should the owner be accredited with and rewarded for any skills or efforts he may bring to the process of land development when it is likely that local authorities will have identified the land on which development should occur and, in this particular sense, have 'created' the rise in value of these properties? Is it equitable *between* landowners that some will benefit from local authority zoning decisions while others will not? On the other side of the coin, what compensation should be paid to those whose properties are subject to compulsory purchase? The owner is not a willing seller and invariably maintains, sometimes quite reasonably, that present compensation arrangements (market value of the land plus disturbance costs) do not amount to the value he would place on his property were he a willing seller (for a full discussion see Corfield & Carnwath 1978). But can such a value ever be determined in a consistent and equitable manner?

While we retain a planning system in which plans have to be realised largely through the initiatives of landowners and developers in bringing land forward, it is clear that the effectiveness with which the system works – which, presumably, has to be measured by the degree to which the plan's specifications are met by development on the ground – depends to some considerable extent on how those owners with property rights respond to the opportunities presented to them by the plan. Most owners will be moved by financial incentives and the greater the incentive, the fuller the response. But this implies that equity between owners and non-owners and efficiency may be incompatible and that a trade-off between these goals is inevitable short of full public control of the development process (Goodchild 1978a). It is perhaps sufficient to note here that the development process and the property markets within which the process operates (see Chs 3 & 4) are more complicated and confused, and their participants more poorly informed, than a mere description of these and the institutional framework might imply. In particular, plans are often not explicit or precise, the planning process itself can be an extended affair (especially with decisions on appeal) and include a considerable amount of informal bargaining and discussion. Uncertainty also pervades the process. Central and local government policies change, interest rates rise and fall, property prices fluctuate and the personal circumstances of landowners alter. Given this situation, and the strength of political and ideological views which are expressed in debates surrounding changes in land policy, it is pertinent to ask why much more research has not been undertaken into the circumstances and activities of the landowner in Britain. For without such information how do the policy makers know what the effect of their legislative changes will be?

A lack of research

There is no one simple explanation for the lack of inquiry, rather several contributory causes. *First* and foremost is the lack of a basic source of data, a matter to which reference has already been made. There is no publicly available land register and associated cadastre giving a mapped definition of property boundaries for England and Wales which also records the beneficial interests of owners or occupiers in particular properties. Establishing who holds the beneficial interests in a particular property is especially significant. These are the financial interests held in property by private or public owners whether these be revenue producing (rent, income) or wealth creating (capital gain, etc). Instead, HM Land Registry holds an incomplete register of legal titles to land, registration of the title normally occurring only on the transfer of a property. But as the Northfield Committee observes, 'For the purpose of registration of title, only the legal owner is relevant; beneficial owners can appoint nominees and thereby draw a "curtain" between themselves and their property' (Northfield Committee Report 1979, p. 112), a widespread practice even in those countries which do have land registers.

Of greater importance to researchers and policy makers, information held in HM Land Registry may only be consulted by those with a 'need to know', such as solicitors conducting conveyancing, and then only with the permission of the owner. In Scotland, the Register of Sasines is open to inspection and contains information broadly similar to that held in HM Land Registry. The Register of Sasines is to be supplemented by a Land Register of Scotland, following the Land Registration (Scotland) Act 1979, but this will also only record legal title although it will remain open for public inspection. This means that in England and Wales, there is no *formal* way in which members of the public can determine ownership patterns as a matter of right. Some information can be obtained when owners seek planning permission or offer their land for sale at public auction, and there is always a large amount of 'local' information available but this inevitably lacks detail and may be of questionable accuracy. Even central government does not have a comprehensive and up-to-date statement on ownership, and where government departments publish data on property transactions they go to great lengths to ensure confidentiality. These market price series are based on data collated by district valuers and the Inland Revenue from individual property transactions, either when properties are sold, transferred to another owner or assessed for probate (see *Inland Revenue statistics*). These data are then used to prepare property market price series such as that for agricultural land published by the Ministry of Agriculture (for a description see Lund & Slater 1979), and those for housing and residential development land as reported in *Housing and construction statistics*. But the degree of disaggregation of the national statistics by type of owner, by nature of property or by spatial unit, is severely restricted.

For those seeking detailed or locationally specific information, the only alternative is to collect data directly from owners, or from those concerned with market transactions, such as land agents. This approach is time-consuming, tedious and expensive, and it represents a major disincentive to inquiry. It is dependent for its accuracy and representativeness on the willingness of those approached to part with information. Many landowners, whether from the aristocracy, the financial institutions (pension funds, insurance companies, etc), charities or public agencies, as well as owner-occupiers, are defensive, or at the very least discreet about the extent of their land holdings. Landlordism in particular has, in the words of Newby, become a 'by-word for self-effacement' associated with a 'cult of inconspicuous consumption' (Newby 1979). Dealers in land, to whom a detailed knowledge of the market represents the basis of their entreprenurial success, also prefer not to disclose 'confidential' information.

Second, until the 1970s, most attempts to explain the pattern of urban growth were based upon neo-classical, micro-economic analysis (see, for example, Muth 1961, Alonso 1964, Mills 1969, Hushak 1975). Partial equilibrium models were developed from assumptions about perfect markets and economically rational behaviour on the part of market participants. Generalised land rent models were evolved in which consumer spending on space (size of site) was frequently traded off against locationally specific bid rents or land prices reflecting accessibility to place of work, shopping and social facilities. By this approach some writers sought to throw light on the efficiency or equity with which the land market operated within given political economies, but the hallmark of almost all these studies, other than their value as a heuristic device, is their concern with demand considerations. Rents bid or land prices paid are regarded as solely attributable to the actual or potential use of the land. Supply considerations, including those resulting from the behaviour of existing owners, are largely ignored. Land is seen as a free gift which has no supply price. Variations in landowner behaviour in the face of fluctuating land prices and uncertain market conditions are treated, if at all, as 'short-term rigidities' in the supply of land. The absence of ownership data is of no great concern.

This position is now being revised in the face of structuralist interpretations of how property markets function and more particularly in response to the growing importance of research into public policy (planning, taxation, compensation and betterment, public land acquisition) in determining land values and the supply of development land. Indeed, there is a large and burgeoning international literature in this field. Yet much of the debate has remained at an institutional level, whether concerned with the relations between property markets and the economy as a whole (see, for example, Ambrose & Colenutt 1975, Neuburger & Nicol 1976, Boddy 1980, Dear & Scott 1981), or, more frequently, land policy comparisons (Darin-Drabkin 1977), the political aspects of changing land policy in Britain (McKay & Cox 1979) or the legal basis of development (McAuslan 1975), discussions in which the landowner is scarcely mentioned. This absence of discussion is surprising in the British context as major changes to capital gains and betterment taxation, affecting the financial prospects of urban fringe landowners in particular, have been introduced since 1965 (see Chs 2 & 5).

Third, in Britain those behavioural studies in which the contributions of the different actors to the development process have been examined are relatively few in number and comparatively recent in origin. They have emphasised the activities of the developer, the planner and occasionally the estate agent and other vested public interests (see, for example, Craven & Pahl 1967, Craven 1969, Hall *et al.* 1973, Robson 1975, Barrett & Whitting 1980, Underwood 1981, Simmie 1981, Ball 1983, Herington 1984, McNamara 1984) in the belief that it is these actors or groups which play the key roles. The developer is credited with most of the initiative in getting development under way and seeing it through to completion; and the local authority planner with determining local housing needs, identifying development land and detailing the pattern and timing of development through the use of development control powers. The effect of this emphasis has been to relegate the landowner to an apparently insignificant role although there is little published empirical evidence to substantiate this perspective or to suggest that it might not be true. In North America, on the other hand, the landowner has received rather more attention (for example, Milgram 1967, Kaiser *et al.* 1968, Brown *et al.* 1981). The planner is regarded as a less influential figure and numerous intermediate owners of land between the farmer and the developer or builder are quite common (Lindeman 1976, Bryant 1982).

We would not deny the value of previous behavioural studies into urban growth processes in Britain, nor indeed challenge the implicit assumption that the landowner is of lesser importance to the development process than the planner or developer in most situations (see Ch. 4). But we do contend that too little attention has been accorded the landowner. The actions of the owner cannot be taken for granted and several studies of the residential development process have been at pains to point out the interdependence of all the actors involved (Barrett *et al.* 1978, DOE/HBF, 1979, Nicholls *et al.* 1980). Except under conditions of compulsory purchase, within the present legislative context *all* the actors have to be in favour of development for it to be able to take place.

A changed emphasis?

Our research shows that the motives and circumstances of landowners are extremely varied and as a consequence owners do not respond uniformly to the development opportunities open to them. Few owners of greenfield sites, we would argue, ultimately refuse to sell their land once it has been identified for development by the local planning authority. But how much of their land to sell, when and at what price, represent momentous decisions for the owner, often to be taken in an uncertain fiscal environment. Development land prices have been very volatile in recent years and the gain accruing to owners has varied dramatically with the passing of new taxation legislation by successive governments. Even so, for the most part, landowners have realised substantial capital gains from selling land for development, drawing attention to the roles of money and property rights in the development process. Landowners tend, therefore, to be more interested in planning decisions and plan implementation than plan making. This concern with plan implementation can also be attributed to the regularity with which planning aims have been overturned by the ups and downs of the economy and to disillusionment over the langour with which structure plans have been produced and approved (Pearce 1980). It is also increasingly evident that policies within plans are constantly being amended in the light of experience and attempts to separate out plan formulation from plan making is to create a false dichotomy (Barrett & Fudge 1981). All these changes have tended to make local planning a more overtly political activity in the sense that the differing interests of the parties concerned (planner, developer, landowner, and the public) have been thrown into sharper relief. One aspect of this is the greater amount of negotiation between applicant and local planning authority which now takes place (see Jowell 1977, Loughlin 1978) and the growth in number and significance of management agreements, including Section 52 agreements, under the Town and Country Planning Act 1971.

Owners and ownership defined

The ownership of property is most usefully seen as consisting of a bundle of rights. For any particular piece of land these rights may be divided between any number of holders, whether they be real or corporate bodies. The most important of these rights confers upon the holder the power to occupy and to use the land, to improve it, to lease or sell certain rights to others, to sell it or to pass it on to one's heirs; and in the last three situations mentioned, to determine which rights are to be transferred, at what price and to whom. In these terms, land as a good may be regarded as having a dual nature. It consists of physical attributes, such as topography, mineral deposits and buildings, and the legal rights (and to a lesser extent obligations) attached to these. 'As a consequence it is more correct to refer to the set of rights in a land parcel as being the object of ownership rather than merely the land itself, as a physical entity' (Pearce 1980, p. 118). It is from the ability to exploit the resource, as conferred or constrained by the rights of ownership, that power, financial benefit and pleasure are derived (see Newby et al. 1978).

The degree to which private individuals and corporations should be able to use and dispose of their property as they wish is an ideological matter that largely determines any evaluation of the relations between private property and community good. As this book is concerned with the regulation of rights in practice and not with any natural rights to land in principle, it follows that property rights are to be treated as conditional and not as absolute. In other words, rights and the benefits derived from these are defined by the political and social structures of the society within which they exist and so are subject to continuous dispute and re-definition (Clark 1982).

Our interest lies with all those who hold rights in land, whether private individuals, statutory undertakers, corporations or charities, where either they or *another* actor in the development process believe their property to be capable of development either now or in the forseeable future. In the urban fringe, this definition includes all those owners whose land, were it put up for sale (but not all at the same time) would realise or would hope to realise a price above its existing use value because of its development potential; i.e. the price would include an element of 'hope' value, however small that element (see Ch. 3). The area of urban fringe land included under this definition is, at any one time, much larger than that for which planning permission has already been obtained. It is also more extensive than the area identified as potential development land on current plans and substantially larger than that which will be developed in any planning period. Some of the land regarded as ripe for development will not be developed, something that was appreciated by the Uthwatt Committee in its discussion of 'floating values' (Uthwatt Committee Report 1942, Leung 1979), and the definition also refers to land belonging to those owners who do not wish to bring it forward although it is earmarked for development. Some owners may gamble on the value of their land increasing substantially in the future because of a further change in zoning to a more valuable use, or an up-turn in the market, or a reduction in the rate of a betterment tax; and a few will have no intention of selling despite the pecuniary gain.

Within the urban area we are concerned with the role of the landowner in the process of re-development. A wide range of owners and development possibilities exist within the built-up area. These include private owners of land in areas of low housing density who seek the subdivision of their properties as a means of re-developing their land at a higher residential density; public utilities owning land, often in large plots, that is surplus to their requirements; private companies holding vacant land adjacent to their existing buildings upon which they hope to expand their premises; and local authorities who have acquired land, perhaps compulsorily, for the purposes of comprehensive re-development and no longer have the resources or the need to complete the schemes. Demand for certain sections of this land is extremely high, as on the edges of the CBD, but elsewhere may be low or even non-existent because of the high cost of rehabilitating derelict or contaminated land (see Ch. 8) or because of strict controls on the density of residential development.

As to the owners themselves, this book is principally but not exclusively concerned with the owner of land that is capable of development yet who does not carry out the development himself. A landowner of this type has been called the 'pre-development landowner' which emphasises the distinction between owners of land and developers of land. This is a cumbersome term, so throughout the book, the term 'landowner' is used without qualification to denote an owner of this type.

The distinction between a landowner and a developer is straightforward where the development process is at an advanced stage and construction work has begun. Then, the developer, whom we regard as responsible for both assembling land and initiating construction upon it, can be readily distinguished from persons or organisations that held a proprietary interest in the land before the developer acquired his interest. Where the development process is at an early stage, distinguishing between a landowner and a developer can be more difficult. Land may be purchased by a developer with the intention of carrying out development but may in fact be sold without any development taking place. Developers may swap land-holdings to mutual advantage, may sell land to other developers to ease their cash flow problems, may decide that planning permission will never be granted and so sell the land back to a farmer, or may sell the land on to another developer or builder so realising a capital gain from the increase in the land's value. These 'landowners' also lie within our definition. Conversely, there are owners who hold land that becomes capable of development during the duration of their ownership. They may then decide to carry out the development themselves, even though the original reasons for acquisition were quite different. They may have acquired or inherited the property with other objectives in mind such as farming, the keeping of horses or as a home. Such owners *are* of concern to us, and the difference between them and the 'developers' referred to above primarily lies in their motives for acquiring the land. Moreover, dealers in land who neither intend to maintain the existing use of the land, unless for taxation reasons it pays them to do so, nor plan to develop the site, but to sell it on to someone else who is prepared to develop it, are also included in our category of landowner.

A descriptive framework

It is with these considerations in mind that we seek an improved account of the development process through an examination of the experiences of individual landowners. Given our general ignorance of how urban fringe property markets function, we believe there is a basic need for such an empirical, process-oriented approach. In this respect our methodological stance is similar to that of Drewett (1973), Craven (1969) and Nicholls et al. (1980) in their various studies of the urban development and re-development in Britain, and to that of Chapin and his colleagues at the University of North Carolina (Chapin & Weiss 1962, Weiss et al. 1966, Kaiser & Weiss 1970). In spite of these earlier studies we still have much to learn.

Our framework draws heavily on the work conducted at the University of North Carolina (see Fig. 1.2). The variables that influence landowner behaviour may be categorised as:

(a)   Contextual factors
(b)   Site characteristics
(c)   Landowner characteristics.

Contextual factors are those over which the individual landowner has no (or very little) influence, for example the general level of land prices (assuming that the owner is not a monopoly supplier) and government policy in relation to development land. These factors may be divided into the state of the land market; taxation policy for revenue, capital gains and development gains; compulsory purchase and compensation policy; and local and national planning policies for the area under consideration. Site characteristics consist of physical considerations such as the topography of the site, its location relative to existing development, its planning status or allocation on the appropriate development plan and its position within the surrounding land-use pattern. Landowner characteristics consist of such matters as the owner's age, financial position, legal personality (i.e. whether held by an individual, company, trust, etc.) and the owner's knowledge and attitude to risk.

In the context of the development process, these constraints on behaviour lead us to a particular concern with three main sets of *linked* decisions that confront all owners of development land (see Fig. 1.2). These may be termed *financial, operational* and *managerial*. All decisions can, in one sense or another, be reduced to a financial dimension, but here we take *financial* decisions to include only those pertaining to what land (its specific location and area) to sell, when to sell it and at what price. *Operational* decisions concern the role the landowner wishes to play in the development process. What dealings do landowners have with the developers and planners? How many owners seek to promote their case by submitting a planning application in association with developers? How is

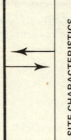

LANDOWNER CHARACTERISTICS

1. **Legal personality** (individual owner, company, public body, etc.)
2. **Occupancy Status** (owner-occupier, landlord, etc.)
3. Sources of income/wealth
4. Family/personal characteristics (age, successor, etc.)
5. **Means of acquisition** (inheritance, purchase, etc.) and **motive of ownership**
6. **Knowledge and Attitude to Risk**

SITE CHARACTERISTICS

1. Size
2. **Current use** and level of fixed investment
3. **Location** in relation to existing development, roads and services
4. **Physical characteristics** (drainage, topography, etc.)
5. **Planning status** (P.P./O.P.P. given, zoned for development, green belt, etc.)

CONTEXTUAL FACTORS*

1. **Land prices** – current state of the land market; activity in the economy and state of the development industry.
2. **Taxation policy** – for revenue, capital gains and development gains.
3. **Land policy** – compensation and betterment (see also 2), compulsory purchase powers, nationalisation of development rights, etc.
4. **Planning policy** – growth or restraint area; decisions on appeal (i.e. reflection of central government attitudes to local policy stands).

* Response to all these factors is significantly affected by **expectations** as to **political** change.

DECISION MODEL

Relating to:

(i) if, and when, the land will be sold (**financial decisions**)

(ii) participation of the owner in the development process (**operational decisions**)

(iii) land management policy during the 'ripening' period (**management decisions**)

Figure 1.2 Landowner behaviour: constraints and the development process.

their approach affected by their previous experience of development? *Managerial* decisions relate to the management policies that owners adopt for their properties whilst they are awaiting, or anticipating, development to occur. What expenditure should be incurred, for example, in the maintenance and effective exploitation of the land while it remains in its existing use? Not all these questions can be answered in the confines of a single book but we will return to them in Chapter 5 and in the context of the case studies

Contents of the book

The next three chapters provide the background within which the actions of the landowner are to be examined. Chapter 2 contains a brief discussion of current and recent changes in land and planning policy in which taxation (especially various development and capital gains taxes) form an important part. Also assessed are the use of compulsory purchase powers and associated compensation legislation. The other part of the chapter sets out current plan-making and development control procedures and the growing importance of bargaining between local planning authorities and applicants in reaching mutually acceptable development proposals. The land market, treated as a forum for the exchange of rights in land, is examined in Chapter 3. The chapter consists of four main sections which describe changes in land prices in Britain, land values in and around cities, the ways in which land values might be expected to change over time and the ability of landowners, either individually or collectively, to influence the price of development land. The development process itself is described in Chapter 4. The description emphasises the different stages in the process and the different roles played by the main actors – the developer, the planner, the financial institution and the landowner. The chapter concludes by establishing key events in the process, in particular the identification of development land and the initiation of development upon it.

Chapter 5 takes the information from the first part of the book and uses it to construct an investment strategy for the owner of either a greenfield or a re-development site incorporating key aspects of the decision areas noted above. The following three chapters provide empirical evidence against which to examine aspects of the investment strategy. The three studies are taken from contrasting situations in terms of the split between public and private ownership, the level of demand for development or re-development, and the attitudes of local planners and central government to development. The three case studies consist of one from an expanding city (Leicester's urban fringe – Ch. 6), one from an area of severe planning restraint (the Metropolitan Green Belt – Ch. 7), and one linked to the problems of re-development within inner cities in Britain. Finally, in Chapter 9 we review the empirical findings and discuss their policy implications.

Note

1   For example, in 1979 the government abolished the Regional Economic Planning Councils and it is perhaps no co-incidence that two recent inquiries into the future roles of regional planning (Regional Studies Association 1983) and land-use planning (by the Nuffield Foundation under the chairmanship of Lord Flowers) have both been initiated and conducted outside government.

2 The policy context

The four contextual factors identified in Chapter 1 fall into two categories. Taxation policy, compulsory purchase policy and planning policy are all imposed for a deliberate purpose by government, while the operation of the land market and the price signals it produces are merely influenced, albeit strongly, by these same government policies. The land market is treated separately in Chapter 3. Here we concentrate our attention on those measures that influence the location and timing of specific developments and their importance for the landowner.

The object of government policy in this field is twofold. The first objective is the orderly development and re-development of land, seeking to balance private and social costs, but in such a way that society can also function efficiently. The second concern is with equity, or the attempt to ensure that the benefits and costs resulting from the development of land are not distributed unfairly among the population. The policy is implemented in the three parts identified above, i.e. planning policy, taxation policy and compulsory purchase policy. Each element is described separately but at the end of the chapter we draw them together for this is the nature of the policy context as it confronts the landowner.

Unquestionably, the policy measures to be described are complex. Some policies have a spatial dimension and are not constant in their effect across the country. Policies also change; the system for taxing sales of development land, for example, has changed eight times since 1945 and each change has resulted in a different approach to calculating the landowner's tax liability. Because of the complexity of these matters, a landowner cannot rely on the popular media to keep him properly informed for although the newspapers do report changes in planning policies, they rarely cover the matter in sufficient depth. Nevertheless, the impression that the media gives of policy changes is extremely important. Usually, the likely effects of new legislation are dramatised and it was easy, for example, to get a totally false impression of the impact the Community Land Act would have on landowners from press reports at the time. Their general tone was to suggest that all owners of development land would have their holdings compulsorily acquired at a low price. This did not happen (see p. 36) but at the time the press reports were widely believed and the possible effects of the media on the landowner's behaviour need to be borne in mind when considering the following discussion. In spite of their complexity we believe it necessary to describe in some detail the contextual factors, especially taxation, if their significance to the landowner is to be fully appreciated.

Planning policy

THE PLANNING SYSTEM

Introduction   The framework of the plan-making system has changed considerably during the post-war period. Most notably, the unitary system introduced in 1947 was abandoned in 1968 and replaced by a dual system based on county (structure) and district (local) development plans, the former providing a general framework for the latter. The content of development plans has also changed. Today, there is a greater emphasis on the social and economic aspects of local planning by comparison with 30 years ago. Nevertheless, the particular purpose of the plan-making system remains much the same at local level. It aims to provide, in local plans, a statutory land-use base against which the merits of individual planning applications may be judged.

Experience shows, however, that the orderly fulfilment of plans' land-use aims are rarely achieved, and planners are well aware of this. There are three main weaknesses with the system. First, plans take time to prepare and they often become out-dated during the period of their statutory existence, and on occasion even while they are being prepared. Second, the planners' powers to implement their plans are weak and implementation is usually much more a matter of what is possible than what might be considered desirable. Moreover, plan implementation is a *separate*, if related, process to plan making and is often conducted by different members of the same planning department (Barrett & Fudge 1981). Third, many of the social and environmental objectives outlined in today's plans are difficult to translate consistently into judgements on the merits of individual planning applications because the policies are often qualitative in nature and contain an implicit political content (Harrison 1972, Davies 1980). It follows that there may be no simple or agreed calculus by which to reach a set of internally consistent and reasoned decisions, and this often leads to the application of routine rules and procedures. These rules may be adequate for minor applications but quite inadequate for handling substantial applications which may contain some aspects of merit, but at the same time challenge the rationale of the plan or the basic reasoning of the planning committee. Increased public consultation in the planning process has only encouraged the questioning.

These three issues go a long way to explain the discretionary nature of the planning system, both in law (McAuslan 1980, 1981) and in practice (Underwood 1981). Discretion increasingly affects the relations between planning officer, planning committee and applicant. Negotiation – formal (as at inquiry) and informal – may take place at all stages in the progress of a planning application and those who are in a position to negotiate from strength will be favoured. The owner with experience of the planning system and its procedures, and the means to afford professional advice, is at an advantage, especially where the application is viewed by the planning committee as marginal to the stated objectives of the plan. In other situations, the planning authority may be able to acquire a substantial planning gain from the applicant or to impose strict planning conditions on the granting of permission.

The plan-making system   There are many other texts which describe fully the town and country planning system that has developed in Britain since the first Public Health Act received the Royal Assent in 1848 (see p. 3). Briefly, it may be argued that the central features of the legislative framework, as they apply to land-use matters, have remained largely unchanged since the passing of the 1947 Town and Country Planning Act. These are as follows:

(a)   Development plans, consisting today of structure and local plans, are prepared for the whole country by local planning authorities.

(b) All development other than for minor works requires planning permission from the local authority.

(c) If consent is refused by the local planning authority, an appeal can be lodged with the Minister.

(d) Only in exceptional circumstances is a local planning authority required to pay compensation if planning permission is refused.

(e) The decision whether to grant planning permission is based primarily on the criteria set out in the relevant development plan(s); and although we shall argue that the granting of planning permission is dependent on many matters, one thing the local planning authority *must* have regard to is the provisions of the development plan (Town and Country Planning Act 1971, s. 29).

Structure plans are not meant to be detailed land-use plans. They are statements of policy or intent to be translated onto a precise land-use base by districts or boroughs in the preparation of their local plans. Progress with the preparation of these detailed plans is extremely variable and clearly they are going to be less comprehensive in their cover than was originally intended (Bruton 1983). This creates difficulties for owners and developers in the preparation of their planning applications and for the planners in seeking to come to a decision on them. This problem is exacerbated where the existing statutory development plan is dated and the structure plan is vague. Statutorily, local plans only have to be prepared where there is a clear need for them – something that is not defined – and where staff resources are available (DOE 1981b, 1984c). Recent reductions in public expenditure have pruned the available resources and there is, for example, no up to date development plan scheme for London and no formal mechanism for co-ordinating the plans of individual boroughs. More generally, Field has noted that

Not only is the preparation of a local plan discretionary, but so too is its scale, with some authorities seeking to prepare plans for the whole of their area, while, elsewhere, other authorities are seeking progressively to cover parts of their area with smaller scale district plans (Field 1983, p. 24).

If the development plan is to give clear guidance for development control decisions, the policies within it must be intelligible, sensible and practical. In too many cases they are vague or impossible to realise, while in others they are simply statements of the obvious (Barras 1979). Policies restricting development to those meeting local needs abound in structure plans, but local needs policies are hard to define and policies to promote them are even more difficult to effect (see Healey *et al.* 1980, Gault 1981). The West Sussex structure plan, for example, permits the allocation of additional residential building land to meet locally generated demand but gives no indication of how the local planning authority can ensure that the houses built on such land are occupied by local people only (West Sussex County Council 1980).

Although considerably more attention is now paid to monitoring development plans than before 1968, it is still very difficult for a county to have a structure plan which is consistently relevant and up to date. Some authorities, notably East Sussex, have attempted to meet this problem by not having a detailed structure plan but instead producing a more simple set of policies which are revised annually. This is the exception, however, and, 16 years after the new development system was introduced, there is still one county without an approved structure plan while others show no inclination for reviewing the existing plan, even though it was prepared in the early or mid-1970s. The approved development plan for the centre of Leicester was, until recently, a plan approved in 1956 (Green 1982), and it is not surprising that the 1956 plan was irrelevant for development control purposes long before the Central Leicester District Plan was approved in March 1982.

In conclusion, development plans do not always provide a clear guide for determining planning applications, even in terms of the particular land-use zones that are designated on the plan. There are three main and interrelated reasons for this. First, the plan is often out of date. Second, the plan does not contain a clear policy towards the type of development proposed. Third, the plan has not anticipated the type of development proposed, such as out-of-town shopping centres or amusement arcades, and therefore has no policy for dealing with it.

To complicate matters further, the range of interests that the local planning authorities are required to consult before deciding planning matters has changed. The 1947 Act envisaged local councils preparing development plans on technical grounds without prior consultation. The public participation requirements introduced in the 1968 Town and Country Planning Act and effectively 'enforced' by the Ombudsman for Local Government ensure that no statutory plan, however minor, is published without comment being first invited from the local population, amenity societies and other interested parties like the House Builders' Federation. As a result political influences are important in shaping new plans even if the pressures they exert are usually less intense than those generated by 'concrete' development proposals.

The relationship between central and local government is more complex now than in 1947. The re-organisation of local government into two-tier authorities has created problems because the counties are responsible for preparing the structure plan and the districts for preparing local plans that conform with it. However, when it comes to determining planning applications, the districts are the planning authority for most types of development and are required to consult the county only when the application materially affects the structure plan. Thus, although the counties prepare the key plan that is approved by central government, the districts have considerable power through their development control decisions and it is clear from recent policy statements (see for example DOE 1981a) that central government intends to down-grade the responsibilities of the counties whilst increasing its own scope to intervene in local matters (See McAuslan 1981). The division of responsibility between county and district has already produced a number of instances of local conflict over planning policy, for example, between Tyne and Wear Metropolitan County Council and the City of Newcastle over shopping provision (see JPL 1983, p. 1, and, more generally, Leach & Moore 1979, Herington 1984, pp. 117–32).

Even so, central government's function is still ostensibly the same. Although not concerned with local plans, structure plans have to be formally submitted to the SOS (DOE) for his approval. To help reach a decision on the plan, including possible modifications to it, the SOS appoints an inspector or panel to conduct a public inquiry. The SOS for the Environment, or more often now, his inspectors, also continues to determine appeals against the refusal of planning permission but not appeals against the decision of the local planning authority to grant permission. The only course for an objector to a scheme which the LPA is likely to approve, and this is true for another planning authority as well as an individual, is to persuade the SOS to 'call in' the application for him to decide it himself (Town and Country Planning Act 1971, s. 35) or to bring a costly action for judicial review through the courts (for example, *Steeple v Derbyshire County Council* (1981)).

The development control system   Statistics of planning applications and appeals make two points clear (see Table 2.1). A very high proportion of planning applications are approved, over 83% on average between 1962 and 1982/3, and the rate of approval increases as the number of applications declines. There are of course many applications for small works and extensions to houses and industrial premises which are not controversial but the rate of approval is still surprisingly high. Figure 2.1 shows the proportion of applications granted for different types of development and it is noticeable that only in the second quarter of 1981 did the success rate for major developments fall below 70%. This was, of course, the first quarter after the introduction of planning fees on 1 April 1981 and a large number of applications were submitted immediately prior to this date to avoid payment. As a result, local authorities determined approximately 20% more applications in that quarter and the success rate fell dramatically. The success rate has, however, increased significantly since the fees were introduced, presumably because developers now submit fewer probing applications designed to ascertain the planning position without seriously intending to develop the land at that time.

The main point that emerges from the planning appeals statistics is the change in the success rate of appellants. Since 1971 the chances of success on appeal have increased from one in five to one in three and it has generally paid the appellant to have the appeal decided by the SOS rather than an inspector because this increases the chances of success still further (see Table 2.2). The number of appeals fluctuated during this ten-year period, with particularly large numbers between 1973–5 and 1980–2. The total number of appeals rose rapidly in 1973–5 as a result of landowners and developers trying to secure planning permission to take advantage of the high level of land values prevailing at the time (see Ch. 3). The extra cost of an appeal was worth the risk of failure. The more recent increase cannot be attributed to the same pressures although land values did rise again in 1978–80. The large number of appeals lodged in 1980–1 (over 20% of all applications refused) and the high success rate of appellants must be due in part to the policies contained in Circular 22/80 (DOE 1980a) indicating that central government had a more favourable attitude to development than most local authorities (see Rydin 1983).

One aspect of planning application procedure is most important for landowners. Planning applications need not be detailed to the extent that they include building floor plans, elevations and the provision of services. An outline application can be submitted to ascertain the principle of development. This will specify the type of development and, possibly, the density of development. As a result, a landowner can submit an outline application without risking

Table 2.1 Planning decisions of local planning authorities: 1962–1983 England and Wales.

Year	Total decisions	Permissions granted	
		Number	Percentage (%)
1962	397 301	333 495	84
1963	411 563	345 651	84
1964	461 715	378 695	82
1965	443 387	364 935	82
1966	415 052	345 799	83
1967	422 553	358 338	85
1968	426 286	359 449	84
1969	402 714	342 889	85
1970	414 301	351 624	85
1971	463 301	385 989	83
1972	614 862	493 097	80
1973	622 652	491 174	79
1974/75	414 900	330 800	80
1975/76	454 206	379 821	84
1976/77	446 142	378 447	85
1977/78	441 612	378 998	86
1978/79	500 901	432 570	86
1979/80	550 122	473 488	86
1980/81	492 000	421 000	86
1981/82	406 000	348 000	86
1982/83	382 000	333 000	87

Source: Department of the Environment.

considerable expenditure on design fees, yet still clarify the planning position for a potential purchaser.

The introduction of charges for planning applications has increased the cost of securing an outline consent for a landowner by a significant amount. The charge for a planning application is not large[1] when compared to the market value of the land with planning permission, but it has to be paid out well before that value can be realised. There is also the risk that the planning permission will not be granted. This can be reduced by discussing the content of the application informally with the local planning authority before the application is submitted. There is also provision in the fee regulations for a revised application to be submitted free if an earlier one has been refused or withdrawn, but the nature of the application and the site it relates to must correspond very closely with the original application. At the present time it is too early to gauge the precise effect of planning charges on the way landowners submit applications. In general, however, planning charges are likely to increase the amount of negotiation accompanying applications by encouraging discussion to start at an earlier stage, namely before the application is submitted, and so reduce the likelihood of receiving a refusal.

Negotiation and planning gain Negotiation is now a recognised part of the development control system, for which there are still no statutory rules or

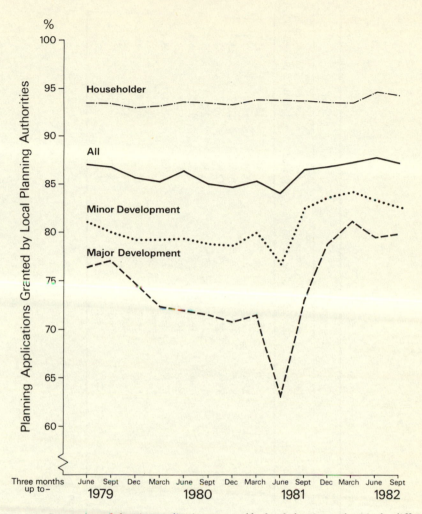

Figure 2.1 Proportion of planning applications granted by local planning authorities by different types of development, 1979–1982. (*Source*: DOE.)

guidelines. Negotiation over a planning application ranges from discussion over the precise siting of windows in the elevation of a proposed extension to a house, to discussions over the size of the residential content in a mixed commercial and residential scheme. It is the latter type that has come to be associated with 'planning gain'.

Planning gain is defined in Circular 22/83 as

... the term which has come to be applied, whenever, in connection with a grant of planning permission, a local planning authority seeks to impose on a developer an obligation to carry out works not included in the development for which permission has been sought or to make some payment or

Table 2.2 Determination of appeals against refusal of planning permission 1971–1983.

Year	Secretary of State			Inspectors			Total		
	No. decided	No. allowed	Percentage allowed (%)	No. decided	No. allowed	Percentage allowed (%)	No. decided	No. allowed	Percentage allowed (%)
1971	2441	698	28.6	3075	546	17.8	5516	1244	22.6
1972	1963	584	29.8	3953	858	21.7	5916	1442	24.4
1973	2387	718	30.0	8495	1659	19.5	10882	2377	21.8
1974	2683	586	21.8	9515	2129	22.4	12198	2697	22.1
1975	2753	692	25.1	8733	2228	25.5	11486	2920	25.4
1976	2273	720	31.7	6980	1997	28.6	9253	2717	29.4
1977	1702	534	31.4	6664	1908	28.6	8336	2442	29.2
1978	1630	501	30.7	7322	2003	27.4	8952	2504	28.0
1979	1503	525	34.9	7430	2077	28.0	8933	2602	29.1
1980	1521	597	39.3	11609	3477	29.7	13130	4074	31.0
1981	1786	644	36.1	12665	4077	32.2	14451	4721	32.7
1982	1100	408	37.1	11815	3595	30.4	12915	4003	31.0
1983	649	232	35.7	10572	3401	32.2	11221	3633	32.4

Source: DOE Chief Planning Inspector's Report.

confer some extraneous right or benefit in return for permitting development to take place (DOE 1983a).

There are circumstances, however, where a developer may voluntarily include an element of community benefit in his original planning application without it being negotiated by the planners. The reason for this is to pre-empt the planner's bargaining position as part of the general negotiations, especially if on the basis of experience the developer knows that this will improve his chances of success. The approved scheme may or may not include additional community benefits. The initial community benefit offered is still 'planning gain' even though it is not actually negotiated. There are many examples of 'planning gain' leading to the provision of a less remunerative but socially desirable use as part of a scheme, such as including residential units in a commercial scheme; dedication of land for public use, often as public open space; giving up a non-conforming use on other land in the developer's ownership; provision of infrastructure, such as improving the sewerage facilities; and payments to the local authority for the provision of parking space in lieu of the developer providing parking spaces on site (see Jowell 1977).

Since the late 1960s planners have been using their bargaining strength to obtain 'planning gain' from developers. The development of this form of bargaining has arisen because of the narrow definition adopted by the courts and the SOS over what may be stipulated as a planning condition. Planning conditions must relate strictly to matters defined in the town and country planning legislation or they are liable to be struck out as *ultra vires*. To get round this restriction local authorities have increasingly used Section 52 Agreements (TCPA 1971) which permit them to strike wide-ranging agreements with owners or developers before they make a formal planning application. Developers have been prepared to negotiate because it has enabled them to obtain a planning consent more quickly than risking an appeal to the SOS. As planners have become more experienced in this process their expectation of the 'planning gain' to be obtained has tended to increase, although these rising expectations can prove counter-productive if the planner does not fully appreciate the state of the local property market (Willis 1982). Planning gain has been realised most often in those parts of London where the shortage of development land is greatest (Stungo 1980).

Disquiet was expressed with the approach of planning authorities to planning gain for a number of years prior to the publication of a report by the PAG in 1981 (see Ratcliffe 1976, Heap & Ward 1980, DOE 1981c). This report crystallised the debate and forced the DOE to issue guidance after a long period of silence. The PAG report argues, for example, that it is permissible for a developer to provide the money for an improvement to a sewage works if, without this improvement, his scheme would be refused because of a lack of sewerage capacity. However, the improvement to sewage works should be limited to the capacity required for the developer's scheme and not be so great that its capacity is increased for the benefit of other schemes as well.

Planners defend the practice and now regard the negotiation of 'planning gain' as an integral part of the development control system. They use it as a way of achieving benefits for their area which would not be achieved, or are not likely to be carried out, by the public sector directly. They do recognise the dangers of allowing local authorities complete freedom to negotiate 'planning gain' but would prefer regulation to be through an approved policy for negotiation and, possibly, a code of practice. This is an important point because the prior negotiation between applicant and officer is usually conducted in private and runs counter to more general attempts to increase public participation in the planning process. The public, and even the planning committee, may then feel that they are being presented with a *fait accompli* when the application is received with supporting comments from the planning officer.

Circular 22/83 (DOE 1983a) is new and this is not the right time (June 1984) to pronounce on its effect. However, the guidance it contains is much more helpful to local planning authorities than the recommendations of PAG (DOE 1981c). The circular recognises that it may be 'reasonable' to impose 'planning gain' as long as either the works are related to the development proposed which would otherwise be unacceptable or, in the case of mixed developments, the imposed use is necessary to secure an acceptable balance of uses. The only sanction it imposes on local planning authorities is the threat that costs will be awarded against them if they are shown to have ignored the circular's advice at a planning appeal. This is of limited benefit to developers because they will not be compensated for the delay to the project as a result of the appeal (Jowell & Grant 1983). The likelihood is that Circular 22/83 will not be the DOE's final word on 'planning gain', particularly if development pressures increase.

A CHANGING CONTEXT

It will be clear from the preceding section that in practice there is more for a landowner to consider when seeking the development of his land than whether the land is designated for a change of use on the relevant development plan. Circumstances alter during the intended life of any plan and many of these will not be anticipated. Changing circumstances may not lead to the complete re-writing of the plan, but may be reflected in the decisions given on planning applications, either by the local authority or, more likely, by the SOS on appeal.

Four kinds of change may be identified. First, there are those that result from significant alterations to local circumstances and to which the planning committee – perhaps under pressure from local interests – feels bound to respond. The provision of increased capacity in the sewerage system may remove one of the objections to a major development scheme. Both the local and the sub-regional planning context may be altered by major public sector investments, such as the building of a motorway, a major bridge, an international airport or the sinking of a coal mine, and decisions over such investments may lie effectively beyond the jurisdiction of the local authority because of their 'national' significance. In each case the development potential of neighbouring land may be changed. Similarly, a loss of development potential may arise from the closure of a major industrial concern, such as when the steelworks at Corby and Consett closed.

Second, there are general changes within the national economy and the structure of society which may be especially marked in particular regions of the country. These will influence central and local government priorities in the planning of particular areas, such as the inner city and the remoter countryside, as well as the general approach of government to a policy of urban containment (for an up-to-date review see Herington 1984). Three such changes of particular concern to the local planners at the present time are:

(a)   The growth in unemployment and the general decline of manufacturing industry
(b)   Changes in the spatial distribution of the nation's population and especially the process of 'counter-urbanization'
(c)   Demographic changes, including the ageing of the population and the continuing decline in the size of the family.
      (For a general review of these issues, see Regional Studies Association 1983.)

In response to these trends central government has sought to assist local authorities in some of the most depressed areas, even if total spending on regional aid has been cut back in line with attempts to reduce public expenditure. The availability of urban development grants, for example, has transformed the economic viability of some private development schemes within run-down inner city areas. Owners of land in these locations have found that their development prospects have increased significantly as a result of government subsidies. Owners of land within an enterprise zone have likewise benefitted and where the two sets of incentives are combined, as they are for a scheme in Salford Docks, a development results which would not have been contemplated five years earlier.

Third, there are, and always have been, marked differences between the major political parties towards the role of planning in determining the optimum use of land. Although the differences are today not so obvious as they have been in certain areas of policy, for example the taxation of development land (see below), the advice local authorities have received and central government's own initiatives have differed. Labour administrations have favoured the development of new towns while the Conservatives have encouraged less planned growth through, for example, the town expansion schemes under the Town Development Act 1952. And, more recently, the two parties' approaches to promoting development in inner city areas have also differed markedly, with Labour relying on public sector activity while the Tories have subsidised the private sector.

Fourth, the inadequacy of the policies in development plans for determining planning applications has led to central government making planning policy through circulars. These circulars have been particularly important in determining whether planning permission should be granted for residential development. The first circular of note on this issue was published in 1970 (DOE 1970) and was followed by six more in the next fourteen years (DOE 1972a, 1973b, 1975b, 1978a, 1980b, 1984a). All have been concerned with ensuring that local authorities have allocated sufficient land for house-building although the precise criteria for ensuring this have altered. The 1980 circular (DOE 1980b), for example, emphasises the need for a five-year supply of land for *private* house-building, a distinction not made in the early circulars or re-iterated in the most recent one (DOE 1984a). A minimum of two years' supply of land has to be available for immediate development. Contemporaneously, there have been discussions between the House Builders' Federation and local authority planners to try to reach agreement over the amount of land to be made available for residential development. The first of these was held in Greater Manchester (DOE/HBF 1979) and has been followed by discussions in most local authorities in England (see, for example, Standing Conference/HBF 1981). The two groups have usually been able to reach agreement at a local level, even if some argue that the 'Manchester method' results in an over-allocation of land (Hooper 1983). Agreement has proved much more elusive, however, when sought at a national scale. The Joint Land Requirements Committee, consisting of representatives of the house-builders and of local planners, has not been able to agree on the amount of land currently available. The planners consider that there is sufficient land identified for development for approximately 220 000 dwellings per annum for the next five years, close to the total of 250 000 identified as the annual requirement in an earlier report (Joint Land Requirements Committee 1982). The house-builders' representatives maintain, however, that there is land available for only 183 000 units (Joint Land Requirements Committee 1983), mainly because they do not accept the number of houses which the planners anticipate will be built on small sites (see Rydin 1983). It now appears that the two sides have agreed to differ, particularly as the latest circular (DOE 1984a) does not offer any assistance for resolving the dispute.

Provision of housing land has always presented a difficult problem for the planning system. The development plans prepared in the early 1950s were based on housing a static population and did not provide for the significant increase that took place up to the end of the 1960s (see Hall *et al*. 1973). Increased public participation in the planning process since 1968 has reinforced the tendency for the system to be used to prevent change and not to release additional land for housing. The political influence of the suburbs is great, even when compared to the skilled presentations of a pressure group such as the House Builders' Federation, and this influence was reaffirmed when the SOS was forced to withdraw his first versions of both the 1983 green belt and housing land draft circulars (DOE 1983b,c; see Ch. 7). The increased demand for housing that is likely to occur as the country emerges from the recession, especially in the outer suburban and rural areas of southern England, after a number of years in which few new houses have been built, will renew familiar pressures on the planning system as local planning authorities try to balance the demand for private housing against the objections of local amenity groups.

To summarise, the planning context for an area can change overtly when a new plan is published, but it is as likely to change covertly as a result of a new circular or a change in local economic circumstances. Recognising the change is not always easy and only the experienced owners of potential development land will spot the change quickly.

PLANNING POLICY AND THE LANDOWNER

The use to which the landowner can put his land is fundamental in determining the land's value (see Ch. 3). Planning policy is, therefore, very important to the owner. As is apparent from the above, planning policy is complex, and may change frequently either with the approval of a new plan or, more subtly, as a result of a change in economic circumstances. The landowner's concern remains the same though; changes in policy only affect him if the prospects for obtaining a valuable planning consent alter and/or the character of the surrounding area is likely to change.

Frequently, a landowner is not provided with a clear picture of the development prospects for his land because either the policy context is changing or the relevant plan is insufficiently specific. Where land at the urban edge is allocated for an urban use in a new plan, the owners of that land are in an unusually straightforward position. But in the absence of a new plan, the same landowners can still try to get their land allocated by submitting planning applications. Alternatively, if the plan allocates other land for development, landowners can still try to get their own land allocated by appearing as objectors at the plan inquiry. Landowners need considerable knowledge of the planning system if they are to assess correctly the likelihood of obtaining planning permission and, perhaps more importantly, the best time to submit an application.

Taxation policy

It is important to preface this discussion by making reference to the social purpose of taxation. In the context of capital taxation, HM Treasury has stated

> Capital taxes are generally seen as having two objectives . . . the first . . . is to relate the burden of tax more closely to taxable capacity. It is based on the view that the ownership of capital (apart from the income it generates) adds to an individual's taxable capacity by giving him a permanent resource of spending power with the security, independence and other benefits, both real and psychological, which stem from this . . . The second objective [is] reductions in the concentrations of wealth (Northfield Committee Report 1979, pp. 213–4).

Three points arise from this statement. First, the objectives of any fiscal system are political and there will be continuing disagreement about them. Second, changes in taxation for social reasons, and primarily for reasons of equity, may have unpredictable effects on the workings of particular aspects of the economy, including the development process. Third, in the absence of knowledge about the wealth and taxation circumstances of individual owners, the introduction of taxes directed at particular policy objectives related to the development of land may prove unsuccessful.

Landowners are affected by a whole range of taxes other than those linked specifically to development gain (betterment). Landowners are influenced by revenue taxes, notably income and corporation tax, by capital taxes, especially capital gains tax (CGT) and capital transfer tax (CTT), and by rates. The incidence of CTT, for example, can influence landowners because it encourages them to hold their assets in a form whose value is hard to measure. Land with some development potential but without planning permission is more difficult to value than land which has already been given planning permission because a number of uncertainties surround its future, the most important of these being the time it may actually take to obtain planning consent (see Ch. 3 below). If the land can be transferred to another owner before planning permission is granted, it will have a much lower value for CTT purposes. The emphasis in this section, however, is on the taxes payable on profits from the sale of land and how these taxes have changed in the post-war period.

All taxes and their marginal rates have been adjusted frequently in recent years with changes of government, and even after each budget. The very frequency of alteration encourages some landowners to try to anticipate legislative change in order to mitigate their tax burden. There is some evidence, however, that smaller owners of agricultural land have a poor appreciation of their tax position – not least because of rapid changes in land prices and the extent to which they can quite legally reduce their tax liabilities (Northfield Committee Report 1979). All landowners have been affected by the increased importance of capital taxation vis à vis income tax since the introduction of CGT in 1965 and the replacement of estate duty by CTT in 1974.

THE TAXATION OF BETTERMENT
The changes that have taken place since 1947 in the 'tax' regime on gains on the sale of development land are considerable. Probably no other transaction has been subjected to so much change, there being no less than five different measures during this period. Even the word 'tax' has to be used cautiously in this context. Two of the measures, the development charge and the betterment levy, were not strictly taxes collected by the Inland Revenue, but were regarded as land reform measures to be administered by special bodies set up partly for that purpose. However, as far as the landowner was concerned, the effect of all these measures was the same, namely to reduce the profit from selling development land.

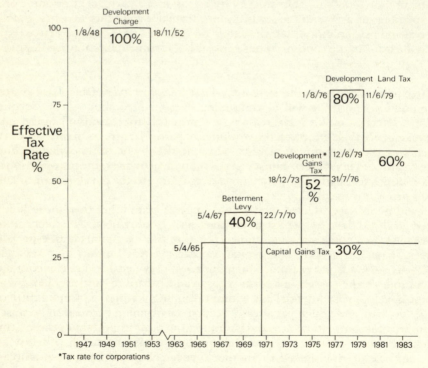

Figure 2.2   Taxes on development land in the post-war period.

The measures that have been in operation since 1947 are set out diagramat-
ically in Figure 2.2 to show how long each was in force.[2] The pattern has
generally been for Labour administrations to introduce new taxes which were
then repealed when the Conservatives regained power (for an historical account
see Mackay & Cox 1979, Ch. 3). The only exception to this is development land
tax (DLT) where the last Conservative government simply reduced the rate of
tax in its first budget rather than abolish it.

Development charge   The development charge was introduced as part of the
package of measures contained in the 1947 Town and Country Planning Act.
The charge differs from subsequent measures in that it was not payable at the
time a transaction in land took place. The charge was payable when development started and was payable by the developer, not the landowner. It was
designed, however, to fall on the landowner because the developer would
notionally deduct the amount of charge payable from the price he would pay for
the land.
   The charge was based on the difference in the value of the land with the benefit
of planning permission and the value of the land in its existing use, i.e. without
the planning permission. All subsequent taxes specifically on development land
have been based on these two valuations although the nomenclature and their
detailed definition have varied. The development charge levy was equivalent to
the *whole* of the *difference* between the development value and existing use value.
At the same time, owners of land with development potential also needed to
establish development rights under Part VI of the 1947 Act. This would then
entitle them to a share of the global sum set aside for compensating owners for
loss of development rights. Although a sum of £300 million was earmarked for
this purpose, no payments were made from it before Part VI was repealed.
Under the provisions of the Town and Country Planning Act 1954, which
dismantled this part of the 1947 scheme, the only owners who received
compensation were those who had established a claim and were subsequently
refused planning permission (see Leung 1979).
   The Central Land Board, a body given the task of administering and
collecting the charge, also had the power to step in and buy land compulsorily to
ensure that owners did not receive more than the existing use value for their
land. These powers were used sparingly and developers were prepared to pay
more than the existing use value to secure a supply of building land. Even so, the
scheme was generally regarded as a failure because landowners were not
prepared to sell land at an artificially low price and the supply of land diminished. The development charge was abolished by the 1953 Town and Country
Planning Act and landowners were then able to receive all the benefit from
obtaining planning permission (see Parker 1954, Cullingworth 1981). It was not
until the introduction of the capital gains tax in 1965 and the betterment levy in
1967 that rising land prices led to new attempts to recoup betterment for the
community (see Lichfield & Darin-Drabkin 1980, Ch. 5).

Capital gains tax   Profits realised from the sale of an investment, including
property, have been subject to capital gains tax (CGT) since 5 April 1965. The
chargeable gain is computed from the difference between the acquisition and
disposal price of the asset and the tax rate is 30%. If the asset was acquired before

6 April 1965, the taxpayer can normally elect to be assessed on either the difference between the sale price and the asset's 1965 value, or by apportioning the sale and purchase prices to the period the asset was held after April 1965. This option is not available in the case of development land, where the chargeable gain is always assessed on the difference between the sale price and the April 1965 value. Expenditure incurred on the asset during the period of ownership, including acquisition and disposal costs, are deductable from the chargeable gain. In addition, following the 1982 Finance Act, capital gains are now index linked, but only from March 1982 and provided that the asset has been held for more than a year.

There are a number of important reliefs for landowners. The sale of an individual's principal dwelling house, including a garden of up to an acre (0.4 ha) in size, is exempt from CGT. A larger area may also be exempted if the Tax Commissioners are satisfied that, by virtue of the size and character of the house, a larger area is required for the reasonable use and enjoyment of the residence. 'Roll-over' relief is available where business assets are sold and replaced. The relief takes the form of allowing the trader to deduct the gain from the cost of acquiring a replacement asset. The payment of CGT is deferred until the time when an asset is disposed of and not replaced. Full relief is available only where the whole sum obtained from the disposal is spent on new assets although partial relief can also be obtained. In addition, the new asset must be in the same class as the old asset to get relief. Thus, where land, formerly occupied for business purposes, is sold as development land by its owner-occupier, the proceeds must be re-invested in land and buildings occupied for business purposes or in fixed plant and machinery to obtain 'roll-over' relief. The replacement asset must also be purchased not more than 12 months before nor more than three years after the old asset is sold. CGT is still payable today (1984) but it is assessed on the proceeds after other taxation payments have been deducted. Between 23 July 1970 and 17 December 1973, however, CGT was the only tax payable on development gains (see Fig. 2.2).

Betterment levy Betterment levy was introduced in 1967 and the Land Commission given the task of administering the levy. Betterment levy was payable on both the sale or the leasing of development land and on the commencement of a project of material development. Where land was sold, the levy was payable by the landowner so there was no attempt to reduce the price landowners received from developers, as had been the case with the development charge. The levy was assessed on the difference between, at the top end, either the sale price or the value of the land with benefit of any planning permissions, and, at the bottom, the purchase price (subject to some restrictions) and the current use value of the land (i.e. its value without planning permission) plus 10%. Where work had been carried out which increased the development value of the land their cost could also be deducted. The levy was charged on the net development value at a rate of 40%, although it had been the intention of the government to increase the rate progressively to 45% and then 50%.

Few exemptions from betterment levy were permitted and this proved to be one of the principal reasons for its failure. No relief was given for small transactions until 1969 and, as a result, the Land Commission found itself with a large number of small assessments which brought the whole scheme into disrepute. This was not helped by the complexity of the legislation which made it hard for professionals to understand let alone the lay public. The reliefs given from betterment levy were limited to the operational land of statutory under-takers, transitional provisions to avoid hardship for developers and to charities as long as the land was used for charitable purposes and not held as an investment. The betterment levy was accepted as a failure even by the Labour administration that created it, and its abolition in 1970 came as no surprise (see Cullingworth 1981 and Hall *et al*. 1973 for further details).

Development gains tax   Development gains tax (DGT) came into operation on 18 December 1973 as an extension of CGT. Where a capital gain had been realised by a land sale, the part of that gain attributable to the development value was taxed as income. An individual could, therefore, pay tax on the proceeds at 83%, the top personal income tax rate at the time. The rules, however, permitted the gain to be apportioned between the four previous tax years, depending on the length of time over which the asset was owned (see Turner 1977). DGT was not levied at the start of a building project, unlike betterment levy, but on the completion of the building, or more precisely, when the building was first occupied – the 'first lettings tax'. As a result, disposal for DGT (and CGT) purposes was deemed to take place following the first letting. Exemptions followed those for CGT with the addition that gains of £10 000 or less by a private individual or gains of £1000 or less for a company were exempt. In addition, development gains could be offset against any development losses – the only time there has been such a provision in a specific tax on development profit. DGT was superseded by development land tax on 1 August 1976.

Development land tax   Development land tax (DLT) has now been in existence for a longer period of time than any of its predecessor taxes on betterment. Since its introduction in 1976 a number of amendments have been made, although its impact on most landowners, as opposed to developers, has not changed significantly.

A charge for DLT arises when either an interest in development land (even an option) is disposed of by sale or lease, or a project of material development commences.[3] DLT is payable by the vendor on the difference between the sale price (or market value) and whichever of the three base values produces the largest amount. Simplifying the position slightly, these base values are calculated as follows:

Base A   Acquisition price plus expenditure on improvements which increase the development value, plus an allowance for the time the property has been owned, plus the increase in the current use value since 1965

Base B   115% of the current use value plus expenditure on improvements which increase the development value

Base C   115% of the acquisition cost plus expenditure on any improvements.

Either base A or base C gives the highest amount where a property has been purchased recently. Where the owner has held the land for some time, base B normally produces the highest figure.

DLT was originally set at a rate of 80%, although the first £10 000 of realised

development value obtained in a single tax year was exempt. This was to avoid
the problems that had been experienced over small claims with Betterment
Levy. The Labour government of the day introduced an intermediate rate of
$66\frac{2}{3}$% for a temporary period, although this had not been included in the
legislation as originally drafted. This lower rate was charged on the first
£150 000 so that the top rate of 80% was not payable until £160 000 of realised
development value had been obtained by a taxpayer in a single tax year. The
intermediate rate of $66\frac{2}{3}$% was originally to end on 31 March 1979 but it was
extended for a further year.

The Conservative Party had made it clear while in opposition that it would
reduce the rate of tax but not abolish DLT (Rossi 1977), and the Chancellor duly
reduced the rate to 60% in his June 1979 Budget. At the same time he increased
the annual exemption from £10 000 to £50 000[4] and stated, 'I do not propose
to make any further reductions in the rate of DLT and the generous increase in
the exempt slice means that it will not need early revision. Owners therefore
have no reason to hold back in the hope of further tax reductions.' These conditions remained until April 1984.

As with CGT, a principal dwelling house standing in a garden of 0.4 ha is
exempt, with the Commissioners of the Inland Revenue permitted to allow a
larger area if additional garden is needed for the full use and enjoyment of the
house as a residence. Charities are now also exempt from DLT, although the
relief given to them in 1976 was only partial. Statutory undertakers,
however, are not given relief from DLT on their non-operational land, a tax
status which is less favourable to them than had been the case with both betterment levy and development charge. DLT bears on developers and builders
because they are liable both when they start a development project and when
they deal in land. A number of provisions were included in the original DLT
Act, and have been added to subsequently, to reduce the impact on them,
particularly where land is purchased and developed within a short period.
Developers can now obtain an assessment of DLT in advance so that they
know their liability before starting work. Residential developers have also
been given a more favourable method of calculating base A (see Finance Act
1981, s. 129).

None of the amendments to DLT, apart from the reduction in the rate of tax,
has been of much help to the owner of a greenfield site. In many cases, the gain
was not sufficient to reach the 80% rate so that the reduction in the rate from
$66\frac{2}{3}$% to 60% is of limited benefit to them and of less significance than the
increased threshold (examples of a landowner's tax liability are given in Ch. 5).
Owners of urban sites, on the other hand, have fared better because the tolerance
levels for 'material development' have been expanded. The calculation of the
current use value for these types of site is complex because the right to carry out
non-material development can be reflected in the calculation. For example,
where a multi-storey factory of 10 000 m^2 is sold for development as offices, the
current use value may well be the value of the property with the notional right to
re-build with, up to, 11 000 m^2 of modern industrial space. Certain changes of
use can also be assumed. A change of use from a shop to an office, for example, is
not material development so that the value of this right can be reflected in the
current use value. The precise rights that can be assumed are not certain,
however, because there is still uncertainty over the interpretation of Schedule 4

Table 2.3 Development land tax: disposals by year of assessment. This table shows the numbers and amounts of net chargeable realised development values (CRDV) of disposals and the associated development land tax in each year of disposal up to the year ending 31 March 1982. In the year 1976–77, tax was charged on disposals on or after 1 August 1976 only. Amounts of CRDV and DLT are in thousands of pounds.

Year of disposal		Assessments made in year ended 31 March						
		1977	1978	1979	1980	1981	1982	Total
1976/77*	Number	36	605	265	76	81	23	1 086
	CRDV	884	17 113	6 988	1 904	1 916	927	29 732
	tax	594	12 020	4 868	1 308	1 378	640	20 808
1977/78	number		230	1 061	491	202	72	2 056
	CRDV		5 740	26 904	11 476	8 185	2 451	54 756
	tax		3 968	18 736	7 976	5 922	1 719	38 321
1978/79	number			313	1 642	846	288	3 089
	CRDV			10 032	50 165	31 768	11 088	103 053
	tax			6 994	35 441	22 786	7 889	73 110
1979/80	number				270	889	427	1 586
	CRDV				12 148	50 118	45 502	107 768
	tax				8 342	31 164	28 352	67 858
1980/81	number					111	593	704
	CRDV					9 682	53 711	63 393
	tax					5 809	32 227	38 036
1981/82	number						102	102
	CRDV						11 126	11 126
	tax						6 675	6 675
total	number	36	835	1 639	2 479	2 129	1 505	8 623
	CRDV	884	22 853	43 924	75 693	101 669	124 805	369 828
	tax	594	15 988	30 598	53 067	67 059	77 502	244 808

Source: Board of Inland Revenue.
* From 1 August 1976.

to the DLT Act.[5] The Courts have not provided guidance on the matter (to date) and, until then, some owners of urban sites may be unable to estimate their DLT liability with accuracy in advance of selling.

Despite being in existence for eight years, DLT is still regarded as a new tax and a subject on which there are few experts. In many cases it is difficult to calculate the owner's DLT liability. This is reflected in the Inland Revenue's statistics showing the yield from DLT (see Table 2.3). From the table it can be inferred that it takes a long time to settle DLT cases and therefore early estimates of the yield from a tax of this type can be misleading. At the end of 1976/7, after one year of the tax's operation, only £594 000 had been collected. Yet by 1982, the figures show that a total of £20.81 million was received from disposals during 1976/7. Once a tax of this type is established, the revenue from it is more stable because delays in settling claims even out.

TAXATION AND THE LANDOWNER

Tax is a personal matter and no two individuals are taxed in exactly the same way because their personal circumstances differ. This is particularly true with the taxation of development land. The price the owner originally paid for the land is important in determining tax liability as is the time when the sale occurs. Because of the speed at which changes in the tax regime have taken place, only the very well informed landowner can expect to be reasonably conversant with the up-to-date position (see Ch. 5).

The assessment of tax on development land is not a wholly arithmetic exercise, as is the case, for example, with the CGT liability on the sale of shares. The tax liability is likely to depend on at least one valuation of the property, probably on an historic basis. Valuers are well used to carrying out work of this type but valuation is more an art than a science so there is always some scope for argument over the precise figures. The initial impact of a new tax on development land is much greater than the subsequent reaction to it because most publicity is given to the new rate of tax not to the reliefs that are available. Means of mitigating the tax liability may not be immediately obvious although there is some scope for avoiding the full weight of every tax. Mitigating taxes is usually an expensive business, however, and is only worth-while when the amount of tax at stake is significant. This does not stop a whole stream of cases going through the Courts and it is noticeable that approximately 10% of the House of Lords cases are on revenue matters (see *Judicial statistics*, HMSO).

The sale of development land usually gives rise to a tax liability under more than one tax. Even if the DLT liability can be minimised, there is still a liability to CGT or to income tax. There may also be CTT implications if assets are to be passed on to other members of the owner's family. Although the taxes do not overlap in the sense that the same 'profit' is taxed twice, the apparent minimisation of one tax is not necessarily beneficial to the owner if another is increased. Generally, however, a landowner wants to minimise his DLT liability because this tax is levied at a high rate (60%) and, more importantly, cannot be 'rolled-over' or offset against other losses.

If a tax is so rigid that it offers little scope for mitigating the liability, it is probably difficult to operate and will catch transactions that it was not really intended to tax. Betterment levy was an excellent example of such a tax because no exemption was given for transactions where the gain was comparatively small. As a result, the Land Commission was inundated with small assessments which were costly to pursue and which brought the whole system into disrepute. This error was recognised and small gains have always been exempt from DLT. The annual exemption of £75 000 (originally £10 000) now offers landowners considerable scope to mitigate the liability by attempting to spread the receipts over a number of tax years.

Tax is a complicated subject generally, but particularly so where sales of development land are concerned. Owners can obtain advice from experts but this is costly and not all owners are in a position to purchase this advice. As a result, ignorance is widespread and this generally leads to owners over-estimating their tax liability rather than under-estimating it because they are not aware of all the reliefs that are available to them. This, in turn, tends to further discourage owners from selling land.

Compulsory purchase and compensation

There is a wide range of policies and powers that affect landowners and which are neither planning powers nor related to taxation. This last section on the contextual factors focuses on the circumstances in which land can be compulsorily purchased and the compensation that is payable to owners as a result. Although this section concentrates on these powers the infinite subtlety of other policy instruments which can affect landowners, ranging from enterprise zones and free ports to smokeless zones, must not be forgotten (for a full discussion and listing of instruments, see Pearce 1980).

The powers whereby land may be compulsorily purchased have been granted to public and private bodies since the end of the 18th century (Lawrence & Moore 1972). Initially, these powers were granted for specific purposes, such as the construction of railways or the improvement of environmental conditions under the Public Health Act 1875, but, as social attitudes changed increasingly to favour the public as opposed to the private interest in property matters, compulsory purchase powers were given to many bodies for a wide range of purposes. In the context of the development process, this progression culminated in the powers of compulsory purchase given to local authorities by the Community Land Act 1975, and now repealed by the Local Government, Planning and Land Act 1980.

Compulsory purchase powers are disliked by landowners because they lose the right to decide when and to whom they may sell their land. Often the dislike stems as much from the psychological costs associated with being an unwilling seller, as from any inadequacy in the financial terms of the compensation payment. Nevertheless, owners may also lose out financially as they can be forced to sell when land prices are low or at a time when it is inconvenient for the owner to vacate the property. In addition, there is considerable distrust of the statutory compensation provisions. Owners generally do not feel that they get a proper sum for their property under the existing compensation code (see Bell 1979).

Owners of development land have been particularly liable to have their property compulsorily acquired during three specific periods. These were:

(a) From 1 July 1948 to 18 November 1952, by the Central Land Board under the 1947 Town and Country Planning Act
(b) From 5 April 1967 to 22 July 1970, by the Land Commission under the Land Commission Act, 1967
(c) From 1 April 1976 to 21 May 1979, by local authorities and the Land Authority for Wales[6] under the Community Land Act 1975.

In all three cases, the compensation paid to owners was the same as they would notionally have received if the land had been sold on the open market at the time. However, the purchase price was paid out net of the tax proceeds operable at the time rather than the gross proceeds with the landowner subsequently paying the tax bill. In the case of the Community Land Act the amount of tax was assessed by the Inland Revenue and this was deducted from the price paid to the owner. The owner did have an opportunity to challenge the assessment but not before the tax had been paid. Any over-assessment would be repaid subsequently but the owner would have lost the use of that money even though interest would be paid.

The difference between these measures, and other Acts granting compulsory purchase powers to government bodies, is their scope. The Highway Acts, for example, permit the compulsory acquisition of land for a specific purpose, namely for roads. Once the need for a road has been established following a public inquiry, the land required can be purchased compulsorily. The important point is that the need for a particular parcel's transfer to public ownership has to be established first. Similarly, land cannot be acquired under the Housing Acts until the local authority has shown that there is a need to improve the existing dwellings or a need to re-develop them which is not going to happen while the land remains in private hands. Acquisitions under the Town and Country Planning Act 1947, the Land Commission Act and the Community Land Act could be justified on much less specific grounds. In the latter case, local authorities were under a duty to consider the desirability of bringing into public ownership all land required for 'relevant' development within the next ten years, and were given powers to do it. Even though relevant development was defined in a narrow way, the apparent threat to private landowners was considerable.[7]

It is important to emphasise that the threat to owners from these measures has proved to be more apparent than real. All three attempts at increasing public sector involvement in the land market have failed because policy makers did not appreciate the difficulties involved and had not allocated sufficient funds to have an immediate impact on the market. And for such a scheme to be successful it needs to show quick results, if only for political reasons. It is noticeable that each scheme only lasted approximately three years. Legislation of this type is complicated and, because it is controversial, does not pass through Parliament easily. As a result, it has not come into force until some way through a Parliament; and yet its financial benefits take longer to achieve than the life of a single Parliament. The legislation then becomes unpopular because it does not live up to its proponents' expectations and the pressures for repeal from its opponents are strong. This was particularly the case with the Land Commission but applies to the other two Acts as well.

The experience of the Land Commission is well documented elsewhere (e.g. Drewett 1973, Cox 1980). Its activities as an assembler of land were always marginal to the functioning of the development land market. In the four years of its existence (1967–71) the Commission only purchased 1133 ha of land and sold about 136 ha. As a central government agency its activities seemed remote from where development was taking place and the Commission did not always work easily alongside local authorities. The mistake was not repeated with the CLA, which was to be effected by the local authorities directly. The details of English local authorities' acquisitions of land under the Community Land Act are set out in Table 2.4. This shows that local authorities spent £12.1 million in 1976/7 but only £9.06 million in 1977/8 following government expenditure cuts announced in December 1976 and a change in the administration procedure for sanctioning loans set out in GNLA/12 (DOE 1977d, see Barrett & Whitting 1980). Activity recovered in 1978/9 only to fall away again as soon as the Conservative government was elected in May 1979.

The amount of land acquired compares favourably with the Land Commission's activity between 1967 and 1970 notwithstanding the effect GNLA/12 had

Table 2.4   Land acquisition by English local authorities under the Community Land Act 1975.

	1976/77	1977/78	1978/79	1979/80	Total
area acquired (ha)	637	268	611	239★	1755
acquisition cost (£m)★	12.1	9.06	22.02	4.54	47.72
spending in land market (£m)†	823	1137	1523	2035	5518
CLA as a percentage of the whole (%)	1.47	0.80	1.45	0.22	0.86

Source: *Community Land Act statistics 1976–77, 1977–78, 1978–79*, CIPFA; *Planning and development statistics 1979–80, Actual*, CIPFA; *Inland Revenue statistics 1980, 1981*, HMSO.

★ This figure is the total purchases by local authorities who supplied information and therefore under-states actual acquisitions slightly.

† Total spending in the land market has been estimated from the Inland Revenue's Survey of Conveyancing series after deducting spending on agricultural land.

on the scheme's momentum. Nevertheless, the local authorities' activity in the development land market was still comparatively insignificant. Table 2.4 shows the proportion that CLA purchases formed to total spending in the development land market and at no time did this exceed 1.5%. It is likely that by comparing the amount of land purchased, local authorities would be shown as having a greater impact on the market because they probably paid a lower average price for their sites. Information on this is not available and anyway it is clear enough that the impact of the Community Land Act on the land market was minimal (see Barrett & Whitting 1980). A great deal more money must be allocated to schemes of this kind if they are to be effective on anything other than a local scale. The Labour Party's latest proposals for a land policy recognise the political necessity for any future scheme to show results quickly but it is less clear whether they recognise the need for very much larger sums of public money to be devoted to it (Labour Party 1983).

The fuss created whenever the Labour Party brings forward legislation of this kind would suggest that the effects on landowners of such policies are substantial. In fact, the reality has proved much less dire. The taxes associated with each scheme have been important but the powers of compulsory purchase have been so rarely used that landowners quickly appreciate they have less to fear than they had been led to expect. The wide powers available under the legislation to acquire land have not been exercised except in rare circumstances so that the number of landowners affected is few, even if at the time it is necessary for each landowner to ascertain the likelihood of his land being acquired.

COMPENSATION

The basic rule relating to the assessment of compensation for the compulsory purchase of land is that an owner has '. . . the right to receive a money payment not less than the loss imposed on him in the public interest but on the other hand no greater' (Scott LJ in *Horn v Sunderland Corporation* (1941)). A landowner should be in no worse a financial position if his land is compulsorily acquired than when it is sold on the open market.

The compensation code relating to development land has broadly followed this basic rule with the notable exception of the period between 18 November

1952 and 30 October 1958. At this time, where the compulsory purchase of a property was instigated, the compensation payable was limited to the existing use value of the land taken, even though the price paid for development land sold on the open market reflected development value. Thus, at that time, one price was paid if land was sold under a compulsory purchase order, while a higher price was paid if it was sold on the open market. This anomaly was ended by the Town and Country Planning Act 1959, which restored open market value as the basis of compensation. Compensation is now assessed under the rules set out in the Land Compensation Act 1961.

The practice of assessing compensation creates many more difficulties than a simple statement of the principle might suggest. The onus of proof is placed on the landowner to establish his claim. The most complicated cases involve the acquisition of premises on which there is a business. The claimant is entitled to compensation for disruption to the business as a result of having to move. It is often difficult to identify the true costs of the move and the Lands Tribunal has frequently had to determine the compensation payable (see, for example, *Appelby and Ireland v Hampshire County Council* (1978)). Although it is impossible to prove, it appears that many small businesses located in inner city redevelopment areas do not survive the effects of compulsory acquisition and are never able to re-establish themselves in new premises (see Fagg 1973, Thomas 1977). The difficulties of re-establishing a business in a new location, following the transfer of staff, the taking on of new staff and general disruption, are all too obvious. The same problem faces a farmer who may be able to buy other land with his compensation monies to replace that lost but cannot immediately replace the intimate knowledge he had of his former land, a matter that can significantly affect his farming profits in the short term. Agricultural occupiers will also experience difficulties following severance, as with motorway construction, and the loss of a part of their holding (Bell 1979, Hearne *et al.* 1977). They may be left with insufficient land to form a viable unit, which will increase the loss to them by more than the land's open market value to a purchaser. Bell (1979) reports that *some* valuers recognise this valuation problem and 'smudge' the issue in determining the amount of compensation payable, but this leads to variable levels of compensation being paid and raises the question of equity. Some kinds of occupier are affected more than others. For example, agricultural tenants are often unable to obtain a new tenancy simply because few new agricultural tenancies are being created (Northfield Committee Report 1979). The tenant, therefore, may be more severely affected than an owner-occupier by a compulsory purchase order, to the extent that he loses the source of his livelihood as well.

Owners of freehold land are usually in a better position. They receive some measure of the market value for the land which they can re-invest. CGT is no longer payable where land is compulsorily purchased (Finance Act 1982), which had previously been a disadvantage. Instead, the gain is carried forward and does not become taxable until the new asset is sold. Even here, though, it may be difficult to establish the actual market value of the property where it is unusual or is the type that is rarely sold, for example, a vet's surgery (see *Wilkinson, Gale and Hall v Middlesbrough Borough Council* (1979)). In the future it is highly unlikely that a government will introduce a basis of compensation that gives less than market value to owners. This principle is enshrined in the European

Convention on Human Rights and, now that litigants have discovered the existence of a Court that will uphold these Rights, no government is likely to contravene it lightly (see Denyer-Green 1984). In addition, it is constantly getting harder for both central and local government to obtain compulsory purchase orders over land. Whether it is required for a road scheme, a reservoir or for re-development, there is always considerable opposition from neighbouring land users and environmental groups, if not from the occupiers themselves.

COMPULSORY PURCHASE POLICY AND THE LANDOWNER
The impact of compulsory purchase policy on landowners is different from planning policy and taxation policy because these policies do not affect the landowner unless he wants to do something different with his land. There is no need to apply for planning permission if the owner intends to continue using the property in the same way. Taxation is relevant only if the landowner is considering a sale of the land. Land policy instruments, on the other hand, are imposed on the landowner from the outside, interfering directly with his use of the land.

Throughout the post war period, the controls on landowners have increased and the circumstances in which land can be compulsorily acquired have also been widened. Planning permission is now required in more circumstances and the conditions in planning consents are more onerous (for example, see the provisions of the Town and Country Planning (Minerals) Act 1981). Attempts to reduce the impact by expanding the General Development Order (SI 1981/245) or repealing the Community Land Act, have not changed the position that much because the scope of permitted development has been increased only slightly, such as allowing extensions of 15% of the floor area of residential property instead of 10%, and there are still powers for a local authority to acquire development land under the Planning Acts to secure the proper development of land (Town and Country Planning Act 1971, s. 112). It is more likely that controls on the users of agricultural land will be increased in the future rather than reduced, and the much criticised Wildlife and Countryside Act 1981 represents a small step in that direction.

Even though landowners are used to the controls imposed on them, the threat of compulsory acquisition is still extremely emotive (Blair 1980). Few landowners actually experience a CPO and to that extent compulsory purchase policy can be seen as the least significant of the three areas of policy described in the chapter. However, their impact on landowners' attitudes is important, especially when a new measure is announced, because compulsory acquisition ends ownership and no owner wants that fate.

Landowners and contextual factors

Owners of development land have to be familiar with a complicated set of controls and taxes if they are to obtain the maximum return from their assets. Ignorance may not only lead to an opportunity for obtaining planning permission being missed, but it can also lead to the compulsory acquisition of land in unfavourable circumstances. Although the policies described above give an outward impression of rigidity with the landowner having little scope for manoeuvre, this is not the case in practice. With sufficient knowledge, an owner can take advantage of the flexibility within the system to increase his return. Whether this is by obtaining planning permissions on appeal, after consent has been refused by the local authority, or by selling land at a time when the tax rate is favourable, the landowner can choose how he wishes to approach matters. He does not, for example, have to wait until his land has been allocated for a new use before seeking planning permission.

Knowledge of the contextual factors is very important, and it would be reasonable to expect landowners who are professional dealers in land to be sufficiently knowledgeable about policy matters to maximise their return. Most owners of development land, however, are not speculators but have purchased or inherited land a long time before it becomes development land. In many cases, they will only own one parcel of development land during their lifetime, so they do not have a chance to build up expertise and are not conversant with the matters discussed above. Even though advice can be obtained from experts, not every owner has the inclination or the means to seek professional advice and does not exploit the system to his best advantage as a result.

The fourth contextual factor, the land market, is discussed in Chapter 3. Land prices are influenced by two of the policy issues discussed in this chapter. The existence of planning permission or the likelihood that a consent will be granted at some date in the future is very important in determining the value of a site, and this relationship is analysed in detail below. Taxes on the sale of development land have an effect on the supply of development land and, as a result, the price of land. This too is considered in Chapter 3.

Notes

1 Planning charges (SI 1983/1674) *Residential development*: outline £47 for each 0.1 ha of site area, maximum £1175; detailed £47 per dwelling, maximum £2350. *Other buildings*: outline £47 for each 0.1 ha of site area, maximum £1175; detailed: £47 for each 75 m^2 of floor space to be created, maximum £2350. *Mineral development*: £24 for each 0.1 ha of site area, maximum £3600. *Alterations or development of less than 40 m^2*: £24. *Change of use*: £47.

2 Land traders, people who make a living from buying and selling land, have been liable for income tax on their profits throughout this period. See Mellows (1982) for further details.

3 'Material development' is defined in Schedule 4 of the Development Land Tax Act 1976 (as amended). Material development is development that is greater in extent than the reconstruction of a building with a 10% increase in cubic content, extensions of up to one-third of the cubic content and changes of use outside broad classes. For example, a change of use from an office to a shop is not material development, but a change of use from a factory to an office may result in a liability to DLT.

4 Now raised to £75 000 as from 1 April 1984.

5 See note 3.

6 The Land Authority for Wales can still acquire land as its powers were re-enacted in the Local Government, Planning and Land Act 1980, albeit on a more modest scale.

7 'Relevant development' was defined in the Community Land Act 1975, s. 3(2) as development in excess of the construction of a single dwelling, an industrial building of 1000 m^2 or any other building of 1500 m^2. In addition, where planning permission existed before the Community Land Scheme was proposed on 12 September 1974, it was not 'relevant development' and so could not be acquired under the CLA powers.

3 Land values and the market for development land

The forum for exchange of property rights

In Chapter 2 the contextual matters of taxation, planning and compulsory purchase policy were examined. Here attention is focused on the remaining contextual factor of special concern to the landowner – the nature and operation of the market in development land. The analysis that follows seeks to draw general conclusions about the following three questions:

(a) What is the spatial pattern of land values in and around a city?
(b) Is the level of land values rising in real terms over time?
(c) To what extent can landowners influence the value of their own land, either individually or collectively?

The peculiar nature of land as a 'commodity' for trading is described by many writers (e.g. Ratcliff 1949, Barlowe 1958). It is not proposed that we should reiterate those points here but simply emphasise that (a) the market deals in property rights, not in the land itself; (b) these property rights are heterogeneous both because they attach to a unique portion of the Earth's surface and because they may be combined together in many different permutations, e.g. leases, rights of way and fishing rights; and (c) the improvements that have been carried out to individual units of land also vary, further emphasising their individual nature. Thus each parcel of land has special physical and abstract characteristics which make it of varying attractiveness to different uses (and users) and which makes the analysis of data on land values difficult (Denman & Prodano 1972). The many imperfections in the land market cannot be ignored either. They result from the peculiar nature of the property rights traded in the market, land's limited supply, and the unequal distribution of property rights among the population (for a full discussion of these subjects see Curry 1978, Harrison 1977).

The value of the property rights in an individual parcel of land is determined at the micro-level by site characteristics. These may be summarised as follows:

(a) Size
(b) Current use and level of fixed investment (improvements)
(c) Location in relation to existing development, roads and services
(d) Physical characteristics, e.g. drainage, topography, which affect its adaptability to alternative uses as well as its maximum productivity in its current use
(e) Planning status – planning consents granted, zoning on the relevant development plan, etc.

These characteristics are all of great importance to owners and to prospective purchasers. But in seeking to answer the general questions listed above, the following analysis concentrates on two of these characteristics – location and planning status – for it is from these that a general pattern of values around settlements can be postulated. But before attempting an analysis of these matters some empirical material is presented on recent changes in land values in England and Wales. This information provides an illustrative context in which to view the more general issues discussed later in the chapter.

Land values in England and Wales

There is not a single market for property rights in land but a wide range of specialised markets. Horticulturalists wanting a site for a market garden would prefer a few acres in the Fens of Lincolnshire to the same acreage in the City of London, while an international banker will want the site in the City of London for his banking hall and office no matter how much cheaper the land in the Fens. And this lack of homogeneity in the land market, resulting from the range of demands placed on land as well as the variable characteristics of individual sites, makes the collection of reliable statistics about land values very difficult. Disregarding the market for dwelling houses, there are only two sub-markets where there are sufficient transactions for a reliable index. These are for agricultural land and for residential building land. Even then it is important to remember that sales of agricultural land may include an element of hope value for an urban use and that the price of residential building land is affected by the proposed density at which the land is to be developed.

The published indices of agricultural land (see the MAFF/Inland Revenue Series) and housing land prices (see *Housing and construction statistics* prepared by the DOE) are disaggregated to a regional level. Even at this level, however, they only indicate a trend in values and are not a reliable guide to the actual value of specific parcels of land or to the conditions of local markets because of substantial differences in value within regions. Within the south-east, this difference is recognised because the figures for residential building land are disaggregated for Greater London, the Outer Metropolitan Area and the Outer South-East. Disaggregation is only possible where there are sufficient transactions – for example, only 57 ha of residential building land were sold in the north of England during 1980 in just 32 transactions (*Housing and construction statistics* 1981) – and there is an inevitable conflict between wishing to subdivide the market and providing reliable data. This conflict affects the *frequency* of publication as much as the spatial disaggregation of the information. Because of rapid changes in land values during the 1970s, both in real terms and as a result of high rates of inflation, there is continual pressure for up-to-date statistics and the MAFF publishes information quarterly and the DOE (*Housing and construction statistics*) twice yearly. No indices of land price are published for other types of urban land although indices are produced for different types of land and buildings. These are based on valuers' opinions of the market and are not normally expressed in absolute terms but as an index only (e.g. surveys by the RICS of City of London office rents).

Despite its shortcomings the DOE's residential building land index provides

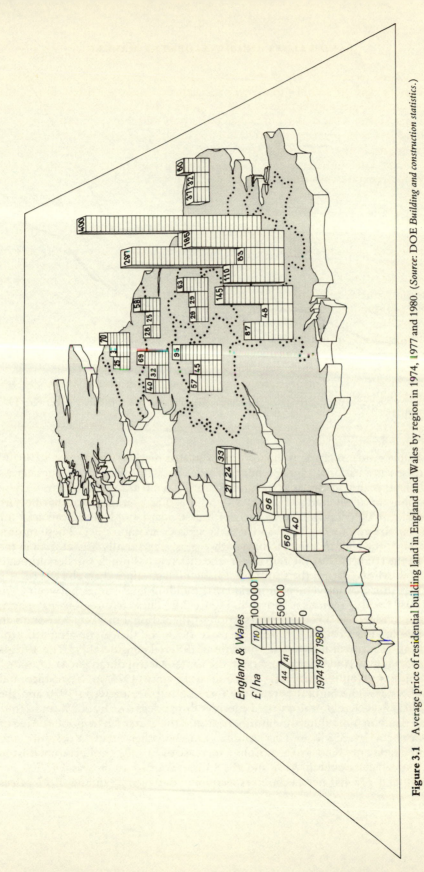

Figure 3.1 Average price of residential building land in England and Wales by region in 1974, 1977 and 1980. (*Source: DOE Building and construction statistics.*)

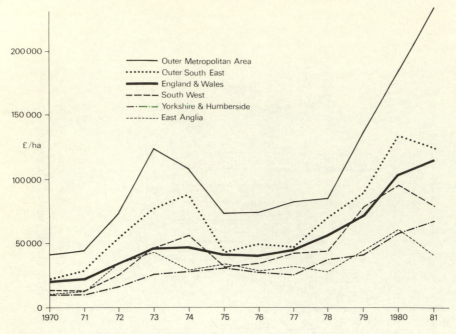

Figure 3.2 Average price of residential building land in a sample of English regions between 1970 and 1981.

a valuable guide to changes in land values in that market. The index is usually expressed as a national average, but this hides wide differences in values across the country and in the way the market moves in different regions. These variations are illustrated in Figures 3.1 and 3.2. The average prices per hectare for residential building land in each of the standard English regions and for Wales in the years 1974, 1977 and 1980 are shown in Figure 3.1. These figures reveal that the level of values in the south-east is substantially higher than in the rest of the country. For the remainder, the difference is much smaller although the West Midlands and the south-west have higher values than elsewhere.

The pattern of movement in residential building land values between 1970 and 1982 for five regions is shown in Figure 3.2. These five regions have been chosen to represent a rough cross-section of the national market. Although an increase in values occurred during the early 1970s and then again after 1977 for all areas, the rate of increase and its timing differed considerably. The 1972–4 property boom saw prices peak first in the Outer Metropolitan Area of London and in East Anglia but prices did not peak until 1975 in Yorkshire and Humberside. The highest percentage increase in price between 1970 and the peak year in each region also varied considerably; prices rose by 202% and 215% respectively in Yorkshire and Humberside and the Outer Metropolitan Area of London but by 353% in East Anglia. On the other hand, Yorkshire and Humberside only recorded an absolute increase of £10 300 per hectare whilst in the Outer Metropolitan Area and the Outer South-East it was £47 700 per hectare and £35 400 per hectare respectively. Between 1975 and 1977 prices remained fairly static in all regions. The fastest rise in 1978 occurred in the Outer South-East where land prices rose by nearly 50% in 12 months. Significant increases took place in all regions during 1979 and 1980 but, like the 1972–4 boom, prices peaked at different times. Prices fell in the Outer South-East, the South-West and East Anglia during 1981 but rose in the outer Metropolitan Area of London and in Yorkshire and Humberside in that year. Values rose again during 1982 and, by the end of the year, had reached a new peak in every region. These figures show that even though a common national trend is apparent in housing land values, local forces are clearly important. Unfortunately, there have been few attempts to analyse the statistical evidence at a regional scale, mainly because of the relatively small number of transactions occurring in some regions in some years (see Neuburger & Nicol 1976). It is with this factual background, and with the problems of providing reliable empirical evidence, that we return to the three issues listed at the start of the chapter.

The pattern of land values

Investigations into the pattern of land values around settlements date from Hurd's study first published in 1903 (Hurd 1970). It could be thought, therefore, that there is little need for further discussion of the subject. It is well known that the level of land values generally declines as distance from the urban centre increases. Our main concern, however, is with the *rate* of decline in values in two key locations of the city – the urban fringe and the inner city. Although both locations have been studied separately there has been no adequate analysis which properly takes into account the effect of development control on values for the whole city; but before this can be attempted some discussion is necessary of the way in which land values are determined in the market.

The demand for development land is a derived demand and the price of land is largely demand-determined, notwithstanding the erroneous assumption that the supply of land is fixed (see Goodchild 1978a); of course, it may be argued that the total area of land is fixed, but the amount offered for sale in the development land market at any one time varies substantially in response to market forces. The demand for development land has two components – the demand from purchasers who wish to *use* the land for a specific and probably new purpose, and the demand from *investors* wishing to enjoy an increase in the capital value of the land (Darin-Drabkin, 1965). We define use to include the development of land whether for owner-occupation or for profit, and therefore the purchase of land as an investment is restricted here to transactions where the purchaser's intention is to hold the property until an appropriate opportunity to sell it at a profit. The distinction between the two types of purchaser can be less clear in practice because the investor may decide to develop the land himself or the user/purchaser sell without developing the land. Nevertheless, the main difference between the user and the investor is that the former is concerned with the value of the land that is derived from its economic rent while the investor is concerned with future expectations of the land's worth which may bear no relation to its current earning capacity (Neutze 1973).

USER DEMAND

The value of land in a city is highest at its central business district (CBD) because that is the area where some users will lose most if they are not located within it. These users are the most sensitive to location. Retailers are prepared to pay high rents to occupy the prime shopping pitch because this is where their turnover will be maximised; head offices seek prestigious addresses; and for many office users there is only one place where business is transacted, for example, the Law Courts for solicitors and barristers, and Lloyds for insurance brokers. They can operate more efficiently if located close to this place and are prepared to pay a rent for that privilege (see also Goodall 1972). But although the advantages of a CBD location remain for many commercial users, rents have been bid up to levels that make it an unattractive location to some of those who have traditionally carried out CBD functions and wish to expand their premises. This applies particularly to manufacturing industry and to some service industries such as wholesaling (Fothergill *et al.*, 1983). These users have less steep bid-price curves (see Richardson 1978) than, say, retailers and the slope of their bid-price curves has declined as the CBD has become more congested.

The demand for residential accommodation in the inner city has reduced because industrial employment is no longer concentrated there. Furthermore, the apparent paradox of those on the lowest incomes occupying the most valuable land, explained most elegantly by Alonso (1964), no longer holds so surely, because much of the employment for that group of workers has moved to the suburbs. As a result, there is no need to bid up land values there simply to reduce the cost of travelling to work. The decentralisation of employment has affected residential occupiers' bid-price curves so that their preference is now generally for a peripheral location rather than a central one (Scott 1982). As a result, the value of land for residential use is higher at the urban fringe than in areas adjacent to the CBD where the quality of the environment is often low. Although it can be argued that transport costs will increase in the future because of the exhaustion of the world's supply of fossil fuels, emphasising the importance of accessibility, the revolution in telecommunications is likely to more than compensate for this and to encourage further the general process of counter-urbanisation. It is unlikely, therefore, that the historic pattern of residential values, one of consistent decline from the CBD to the fringe of the city, will return.

INVESTOR DEMAND

Investor demand represents the 'pure' speculative element in the demand for land. Two types of speculator can be identified in the market for development land. The first type aims to achieve a short-term profit by purchasing land with planning permission (or land where a consent can be readily expected), holding it until the value has increased and then selling. The second type of speculator is prepared to wait longer by purchasing land without planning permission and selling it once consent has been granted. Such speculators may have to wait ten years or more before this happens and will often purchase the land at little more than its value in its current use. This latter type of speculation can occur in any of the sub-markets for development land (including land for re-development) and at any time. Short-term speculators are attracted into the market when prices begin to rise more rapidly than in other investment markets and are expected to continue to do so. Short-term speculators do not exert much influence over the spatial pattern of land values, although they may increase the value of short-term hope land proportionately more than long-term hope land, but they do affect the way land values move over time (see below).

The demand for land from long-term speculators, on the other hand, may consistently affect the pattern of values because they can out-bid 'users' in the two locations under consideration. Where land at the urban fringe does not have planning permission for an urban use, the only user demand will be from agricultural or other rural occupiers. They are likely to be out-bid by investors speculating that planning permission will be granted at some date in the future. The only serious competitors may be hobby farmers, who are primarily buying themselves a country life-style rather than a commercial farm, and mineral operators, who themselves may have long-term speculative goals with the development of their reclaimed mineral land. In the inner city beyond the CBD the demand from users is often weak, although investors may be prepared to speculate that the CBD will expand and so out-bid any users who are interested in the current use of the site. It is now necessary to examine in more detail the ways in which values are determined in these two key locations.

THE URBAN FRINGE
The *detailed* pattern of land values at the urban fringe is important because there is a considerable difference in value between agricultural land and the greenfield

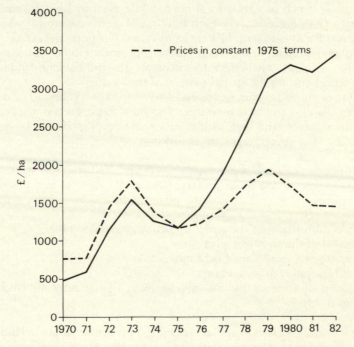

Figure 3.3 Average price of vacant possession farmland in England and Wales between 1970 and 1982 (solid line). (*Source*: MAFF/Inland Revenue Agricultural Land Price Series (allowing a 9-month time lag).)

site with planning permission for residential development. The price of residential development land in various regions is shown in Figure 3.2 and that for vacant possession farmland in England and Wales between 1970 and 1982 is contained in Figure 3.3. Agricultural land prices rose from under £500 per hectare in 1970 to over £1500 per hectare in 1973 before declining to £1080 per hectare in 1975. Between 1975 and 1980 they rose rapidly to £3304 per hectare but have declined in real terms since then. As with residential development land prices, there are significant inter-regional differences in price and the timing of price increases and falls (see Munton 1976). In 1980, for example, average prices ranged from £2214 per hectare in the four most northerly counties of England to £3565 per hectare in the South-East and £4017 per hectare in East Anglia.[1] These differences are small, however, compared to the difference between agricultural land prices and residential development land prices. In the Outer Metropolitan Area of London, for example, the gross difference was approximately £40 000 per hectare in 1971, £112 000 per hectare in 1974, £75 000 per hectare in 1977 and £151 000 per hectare in 1980. Put another way, in 1974 residential development land prices were about 100 times higher than agricultural land prices but only about 50 times higher in 1980. These figures must be treated with caution as they do not refer to identical areas but they do provide a useful general guide to price differences. More specific data for London's Green Belt, as a special case, are given in Chapter 7.

The south-east of England as a whole represents an extreme case by national standards but residential building land around Leicester, for example, is worth 20–25 times as much as agricultural land, while even in Lincolnshire where agricultural values are relatively high in national terms and residential values low, there is still a five- to tenfold increase in value. The potential capital gain for a successful speculator in urban fringe land is enormous. Given the considerable incentive to speculate, what effect does investor demand have on land prices at the urban fringe and on the spatial pattern of land values?

The value of rural land can be expected to rise as the likelihood of development taking place on that land increases. The Sheaf Report sets out seven stages at which the value of land that is ultimately to be developed may be enhanced (DOE 1972b). The seven stages are as follows:

(a)   Identification of a sub-region as a growth area by a regional strategic plan
(b)   Identification of the main preferred zones for development within the sub-region by a draft structure plan published as a basis for public participation
(c)   Formal submission of the structure plan to the SOS (DOE)
(d)   Approval of the structure plan
(e)   Publication of local plans (including action area plans)
(f)   Formal adoption of local plans
(g)   Provision of services for the development of the relevant land (DOE 1972b, p. 49).

Although it is unlikely that proposals affecting a particular parcel of land will be made at each of these seven stages, the probability that planning permission will be granted increases at each stage. A speculator will be prepared to offer a greater percentage of the final value of the land with planning permission as each stage is reached, and as recent research in North America demonstrates, the proportion of rural land owned by investors and developers grows as the prospect of development in the near future increases (Brown *et al.* 1981).

It is a widely held opinion that there is a large amount of market activity between the stage when urban interest is first shown in a site and the stage when planning consent can be obtained (see, for example, Brocklebank *et al.* 1978), and this is frequently the case in North America (e.g. Brown *et al.* 1981, Bryant 1982). Other evidence suggests, however, the opposite conclusion. Drewett, for example, concludes that there is one market in agricultural land with no, or very little, prospect of development taking place and another in greenfield sites with planning permission for development, including sites that are virtually certain to obtain a consent within a reasonable length of time (Drewett 1973). Intermediate markets are regarded as of small importance in the British context of comprehensive land-use planning. It is reasonable to assume, however, that the amount of speculative activity (or the size and importance of 'intermediate' markets) depends on the degree of urban restraint being imposed around the margins of cities, by green belt restraint for example, and on the general state of the property market. At times of property boom and rapidly rising land prices when development land is much in demand, such as between 1971 and 1974, speculative activity increases. Indeed, the imprudent purchase of land with limited development prospects at inflated prices was one reason for the collapse of a number of development companies during the mid-1970s. Our own research, though confirms Drewett's view. Our study of landowners in Leicester revealed very few sales and acquisitions of greenfield sites while the planning status of the land was uncertain. The results from our study of the sales of land in the Metropolitan Green Belt show a similar picture. In no year did sales of land with 'hope' value exceed 10% of the total area of land sold and in three of the five years it was less than 5% (see Ch. 7). The conclusion we drew from the data was confirmed by the opinions expressed by district valuers practising in the Metropolitan Green Belt area. These findings are developed later in the book and were undoubtedly influenced to some degree by the firm imposition of restraint.

This conclusion is surprising given the incentive to speculate. The most likely explanation for the relatively few transactions in land with 'hope' value is that most landowners are not willing to sell their land until there is a real prospect of planning permission being granted, because they seek all or most of the development value in their land for themselves. The value of a greenfield site with long-term development potential depends on an estimation of its value if consent is immediately obtainable, less an allowance for risk because it is uncertain when consent will be granted (this affects holding costs or the opportunity costs from having capital committed in this way), or whether it will be granted at all. As a result, the difficulties many developers and land dealers experienced in the mid-1970s has encouraged them to take out options or conditional contracts with landowners rather than to purchase the freehold ahead of obtaining planning permission (see p. 70).

Theoretically it is possible for an owner to determine the present value of his land by summing the expected future income from its current use (say farming) until it is developed, by estimating the land's future development value (in current terms), by determining the expected date of the sale, and by discounting these values back to the present at a rate of interest that reflects the opportunity cost placed on these sources of future income (see also Clonts 1970). In its simplest form, this approach to determining the present value of potential development land may be formulated as follows:

$$V = \left(a - \frac{a}{(1 + i_a)^t} \right) \bigg/ i_a + \left(\frac{c}{(1 + i_c)^t} \right)$$

where V is the present value per hectare, a is the expected annual agricultural income per hectare, i_a is the discount rate applied to future agricultural income, c is the expected sale price of the land when sold with planning consent for urban development per hectare, i_c is the discount rate applied to the expected sale price of the land, and t is the time (in years). This formula allows for the use of different discount rates for future agricultural income and the expected sale price of the land as the owner's assessment of the risk attached to these different sources of future income may well vary. In particular, the owner may attribute a higher risk, and thus impose a higher discount rate, to the sale value of the land than to future farming income.

The value of V is largely dependent on the discount rates adopted, the expected value of c and the length of time (t). As a theoretical approach to determining the value of V, the method implicitly assumes that buyers and sellers agree on the values to be attributed to the terms in the formula. But these values depend a great deal on judgement, expectation and knowledge, and ignore the bargaining that will inevitably ensue between purchaser and vendor over the sale price of the land. It is more realistic to assume, therefore, that the owner will in practice calculate the lowest price at which he is prepared to sell and that the potential purchaser will calculate the highest price which he is prepared to offer, each making due allowance for their own attitudes to risk (see Raiffa 1968). The agreed price may differ substantially from either of these figures but it has to fall within their range. The comparatively small number of transactions that take place in these circumstances in Britain suggests that either owners are more prone to take risks than potential purchasers, or, more probably, that owners' estimates of the probability that planning permission will be granted are more optimistic than the potential purchasers' estimates. As a result, the potential purchaser is rarely prepared to offer a sufficient sum for the landowner to be willing to give up his freehold interest.

This analysis suggests that the price of land in the urban fringe begins to reflect 'hope' value only when there is a good prospect that planning consent will be granted in the near future. Once the development potential crystallises, however, the value of the land increases very rapidly. Hope value is concentrated close to the edge of the urban area and land values decline sharply to agricultural levels beyond this point. This is especially the case in areas of firm planning restraint, as Boal has sought to argue from his study of Belfast (Boal 1970). He was concerned, at a theoretical level, with the effect on land values of the imposition of a green belt around the city and he recognised that there would be a large disparity in values on either side of the green belt's inner edge. He imagined, however, that speculative pressures would be totally removed from land within the new green belt, although this is not completely so in practice. For example, speculative pressures will remain where development land prices are high, as in the area of the Metropolitan Green Belt, because no area of restraint can be fully effective. It requires the grant of very few planning permissions to maintain an owner's belief that he will obtain planning permission one day too, no matter how severe the stated restraint policy. Speculation then takes the form of investors and dealers offering to purchase options (see Ch. 7) on such land and in the submission of optimistic planning applications.

The reverse can be said to be generally true when planning is less effective, as in the United States. The work of Brown *et al.* (1981) reveals that around cities in North America, 'urban' ownership features – such as the acquisition of an interest in land by investors – begin to arise in locations where the investor does not anticipate development occurring for many years. Indeed, the whole thrust of their argument, based on their empirical research, is that

> Because of the opportunity for speculative profits from appreciation in land values, the character of both rural land and of its ownership begin to change more than 20 years before an area is actually urbanised, and long before public policy efforts to influence urban development typically take form (Brown *et al.* 1981, p. 131).

However, in Canada where controls on new development are more effective than in the USA, Brown *et al.* (1981) found fewer speculative purchasers. Thus, the absence of speculative purchasers in Britain prepared to acquire the freehold appears to be due to the certainty created by the planning system. Although speculative pressures do exist, they are simply expressed in a different way, mainly through the purchase of options.

The value of land at the urban fringe in Britain is determined largely by its planning status, whether planning consent has been granted or whether the site is allocated for an urban use in a development plan. The demand from users for residential building land does vary but it is always likely to produce an offer well in excess of the agricultural value. This is the crucial difference between the determination of land values for greenfield sites and for urban re-development sites, as is shown below.

INNER CITY AREAS

Attention has focused on inner city areas recently partly because of the amount of vacant and under-used land that is to be found there. The explanation for this phenomenon cannot be expressed simply in terms of the change in the location preferences of certain users originally found close to the CBD and the effects of this change on land values. Institutional and structural factors are also important.

As Hallett points out, there is inevitably going to be *some* vacant land and property within an urban area because a city is a living organism that must adapt to changing circumstances if it is to survive and prosper (Hallett 1979). While the change is taking place the former use must vacate the property before it can be replaced by a new one. The more serious problem occurs, however, where there are no uses which want to replace the former ones. In many inner city areas there has been a considerable reduction in manufacturing employment since the 1950s as a result of positive attempts by local and central government to re-locate such employment outside the city, because of the congestion associated with inner city sites and the inability of firms to expand there, because of the preference of new firms for medium-sized towns in more rural parts of Britain (see Fothergill & Gudgin 1982, Massey & Meegan 1982) and as one consequence of the general economic recession of the late 1970s and 1980s. In a few locations, however, manufacturing employment has been displaced by commercial development, partly, it is suggested, because factory owners have been able to sell their premises for a substantial profit. Owing to the strength of demand for offices in London, developers have been able to offer large sums for office development sites which exceed the value of the factory premises in their existing use.

Even within less dynamic cities than London, where the demand from commercial users is less buoyant, changes of function still occur. The development of covered shopping centres since the mid-1960s within the CBDs of many towns and cities has had a major impact on the pattern of values within the CBDs. The development of two new shopping centres in Nottingham provides a good example. They opened in the early 1970s and have not only caused a reduction in trade (and therefore in value) in some previously good secondary retailing locations, but they have also caused the prime shopping area to move from Lister Gate/Albert Street to Clumber Street. The effect of the two new centres has been to shift the principal shopping route to the east, raising values in, for example, Bridlesmith Gate by a substantial amount and reducing them to the west of Old Market Square (see Fig. 3.4). This is not an isolated example, as the development of shopping centres at Leeds and Newcastle-upon-Tyne demonstrates (see Davies & Bennison 1977).

The value of an inner city site can, therefore, be expected to alter over time. Although its location is fixed in a geographical sense its relative location can be altered in an economic sense by improvements to the transport network, to the infrastructure or by the re-development of a neighbouring site. Location can also be 'altered' by the gradual expansion of the CBD so that a site that would have been regarded as too peripheral for a CBD function a few years previously, such as Whitechapel as part of the city of London, now assumes one.

Changes in the value of urban sites usually take place gradually. It is difficult to predict both the speed and magnitude of that change because demand is not constant. An increase in value is not so dependent on the granting of planning permission as in the urban fringe, except where consent is obtained for a use which is restricted, as, for example, with offices in central London. The value of an urban property in its existing use with its existing buildings (if any) is independent of its development value and there is no guarantee that the property is more valuable as a re-development site. It can be expected, therefore, that there will be more speculative activity in the market for urban sites because there is less certainty that development values will increase, so the incentive for the existing landowner to hold on to the property is less obvious. Where the level of user demand is low or non-existent, however, the landowner may not be prepared to sell for a nominal sum, simply because he anticipates that someone will want to use the land at some future time. Indeed, he may have little to lose by holding on to his land, and possibly much to gain.

As with idle land on the urban edge, the value of a vacant urban site is determined by the expectation of its future worth rather than its current

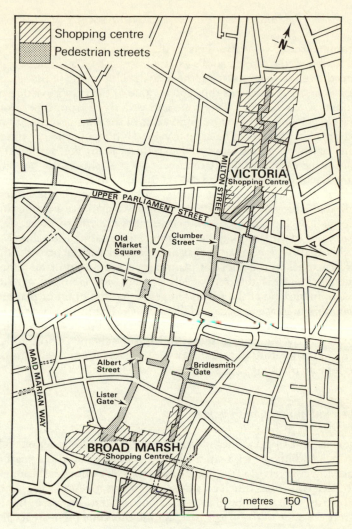

Figure 3.4 Shopping centre development in Nottingham.

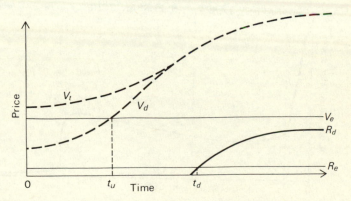

Figure 3.5 Change in value of a vacant urban site awaiting development.

income-earning capacity. This is illustrated in Figure 3.5. R_e represents the rental obtained from the land's existing use as, say, a surface car park. R_d represents the rental obtained from the new developed use of the site net of development costs. V_e represents the capital value of the land's existing use which, like the rent R_e, is constant over time and is derived from capitalising the income flow (R_e). V_d represents the capital value of the land assuming that development takes place at time t_d. The capital value (V_d) at a particular time is the present value of the expected flow of net returns from the developed use (R_d) and ignores the capital value attributable to R_e. V_t shows the capital value that the market would offer for the land on the assumption that the development can profitably be undertaken at time t_d and it allows for the future income flow realisable from R_e. Development will not start until income flow R_d exceeds income flow R_e, i.e. at t_d, but, because it is *expected* to exceed R_e, the development value of the land (V_d) is greater than the existing use value (V_e) after time t_u.

This analysis is similar to that noted earlier for the urban fringe but the key difference lies in the effect of planning permission on land values in locations experiencing very different levels of demand. Demand generally exists for development land at the urban fringe so that the grant of planning permission *allows* this increase to occur (Hallett 1977). The same need not apply to urban sites. Planning permission may be obtainable but re-development will not be underaken by the private sector unless the scheme is profitable. The level of demand is therefore the crucial factor in determining the value of an inner city site, not its planning status.

The resultant pattern of values

The pattern of land values indicated by this analysis is set out schematically in Figure 3.6. This shows a rapid fall from a peak value at the heart of the CBD to much lower levels of value in the inner city. The values in the inner city are likely to be determined as much by investor demand for future uses as by demand for current uses. In the suburban zone, values tend to rise very slightly to approximately the edge of the urban area. Within this zone there are local peaks in value

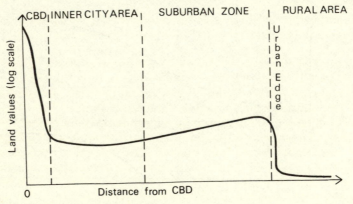

Figure 3.6   Land values in and around a city.

where there are local commercial centres or land suitable for industrial use, or high-class residential areas with local amenities (these are not shown in Fig. 3.6). At the urban edge, land values fall away sharply to agricultural values.

This analysis of the pattern of values within the city is similar to the one put forward by Hallett (Hallett 1979) which in turn is based on research by Bourne (Bourne 1967). Hallett, however, does not analyse the pattern at the urban edge. Where consent can be obtained for, say, residential development in a village in the urban fringe but a short distance away from the urban edge, the level of value is likely to differ little from that at the urban edge. The traditional concept of a declining pattern of land values for residential development may still hold, but it only becomes readily apparent some way from the edge of the city. This is not only because levels of private mobility have improved but, as the 1981 Population Census shows, more people now appear keen to live in rural surroundings and in small to medium-sized towns.

The level of land values and time

It is widely assumed that land is a good investment because it increases in value at a faster rate than inflation. This notion goes back to J. S. Mill's famous comment that 'landowners make money, as it were, in their sleep' (Mill 1871). Certainly, the value of land has risen faster than most other forms of investment, including equities, in the post-war period in Britain. Land prices rose almost continuously until the early 1970s when the property crash of 1974–5 showed that land values could fall. Land prices have risen again since the mid-1970s, but high rates of inflation have tended to obscure the real pattern of recent change, which is best described as cyclical and uncertain rather than confidently upward. This is illustrated particularly well by changes in agricultural land prices when these are measured in constant terms (see Fig. 3.3).

Of greater interest are the longer-term movements in values. Hallett argues that land values do not grow at a faster rate than inflation. He bases his conclusion on an analysis of three separate sets of statistics:

(a) Official or unofficial figures of land prices, deflated by income, construction costs or retail prices
(b) The proportion of site costs in the total costs of new housing
(c) Estimates of the share of 'pure' land rent in the national income.

Unfortunately all the statistics he quotes are open to doubt in one way or another (Hallett 1979, pp. 83–95).

Hallett relies largely on Vallis's series, which provides an index of values between 1892 and 1969, for his data on land prices (Vallis 1972). It is the only index that compares values for a variety of land markets in England over such a long period and it is very valuable for that reason alone. The actual figures do, however, need to be treated with caution. This is because they are based on auction sales data only up to 1964, depend on a relatively small number of observations for such a long period, and cover a period for which there is no single, agreed deflator of general price changes. Nevertheless, Vallis aggregates his figures into five main time periods (see Table 3.1) and these portray

Table 3.1 Land prices in England by type of property 1892–1969 (in thousands of pounds per hectare). Price medians, as recorded in columns A and as deflated to constant 1900 prices (columns B). Decimals rounded to the second place and values converted to metric figures making some of the percentage change figures, which are the original, slightly inaccurate.

Year group	Industrial land A	B	Commercial land A	B	Residential land A	B	Agricultural land A	B
1892–1916	3.30	3.30	50	50	0.62	0.62	0.05	0.05
1917–1930	0.70	0.35	44	25	0.77	0.40	0.06	0.03
1931–1945	3.14	1.80	52	30	2.20	1.28	0.07	0.03
1946–1963	10.25	2.47	346	86	11.12	2.47	0.21	0.04
1964–1969	29.40	4.69	576	91	26.19	4.20	0.49	0.07
percentage change in price between first and last year groups	+795	+43	+1065	+85	+4140	+580	+900	+50

Source: Based on Vallis (1972, pp. 1211 & 1406).

reasonably consistent trends. Values in all the property sectors rose faster than retail prices over the *whole* study period, and have risen further in real terms since, but values fell in all sectors after the First World War. Land values also rose as fast as average earnings between 1890 and 1976 and many would regard an investment very highly if it appreciated at the same rate as average earnings over such a long period. They might well consider that Mill's comment was justified and Hallett's position open to some doubt.

Hallett's use of the other two indicators in support of his proposition is open to more serious criticism. Although the widely respected Nationwide Building Society's estimate of the site value of a dwelling as a percentage of the total cost of new houses shows that the percentage remains to this day slightly in excess of 20%, this measure ignores the fact that plot sizes have declined, particularly in the post-war period (see Drewett 1973). Thus, although the proportion of land value in the finished house price may not have altered, this is only because plot sizes have been reduced and housing densities increased. It is noticeable, too, that Vallis's figures show a large difference in the growth rates for residential land prices and building plot prices. The former increased by 580% in constant terms (see Table 3.1) but the latter by only 111% in the first seven decades of this century. Hallett also quotes the low proportion (4.4%) of factor income rent in the national income statistics for the UK as indicative that there has been no long-term upward trend in land prices in relation to national income. The basis on which this proportion is derived for the Blue Book statistics is itself open to doubt, particularly as it purports to include the imputed rent received by owner-occupiers.

Hallett's analysis of the movement of land values over time is most helpful, however, because it is an attempt to study an emotive issue objectively by adopting a long-term perspective. Yet the land price data he employs, *over the time period he uses*, do not seem to support his position. Land values *have* risen in real terms during the 20th century and it may be argued that the difficulty in increasing the amount of land available will, with rising demand, lead to land having a scarcity value unless it can be used more efficiently. It may, then, remain a particularly attractive investment, especially at times of inflation. But taking a long-term view, we would be in broad agreement with Hallett. The demand for the goods and services supplied by the use of land largely determines the land's rental and capital value. This is clearly demonstrated by the cyclical pattern of values during this century, largely in line with the state of the national economy (see Table 3.1). Unless those goods and services that are particularly dependent on land gain in *relative* importance within the economy – and we see no particular reason why this should occur – then we would not expect land prices to rise in real terms indefinitely. Within this broad picture, however, there may well be periods and places in which particular sectors of the land market will exhibit substantial rises in value, perhaps in response to changes in public policy stemming from, for example, even more severe restrictions on the supply of development land (see below).

The supply price of land

There are two opposing positions which have been put forward regarding the supply price of land. The traditional view, simply expressed, is as follows: land exists in the natural order of things and costs nothing to produce. It is also limited in supply and users are prepared to offer rent to occupy it because there is not enough to go round. In most cases, it is more worthwhile for the owner to allow his land to be used in return for rent than to leave it vacant. The decision whether to let should not be influenced by the amount of capital invested in the land because the expenditure on the capital improvement cannot be recovered (Ely & Wehrwein 1940). In this analysis, therefore, (which assumes that landowners do not have monopoly power but are competing for tenants) the landowner has no influence on the level of rent that he can obtain from his land and has to accept the level of rent the market offers.

The alternative analysis is more recent in origin and focuses on the sale price rather than the letting price of land (see, for example, Lichfield & Darin-Drabkin 1980, Evans 1983). The analysis emphasises the monopoly power that each landowner holds because his parcel of land is unique. It is argued that landowners can withhold their land from the market until the price has risen to a level acceptable to them. Even if this means keeping the land vacant, the landowner does not necessarily lose. The land does not deteriorate with the passage of time and leaving the land vacant may ensure that the most advantageous development proposition is not missed (Neutze 1973). The conclusion drawn, therefore, is that landowners have considerable monopoly power and can effectively determine the sale price of their property by withholding it from the market until they decide to sell (see also Drewett 1973).

Which of these opposing views is correct or more nearly accords with reality? Before this can be considered, it needs to be established whether the landowner has a minimum supply price below which he will not sell. This is in fact the case because under normal circumstances the landowner will not sell unless he is offered at least as much as the land is worth in its current use. In the urban fringe, land will not be converted to an urban use from agriculture unless an amount exceeding the agricultural value of the land is offered. Similarly, the supply price for an urban site must exceed its existing use value if its owner is to sell. There is, however, an important difference between the supply of greenfield sites and of urban sites. The existing use value of most greenfield sites on the edges of settlements does not vary greatly, at least in relation to urban development land values (see above). However, the existing use value of urban sites does vary widely because of the differing uses being carried out upon them, the different sizes of buildings and their state of repair. In consequence there is a greater variation in the supply price for urban than for greenfield sites, and the higher the price offered by a prospective purchaser the greater the number of urban sites whose owners' supply price will be exceeded.

'Costs of supersession' also prevent land from moving freely from its existing use to a new use. A bare margin between its value as development land and its existing use value is insufficient, and not just because there are transfer costs involved in the transaction, such as solicitors' fees. The proprietor of an old factory, for example, requires from its sale a sum that will enable him to re-establish his business at a new location, including a sum to cover the inconvenience of the move. The same kind of analysis applies to greenfield sites but in a slightly different manner. The acquisition of a whole farm for development is relatively straightforward. The farmer should be able to acquire a new unit with the sum received from the sale and have plenty of capital left over after allowing for removal costs. The position is not quite the same where part of an agricultural unit is sold for development. It may be difficult for the farmer to acquire a similar area to that sold if the land is to be contiguous with his existing unit as less than 2% of all farmland in Great Britain is sold each year. If he cannot purchase additional land nearby, the land remaining after the sale may be insufficient to form a viable holding and it may be more difficult or costly to manage. It follows that the farmer, part of whose land is to be acquired, is likely to have a higher supply price per hectare than one who sells his whole farm for development (for a discussion of this issue see Bell 1979).

There is a further factor that needs to be considered. Amenity considerations which cannot readily be measured in pecuniary terms are important to some owners. A residential owner-occupier may well not be prepared to leave a home in which he or she has lived for many years even though offers have been submitted for the property which substantially exceed an objective assessment of its current market value. The costs of supersession in this type of case can be considerable and a sale may only take place for reasons unrelated to the financial gain obtained from the transaction. It is clearly erroneous, therefore, to regard the landowner as having no supply price. However, further analysis is necessary to determine whether landowners can and do influence land values more generally. This depends on the nature of the supply curve for land and how changes in the supply curve influence the quantity sold and the price of those sales.

Pennance has argued that increases in the supply of development land have no effect on the sale price of new houses because their selling price is independent of land and building costs (Pennance 1969). This is because the number of new houses offered for sale at any time forms only approximately 10% of the total number of houses on the market, as the annual supply of new dwellings is very small compared with the existing stock of dwellings (see Neuburger & Nicol 1976 and Goodchild 1978a for a more detailed exposition of house price determination). As a result, developers have little control over the price at which they can sell new dwellings and are, in fact, operating under conditions of monopolistic competition (see Lipsey 1983). The demand curve facing residential developers is very elastic because a small change in price will lead to a large change in the number of houses sold. If prices are increased, sales will fall off rapidly because home buyers will switch to the second-hand market. A small reduction in price, however, will lead to a significant shift from the second-hand market because new houses will then be cheaper.

The same analysis applies to the value of new commercial buildings even though office occupiers are prepared to pay a premium for new office accommodation. It may not be appropriate, however, for industrial building land where the preference shown by users for new industrial accommodation is much stronger and accounts for the paradox that in 1981 there was still a boom in industrial development despite the severity of the recession and the large amount of industrial space that was vacant (see King & Co. surveys).

Concentrating on the residential sector for the time being, developers have a maximum price that they can offer for land. This is determined by the price at which they can sell the finished house, the cost of building it and their profit margin. Even though developers may rely on inflation to help them out, they cannot automatically pass on increases in costs to the house purchaser because he will either buy an existing dwelling instead or not make a purchase at all, if the price of the new house rises. Thus, if the developer pays more than his maximum price for the land it will either reduce his profit margin or the houses will remain unsold. Developers, therefore, will not offer landowners a price that exceeds their maximum figure unless they are desperate for land and are prepared to reduce their profit margins. If landowners are not prepared to sell at this price, and they may be under no pressure to do so, they cannot be sure that the developer will be prepared to offer a similar price in the future as this will depend on what happens to house prices. Even though the landowner may anticipate that values will rise in the long run, there may be no immediate increase in the price offered because of short-term fluctuations in the housing market.

There is, therefore, at any one time, a maximum price which developers can afford to offer for a parcel of land and a minimum price below which its landowner will not sell. Where the bargain is struck depends largely on the amount of residential building land available for sale. As planners have attempted to restrict the amount of development land (see Ch. 2), so developers have often been forced to bid up to their maximum price simply to secure land. As a consequence the market price of development land is often well in excess of the landowners' supply price, but this is so because of the high price purchasers are prepared to pay for housing rather than the ability of the landowner to bid up the price of his land. The landowner is therefore, at any one point in time, a price taker unless he controls so much development land that he has monopoly power. In practice this is unlikely, particularly as there is nothing to prevent other landowners or developers attempting to break the monopoly by seeking planning permission on other land (see also Brown et al. 1982).

It will now be apparent that there is an important difference between the argument put forward at the start of this section and the one contained in the previous paragraph. The argument at the start of the section, which suggests that the landowner is a price taker, is based on the renting of land and not selling it outright. It does not pay to leave land vacant for long if it can be let, and a rent is money valuably received if it covers the variable costs of letting and makes a contribution to the fixed costs of holding the land, as long as the letting does not severely prejudice what the land can be used for in the future (see Ch. 6). A sale, however, is a final action. Land can be sold by its owner only once, unless of course he buys it back. If the landowner feels that the price offered is not sufficient he can refuse it and withhold the land from the market.

Can landowners simply wait until values rise to a level where their expectations regarding its market price can be realised, as Lichfield and Darin-Drabkin suggest? Theoretically this is possible because there is nothing to stop an owner withholding his land for as long as he wishes unless powers are obtained to acquire his land compulsorily. Whether his act of withholding will actually cause land values to rise because of the monopoly he holds over the supply is less likely. Even though each parcel of land is unique by virtue of its location, there are likely to be other sites which are close substitutes so that the degree of monopoly power held by an individual landowner is rarely significant, and in the last analysis developers will not consciously and repeatedly build houses at a loss. But what happens to land prices if a number of landowners decide to withhold their land at the same time?

To answer this question it is necessary to investigate the nature of the supply and demand curves of building land and, to simplify the matter, the analysis is restricted here to the supply and demand curves for residential building land. In the short term the demand curve for residential building land at a given level of values for housing accommodation is likely to be elastic, i.e. a small decrease in the price of land will result in a large increase in the amount of land demanded by developers because their profit margin on each house will increase encouraging them to build more houses and new developers will also be attracted into the market. This conclusion on the elasticity of the demand curve for land is confirmed by Lipsey's analysis (1983). He argues that the elasticity of demand for a factor of production is determined by the elasticity of demand for the industry's product, the proportion of total cost made up by payment to the factor and, lastly, the ease with which other factors can be substituted for the one in question. Although there is no easy substitute for land, the elasticity of demand for new houses is high and land forms a significant part of total costs, typically 20% of the total.

The demand for land is a derived demand where the amount of new housing produced is small, relative to the total stock of houses, with future expectations playing an important part in developers' decisions. Demand is, therefore, volatile and liable to move rapidly; but as the aim of this analysis is to ascertain the effect of owners withholding their land and refusing to supply, it is assumed that the level of demand is stable. This is a realistic assumption in the short term while house prices and building costs remain reasonably constant.

According to Neuburger and Nicol (1976), the supply curve for development land is more inelastic than the demand curve. They estimated a supply price elasticity of 0.4. This indicates that more owners are prepared to sell their land as the price increases but because the supply is limited, by the amount identified on development plans for example, there is not that much more to offer. This is illustrated by the number of housing plots sold during the property boom in the early 1970s (see Fig. 3.8 below).

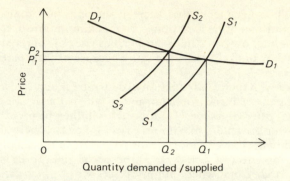

Figure 3.7 The effect of changes in supply on the price of development land.

The effect of a reduction in supply on the price of development land is illustrated in Figure 3.7. D_1–D_1 represents the demand curve for development land; S_1–S_1 represents the original supply curve; OP_1 and OQ_1 represent the initial price and the quantity of land sold respectively. When the supply of development land decreases to S_2–S_2 the effect is both an increase in price to OP_2 and a reduction in quantity sold to OQ_2. Because the demand curve is elastic, the greater change takes place in the quantity sold with only a small increase in price. Thus, owners are unable to get either an immediate or a significant increase in the price a developer is prepared to offer for their land by with-holding it.

In the longer term, however, land prices are likely to increase because fewer new houses will be built as the supply of land is restricted. In time, assuming that the demand for housing does not decline significantly with the price increase, house prices will increase because of the shortage of supply. This will allow developers to increase their maximum price and move the demand curve for land upwards. Landowners will then be able to get the higher price they wanted. Thus

> It is not easy for landowners to force up prices. This is possible only if their withholding of land so affects the amount of new development being carried out that the value of existing accommodation increases. Then developers will be able to obtain higher prices for new space and conse-quently have a larger sum to offer for the land (Goodchild 1978a, pp. 26–7).

Evans (1983) reaches a similar conclusion which is that landowners can influence land prices, but he does so by a different approach without distinguishing between short- and medium-term effects. This conclusion is reached mainly because he does not specifically consider the elasticity of demand for develop-ment land.

If landowners can influence land prices by withholding land collectively, in what circumstances are they likely to do so? Although it may appear to some that landowners are a tightly knit group with a common outlook, this is not the case, particularly when each owner devises his own investment strategy. An investment in development land can only be realised by selling that land and it will be argued in Chapter 5 that there is an optimum time at which each landowner should sell if he is to obtain the maximum return from his investment. Although all owners gain if land values rise, the optimal time at which each should sell is unlikely to be the same because of their particular financial circumstances.

More generally, if there is a reduction in demand for new houses, there will be a reduction in the demand for land and a fall in the maximum price that developers will offer, and fewer landowners will then be prepared to sell their land at the lower prevailing maximum price. Likewise, there are other events that alter landowners' expectations, causing a shift in the supply curve. Take, for example, the effect of a new tax imposed on the proceeds of the sale of development land. Landowners' supply prices will be increased because their proceeds net of tax will be reduced and, as a result, they will require a higher minimum price. In Britain, the imposition of taxes on development land has always been regarded as controversial. The main political parties have disagreed on this aspect of land policy (see Ch. 2) and the party in opposition has usually promised to repeal the measures introduced by the Government. As a result, when a new tax has has been introduced (or repealed) landowners have been encouraged to speculate on a change in government, and to sell or withhold their land accordingly.

While the development charge, betterment levy and development land tax were in operation it was widely reported that the supply of development land was reduced. Evidence of the development charge's effect on supply is largely anecdotal even though those sympathetic to its purpose accepted that supply was reduced by it (Parker 1954). More detailed evidence is available about the effect of betterment levy on the supply of land. Neuburger and Nicol (1976) conclude from their study of house and land prices between 1963 and 1973 that land prices were a function of house prices in both the current period and the previous period, while the volume of land sold was a function of current land prices and the presence or absence of the betterment levy. While the betterment levy was in operation they estimate that the supply of land was reduced by 30%, but they did not find that betterment levy affected land prices. The immediate effect of the introduction of betterment levy in 1967 was to reduce the supply of land. Land prices rose quite rapidly between 1968 and 1970 (Drewett 1973), even if the increase was subsequently made to appear insignificant by the rise that occurred during the period from 1971 to 1973 (see Fig. 3.3). But the increase in land prices was also associated with an increase in house prices and Neuburger and Nicol do not say whether the introduction of betterment levy had any effect on house prices either immediately or in the future. It would require very sophisticated statistical analysis to prove this hypothesis and the data available on house and land prices are almost certainly too imprecise to be subjected to such an analysis. Analysis of the effect of development land tax on the supply of development land is also limited apart from our own research. While DLT was levied at a maximum rate of 80% between 1976 and early 1979 a significant volume of land in Greater Leicester was unlikely to be offered for sale (see Ch. 6).

The aggregate position for England and Wales, based on an index of private sector housing land prices adjusted for inflation between 1970 and 1981, together with the number of transactions in housing land, is shown in Figure

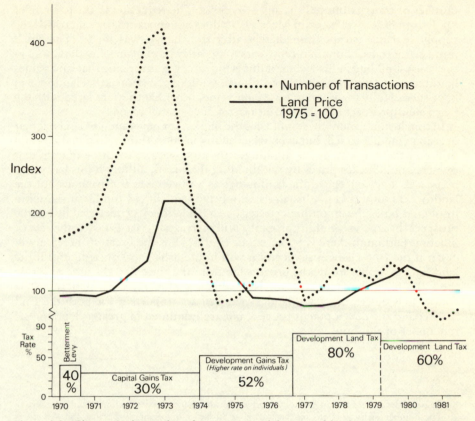

Figure 3.8 Changes in the number of transactions and the price of development land in relation to capital and development gains taxes, 1970–1981.

3.8.[2] The boom of the early 1970s stands out. The volume of transactions increased rapidly during 1971 and 1972 as soon as betterment levy was removed, although capital gains tax remained. It is noticeable that the supply increased before land prices had begun to rise in real terms, even if both prices and the number of transactions reached their peak in the first half of 1973.[3] The rapid fall in the number of transactions from that peak was well under way before development gains tax was introduced on 18 December 1973. The introduction of DGT appears to have helped this trend but the market was collapsing anyway.

The position in 1976, however, is more interesting. The Labour government announced its intentions for land policy, including a development land tax, in its White Paper *Land* (DOE 1974) published on 12 September 1974. Because of Parliamentary pressure of business, the Government was unable to introduce DLT at the same time as the Community Land Act. As a result, a number of owners sold during 1976 before DLT came into force on 1 August, to avoid the higher tax rates payable under it, despite the fact that the market price was comparatively low. In the half-year following the introduction of DLT, the number of transactions fell sharply – by 50%. The reduction in the top rate of DLT from 80% to 60% from March 1979 does not appear to have increased the supply of land, except immediately after the change was made. The small numbers of transactions in recent years may partly be explained by the slump in the house-building industry but, if this is the case, it is surprising that land values have remained as high as they have. One possible explanation is that landowners have successfully managed to raise land values now that they are faced with the permanent prospect of a significant tax on development land.

In conclusion, landowners influence the market for development land by their decision whether to sell, but even when acting in concert they do not affect land prices in the short term. In the longer term, however, theory suggests that owners can influence prices by withholding their land, although this has yet to be *proved*. The concept of the landowner as a price taker is erroneous but the landowners' power is not usually as extensive as Lichfield and Darin-Drabkin imply. As far as the investment strategy of a landowner is concerned he has the prospect that the value of his property will increase at least as fast as the rate of inflation (although there is no certainty of this), but the greatest increase will occur if the land changes its position within the urban spatial structure. If the land 'moves' either inside the urban edge from the agricultural fringe or inside the CBD from the inner city, the land's value will increase dramatically. The factors that determine when landowners sell are important for both the land market and the development process and are examined in greater depth in the remainder of this book.

Notes

1 Regional definitions are not exactly the same as for the residential development land price series.
2 The number of transactions has been used as an indicator of supply because this statistic is available for each half year while the actual number of plots sold is available for whole years only. The number of transactions tends to understate slightly the variations in the number of plots sold but it shows the general pattern quite clearly.
3 There is a time lag of approximately 4 months from a transaction taking place and it being reported in the housing land statistics.

4 The development process

The policy context and the operation of the land market are analysed in the previous chapter. These have an important bearing on how development takes place and how those involved in this process behave. These aspects of the development process are analysed below so that a greater understanding of the landowner's role in this process can be provided.

Stages in the process

The development process begins when a parcel of land is considered suitable for a different or more intensive use, and is completed when the necessary changes have taken place and the land re-occupied. Lichfield (1956) provides one of the best known accounts which can be summarised as follows:

(1) The 'maturing of circumstances' that make possible a change in the use of land, for example the construction of a new road or the selection of a settlement for expansion
(2) Purchase of the land by a person prepared to develop it
(3) Preparation of the land for development, including both 'physical' construction work and 'abstract' operations such as establishing legal title to the land
(4) Preparation of the development scheme, including obtaining all the necessary consents, especially planning permission
(5) Arrangement of the finance to carry out the development
(6) Construction of the development scheme
(7) Its occupation by either the developer, a new owner or a tenant.

This description pertains primarily to the development of a greenfield site on the urban edge and there is no comparable outline for the cycle of re-development. There is, however, a reasonably well-defined course that a site follows once it is in urban use (Bourne 1967). Bourne suggests that the first stage of the cycle occurs when the original structure is used for a new function, or for the same function but more intensively. Examples include the conversion of a suburban house into a number of flats or its occupation as offices. The next stage involves the partial alteration of the original structure to improve its utility in its new use. The final stage arrives when the structure is demolished and replaced with a new building. The cycle may then start again, but it will not necessarily progress in a uniform manner. Deterioration in the original structure is universal but demand from new uses or a more intensive use will not manifest themselves everywhere and some parts of the city will experience a general deterioration of its built structures with no compensating re-development, leading eventually to derelict buildings and vacant land.

A revised account of the development process for the urban fringe is provided

Table 4.1 The land development process after Drewett (1973).

Stages of development	Non-urban use	Non-urban use; under urban shadow	Urban interest	Active consideration (1): planning permission	Active consideration (2): purchase of land	Active development	Purchase of development
description	in agriculture, or woodland, or other non-urban use; possibly idle	changed use: greater intensity of use, multiple use, recreation, idle	decision agent recognises land has potential for a time period	agent contacts planning authority and/ or government for development permission	agent contacts another agent re possible land sale	physical development of land	purchase of property and occupation
decisions	opportunity costs lower than present use	relative location change or pressure of opportunity costs	decision to consider land	decision to purchase land	decision to purchase land	decision to develop land	decision to purchase
decision agent	landowner, speculator, developer	landowner, developer, speculator	planner, developer, landowner, speculator	developer, planner	developer, planner	developer, planner	consumer
financial support	unchanged	agricultural mortgage corporation	preliminary arrangement of financing	preliminary arrangement of financing	purchase of raw land loan	construction loan	mortgage local authority

Source: Drewett (1973).

by Drewett (1973; Table 4.1). It is adapted from a description of the American situation portrayed by Weiss *et al.* (1966). Drewett's description emphasises the importance of the pre-construction stages, equivalent to Lichfield's 'maturing of circumstances'. He lays greater stress than Lichfield on the developer's decision to purchase the land and the need for planning permission. This may reflect the different timing of the two accounts. Lichfield was writing in the mid-1950s when the development control system was still in its early years, although he does reiterate his 1956 description in his later work (Lichfield and Darin-Drabkin 1980). By the time Drewett wrote his account, the importance of development control and the need to obtain planning permission was not in doubt. An even more recent study seeks to qualify Drewett's account by arguing that Drewett over-systematises what, in practice, is a complicated sequence of events (Barrett *et al.* 1978). The sequential nature of the development process is not contested, but Barrett *et al.* maintain that the stages can be reduced to no more than three broad *sets of events* – development pressures and prospects, development feasibility and implementation. These sets of events correspond approximately to stages (1)–(2), (3)–(5), and (6)–(7) respectively in Lichfield's process, but the authors say that within each of the three broad phases the more specific events described by Lichfield and Drewett will not occur in any prescribed order. Their development pipeline is a useful aid for categorising aspects of the development process. They do not claim, however, that it is a model for showing the significant relationships between the actors involved and it is towards this aspect that this chapter is directed.

It is essential to recognise that the development of land cannot proceed unless agreements are reached between a variety of actors, and agreements may only be reached after considerable negotiation. The developer, for example, has to agree to purchase the land and the landowner agree to sell. Planning permission has to be obtained and this may involve the planner in lengthy discussions with applicants (see Ch. 2). In order to illustrate this perspective the chapter focuses first on the principal actors involved, and then draws aspects of the development process together by examining the way land passes through the development pipeline and by re-defining the development process in terms of its key *events*.

The actors in the process

A large number of actors can be involved. Lichfield includes:

the original landowner or any subsequent purchaser of the land; the developer who undertakes the process; the building industry, including the professions connected with it; the legal profession; the public authorities; the persons lending money; the ultimate consumer who may be a tenant or owner of the finished development (Lichfield 1956, p. 4).

The crucial decision in bringing about a development may be taken by any of these actors, although the developer is usually regarded as playing the key role in both the English and American development processes (see Craven & Pahl 1967, Clawson 1971, Lichfield & Darin-Drabkin 1980, McNamara 1983). Craven and Pahl attribute the key role to the developer because he is responsible for carrying out the development scheme and may also persuade owners to sell land by approaching them directly. In the American case, Clawson regards the developer as 'the innovator, the one who starts the change' (Clawson 1971, p. 75), although others highlight the importance of land dealers in the purchase of farmland, often years before this is sold to developers (Brown *et al.* 1981, Bryant 1982). The choice of the other principal actors is more difficult. Drewett, for example, includes the landowner, speculator, planner and consumer (see Table 4.1). Massey, on the other hand, includes the planner, financial intermediaries and property owners (Massey 1969).

In this case we intend to exclude the consumer from the discussion because of our overall concern with the supply of development land and the landowner's role within this. The landowner's decisions rarely impinge directly on the consumer, although changes in consumer demand influence land prices to which the supply of land responds. Consumer demand, however, is not for the land itself but for the buildings constructed upon it. The consumer is not, therefore, a principal actor within the development process, although his behaviour does influence it.[1]

The roles of the principal actors

THE DEVELOPER
The developer and those who loan him money are the risk takers in a development project. Three types of project may be distinguished:

(a) Development for sale, for example dwellings for owner-occupation
(b) Development for letting, such as local authority housing, and shops, offices and industrial buildings for occupation by tenants
(c) Operator's own development, i.e. development for occupation by the developer himself.

Development of all three types is carried out by both the private and public sector, but the amount of public sector development for sale is limited. Different factors are important for public and private sector developers. Public sector developments are not normally undertaken solely for financial reasons. A local authority may make a profit from carrying out a central area re-development scheme but the scheme is undertaken with the main aim of improving facilities for the local community. A private sector developer is primarily seeking a profit from a scheme, although prestige obtained from carrying out a particular development may be a subsidiary consideration. Public and private sector developers tend to approach their tasks differently. The public sector developer proceeds more slowly because of the need to consult the public and to have decisions approved by political masters. The private sector developer attempts to complete the task as quickly as possible, unhampered by such consultation unless imposed by public bodies (for further details see Cadman and Austin-Crowe 1983).

The developer's key area of activity is widely regarded to be his decision to purchase land (Drewett 1973) and, in the English context, this decision has been widely studied (e.g. Craven 1969, Harloe *et al.* 1974, Bather 1976, Economist

Intelligence Unit – see DOE 1975b, 1978c). Drewett (1973) acknowledges the need for additional skills, including technical and management skills, in construction, the ability to tap sources of finance and competence in marketing the final product. The developer is faced with intense competition. In 1983, 9127 separate 'firms' completed at least one house in Britain while there are currently (1984) approximately 3800 members of the House Builders' Federation. The large builders, however, produce a significant proportion of the total output. Both Barrett and Wimpey each build close to 10% of the new houses completed annually and the top 25 developers produced 41% of the 1983 total (NHBC 1983). However, despite a tendency for the large companies to increase their share of the market there are still many builders producing less than 10 houses per annum. The size of the development company and its links, if any, as a part of a conglomerate, affect its land acquisition policy and its ability to ride out difficult market conditions in an industry that is renowned for its cyclical pattern of activity (Ball 1983).

Acquiring land   The developer needs to acquire land regularly to maintain a production flow of dwellings and other properties, and to retain the full employment of his labour force and other factors of production. This land needs to be suitable for the type of dwelling that the developer specialises in building, and it must not be purchased in excess of a price that allows the developer to make a profit having regard to anticipated building costs and the sale price of the finished houses. Lastly, the sites must either have planning consent already or the developer must anticipate that planning consent will be granted before he wants to commence development.

   There are a number of methods by which developers acquire land. Drewett (1973) suggests seven, namely

(a) *Lobbying*   The developer contacts local estate agents and surveyors, obtaining particulars from them of sites, if and when these become available.
(b) *Saturation*   The developer employs a research team to identify the likely areas of future growth from a local planning authority's policy documents and then contacts the appropriate landowners to negotiate terms.
(c) *Personal*   Contact with local solicitors and building societies who through their own contacts introduce the developer personally to dealers in land.
(d) *Contact with area planning officers*   Area planning officers are asked to indicate the land that is available for development in planning terms.
(e) *Auctions*   Although use may be made of them, developers prefer not to purchase land at auction because prices tend to be higher than at sales by private treaty.
(f) *Direct approaches by landowners*   Landowners may consider their land suitable for residential development and approach developers directly. This method can result in land being purchased at a lower price than if it is bought through estate agents.
(g) *Land acquired from other development companies*   This is land which is sold for one of the following reasons: where the developer can no longer afford to hold the land or decides to cease trading altogether; where the land is

surplus to requirements; or where the developer considers it more profit-able to sell the land rather than to develop it himself (see also Ball 1983).

Evidence of the relative importance of each method is provided by Bather (1976). He found that most development land is offered for sale by the landowner, often through an estate agent. Developers, however, do obtain a significant proportion of their land by approaching the landowners directly, although only 2.8% of Bather's sample relied exclusively on this method. The amount of land obtained in this way appears to be declining partly because owners are now more aware of the market value of their property, so that this is no longer a means of buying land cheaply (Weinburg 1976). The extent of land trading by developers appears to be limited and for most developers is a small part of their activity (DOE/HBF 1979). This aspect of developer behaviour is specifically considered below (see Ch. 6).

Type of land purchased   Developers have a choice of purchasing either land that has been allocated for development, or on which planning permission has been granted, or land which is not programmed for development known as 'white land'. The advantage of buying 'white land' is that it can be purchased much more cheaply than land which is allocated for development because there is a real risk that planning permission will not be granted. Costs will be incurred in obtaining planning consent through both the charges for applying for planning permission and for appearing at an inquiry if an appeal is lodged against a refusal of consent by the local planning authority. These costs will need to be reflected in the price that the developer pays. Even more important, where consent is granted it may take so long to obtain that the holding costs incurred from interest charges result in a higher effective purchase price than for land that already has planning permission. Not all developers are prepared to take this risk, and in Bather's survey in Reading 43.7% of the sample said that they never purchased 'white land' (Bather 1976).

The most common way in which the purchase of 'white land' is undertaken today is through an option or conditional contract. An option is an agreement that allows a developer to buy land at an agreed, fixed price by serving notice on the owner at any time within a specified period, normally two years. A conditional contract is one that does not take effect until a specific event occurs, usually the granting of planning permission. A time limit is imposed by which date the event making the contract unconditional must have taken place. The difference between the two is this. A developer who holds an option *can* buy the land at any time during the duration of the agreement. A developer who holds a conditional contract *must* buy the land if the event on which the contract is conditional occurs. Thus, if planning consent is granted, the developer must purchase the land.

These arrangements reduce the developer's risk because the purchase monies are not paid to the landowner until planning permission is obtained. In addition, the purchase price is usually less than the price the developer would have to pay if the land already had planning permission and a discount of approximately 10% can be expected (DOE 1975b). The developer also benefits from this arrangement because his potential land bank is increased without committing a large amount of capital to an asset which may not produce a profit for some time. He usually only has to put down a small non–returnable sum at the time that the option or conditional contract is granted and bear the cost of obtaining the planning consent. The DOE's study concludes that: 'The widespread use of options on purchases of land without planning permission suggest that the time scale and problems [of buying "white land" outright] are such to exceed normal commercial prudence' (DOE 1975b, p. 44).

The latest information available suggests that developers are buying less 'white land' in the urban fringe than was the case during the 1950s and 1960s. This is probably due to the higher interest rates that have prevailed since the early 1970s, the existence of development land tax since 1976 and the reduced amount of land that has been released for development in the urban fringe with the onset of recession in the second half of the 1970s.

Developers have a further choice in their site selection which has become important to policy makers recently. It was widely thought that they were not prepared to develop inner city sites because of their poor environment (DOE/HBF 1979). However, a recent study has found that a significant proportion are prepared to develop such sites (Nicholls *et al.* 1980), a further example of local authorities confusing their physical planning criteria with the developer's wish to make a profit. The key criteria appear to be the size of the site and its environment, and that the vendor (normally a local authority) should not ask an excessive price for the site, whatever they had paid for it previously. Those sites which no developer would consider suffered mainly from the poor quality of the local environment. There is therefore no blanket objection by the private sector to residential development in the inner city as estates built by Wimpey and others in Liverpool show (see also Anderson *et al.* 1983).

Little detailed information is available about the ways in which developers of different size acquire land. Generally, only the large companies are able to employ specialist site finders, while the smaller companies rely on hearing about sites from their contacts. Large companies are also able to consider purchasing 'white land' more readily because they have the resources to spread the risk involved. Some large companies, however, do not acquire 'white land' as a matter of policy even though they have the resources to do so. Likewise, residential developers also differ in the degree to which they concentrate on building dwellings speculatively to sell to owner–occupiers. Some also carry out commercial and industrial schemes, and engage in land trading and general contracting. Some do not carry out their own construction work but subcon-tract it to a builder and take a profit by dealing only in the completed houses and the land. It is questionable, however, whether this distinction is important for understanding the development process as the key role of the developer stems from his initiating action on a site and risking capital by purchasing the land. The largest residential developers do, in fact, carry out their own building work unlike their principal counterparts among non-residential developers, such as Land Securities, Hammersons and MEPC. Residential developers who do not carry out their own building work proliferate only in those periods when such development is very profitable (DOE 1975b). This is partly due to the speed with which they can enter and leave the market, and partly because they cannot afford to buy land when the demand for new buildings is slack when builder–developers are prepared to undertake schemes for a builder's profit only.

Table 4.2 Private sector residential developers: estimates of stocks of land with planning permission for housing, number of private sector starts and number of years' supply of land 1977–1980.

| | | Number of 'starts' in previous 12 months | Land with planning permission (outline or detailed) | | | |
			Plots with main services available	Years' supply	All plots with planning permission	Years' supply
1977	February	144 000	310 000	2.15	350 000	2.43
	June	135 000	290 000	2.15	350 000	2.59
	October	132 000	270 000	2.05	310 000	2.35
1978	February	139 000	230 000	1.65	280 000	2.01
	June	147 000	240 000	1.63	270 000	1.84
	October	150 000	270 000	1.80	320 000	2.13
1979	February	150 000	240 000	1.60	270 000	1.80
	June	146 000	280 000	1.92	320 000	2.19
	October	145 000	230 000	1.59	270 000	1.86
1980	February	140 000	210 000	1.50	230 000	1.64
	June	133 000	180 000	1.35	210 000	1.58

Source: DOE.

Land banks To ensure a constant supply of building land a developer can either try to buy land as he needs it or maintain a 'land bank'. Even though interest charges have to be borne (whether notional or actual) and the demand for houses may change, the advantages to a developer of holding land are considerable. A land bank allows a company to plan a continuity of operation and, in rare cases, where they have a monopoly or are in an oligopolistic situation over the supply of development land, it may enable them to influence zoning, local development plans or even the price of development land (for discussion see Markusen & Scheffman 1977, Rydin 1983). The developer also benefits from any real increase in land values and avoids the necessity to buy land just to stay in business when land prices are high. There is no agreement, however, on the size of the minimum land bank required. In responding to Drewett's (1973) enquiries, developers maintained that the minimum required was 2 years' supply of land, while a survey by Shankland Cox (1972) found that most developers wanted less than a two-year supply and only 12.5% of their sample considered that more than this amount was necessary.

The actual, as opposed to the preferred, policy that developers adopt toward a land bank appears to differ widely. Studies of developers' land banks show them to be small or non-existent by comparison with the ideal of two years' supply of building land – an ideal that some developers relate to the length of time it usually takes them to get planning permission which often necessitates going through the appeals procedure. However, the picture shown in Table 4.2 indicates that developers held a minimum of approximately 1.7 years supply of land between 1977 and 1980. This is surprising as two recent studies found that, in one case, 40% of their sample of developers did not have a land bank at all and, in the other, 50% had less than a year's supply of land (Nicholls *et al.* 1980, Federation of Master Builders 1981). Table 4.2 is derived from evidence collected regularly by the DOE from a sample of house builders until 1980 when the survey was discontinued. The table shows the amount of undeveloped land with planning permission owned by builders at the relevant dates and these have been compared with the number of dwellings started by the private sector in that calendar year so that builders' land banks can be expressed in terms of the number of years supply, i.e. how long the land would remain undeveloped at the prevailing rate of construction. It should be emphasised, however, that for land to be included in the survey it must have both planning consent and be owned outright. Land without consent and/or 'owned' through an option or conditional contract is not included. It suggests that developers' land banks are larger than most surveys have revealed. This is probably due to the large proportion of undeveloped land being owned by the large house builders while the small developers own little (Smith 1982). The housing division of Tarmac PLC, for example, the third largest house builder, had a land bank amounting to 11 500 plots at the end of 1982, approximately 2.3 years supply (Tarmac 1982), well above average according to Table 4.2. Small companies can rarely afford to hold such a land bank, especially when interest rates are high. When interest rates fall the demand for housing increases because mortgage repayments are lower and the demand for building land increases. The developer then has difficulty in buying land to maintain production, let alone buying land for development in the future.

It is not clear to what extent developers are circumventing the problem of holding land by obtaining options or conditional contracts from landowners. It is known to occur on a significant scale in the Metropolitan Green Belt (see Ch. 7) and elsewhere, but the extent of individual developer's holdings has not been established, nor whether they regard such holdings as a substitute for owning land outright or as a complement to provide a balanced 'portfolio' of land.

The extent of developers' land banks is crucial to the development process if a steady stream of dwellings is to be produced. Developers vary the speed at which they develop sites to meet changes in demand (DOE/HBF 1979) but their flexibility without a land bank is limited. Without land banks a steady stream of production can occur only if land is allocated for residential development in a regular manner and if this land is supplied quickly by landowners.

THE PLANNER

Planners stand out from the other principal actors because they are the only group that, in the main, is not seeking to profit financially from the development process. Their aims are quite different and are defined principally by the ends to which they believe planning is directed and by how they should act out their professional roles as planners. Their impact on the way the development process operates thus depends on three related matters. First, in broad terms, it depends on the general scope and objectives of the planning system and the esteem in which the system and its officials are held by government and society. Second, it depends on the nature of the planning system itself, not only in terms of its statutory functions, but also in the discretion afforded to the officer in his day-to-day dealings with the other actors in the development process. The extent of discretion depends on what decision-making functions have been devolved to him by the planning committee, a matter of some importance with the growth of negotiation and bargaining between interested parties in recent years (see pp. 23–4). Third, it depends on how the planner sees his role within the system and, although we are primarily concerned with the local authority planner, the same point arises with officials from the DOE.

Although the scope of the planning system has not changed substantially since 1947 (see Ch. 2, pp. 16–17), the role of the planner in the development process is not the role that was envisaged by the architects of the 1947 Town and Country Planning Act. Their intention was that development would follow development plans and be carried out largely by the public sector. The planners would therefore determine the pattern of development and play the key role in instigating development. This has not, of course, happened because most new development has been undertaken by the private and not the public sector. Planners' expectations, however, have not changed. They believe that they should be able to influence development decisions more directly and have frequently called for more powers to achieve this (see, for example, RTPI 1976), instead of considering how their existing powers could be used more subtly to manipulate market forces (see Moor 1983).

The demand by the planning profession for a broader remit comes at a time when planners are subject to considerable public criticism, some of it mis-informed. The level of criticism does not appear to have been reduced, and if anything it has been reinforced by increased public participation in planning decisions. Moreover, to the public antipathy that local authority planners experience must be added the antipathy of central government. The present Conservative government has made it plain on several occasions that it believes local planning to be hindering the implementation of the Government's economic and social policies, and that therefore the local planning authority's powers should be trimmed in a variety of ways.

The planners exert their main influence over the development process through the development control system, but these powers have been closely circumscribed. In his modification of structure plans, for example, the SOS has struck out many promotional policies where these would affect the provision of educational and health services, services which other central government departments wish to determine (see Jowell & Noble 1981). Elsewhere, the Courts have interpreted the scope of the planning system narrowly, striking down planning conditions where local authorities have attempted to extend the notion of what constitutes a 'material consideration' (Purdue 1977). In the context of development control, local authorities are accused by government of delaying planning applications unnecessarily and thereby adding to the con-struction industry's costs while at the same time inhibiting the establishment and growth of business (House of Commons 1977, DOE 1980b, 1981a).

At a more detailed level, the General Development Order has been amended to permit the construction of extensions to residential property of up to 15% of the floor area without the need to obtain planning permission. This has been done to reduce the number of 'minor' planning applications with which the development control system is required to cope, particularly as very few of these are refused (see Ch. 2, pp. 19–20). It is quite clear though, that the need to obtain planning permission has been responsible for a better standard of design, and, more importantly, has ensured consultation with neighbours likely to be affected by development proposals. Like so many other areas of regulation in a mixed economy, the degree of control to be exercised is a political value judgement (see Lichfield & Darin-Drabkin 1980). On the one hand, the system of control requires a bureaucracy to administer it but on the other, without control, development will occur that has adverse effects on others not party to that decision to develop. At present, the planning system can fairly be said to be in retreat, despite the broader social and economic remit demanded for it by the planning profession during the 1970s.

This conclusion notwithstanding, the planner's influence on the development process is still clearly exerted both during plan preparation and when development control decisions are being taken. Developers are guided by planning policy documents because they cannot develop land without first obtaining a planning consent. Even though the developer may appeal against a refusal by a local planning authority, the SOS, or more likely his inspector, will decide the appeal having regard to the same planning policy framework. Indeed, it is through the local policy framework that the planner is able to indicate to the other actors those sites on to which 'urban interest' falls (see Table 4.1). Guidance may be direct or indirect. It will be direct where the land is precisely allocated for a new use on a local plan, slightly less so where a structure plan indicates that a settlement is to expand by a specific population. Even where there are no plans, landowners and developers must take into the account the likelihood of obtaining planning consent either from the local authority or on appeal in determining where urban interest is to fall.

The grant of planning permission depends on a number of factors which each party can recognise, such as the availability of services, site access and the degree of intrusion into the open countryside of the proposed development. As a result, planners have had some success in controlling the location of new development, especially at the urban fringe, and preventing scattered development in the countryside (Blacksell and Gilg 1981). They have also been relatively successful in preventing development taking place where they do not wish to see it (Wood 1982). The planners' policy framework, however, has not prevented the submission of planning applications on a considerable amount of land not allocated for development (see, for example, JURUE 1977). Although the vast majority of these applications have been refused, and most refusals upheld on appeal, this does not always remove speculative pressures and the expectation that consent will be granted eventually. The management of some urban fringe land has suffered in consequence.

There is a growing literature in which the discretionary nature of the development control system is emphasised[2] and, in particular, the difference between policy as formulated and policy as implemented (see, for example, Barrett and Fudge 1981). Contributing to these issues is the widespread use today of planning conditions and Section 52 Agreements (1971 Town and Country Planning Act) (see Ch. 2). Negotiation, or at least discussion, between applicant and officer now takes place regularly before a formal planning application is submitted. Officers see it as one way in which they can take advantage of the increasingly *ad hoc* nature of the development control system, in which less attention than formerly is paid to local planning policy and more to the merits of the particular case. Discussion provides the officer with an opportunity to persuade the applicant to amend the scheme so that it conforms more closely with the planner's own ideas of the most suitable form of development for the site in question (Caddy 1978, Underwood 1981). On the other hand, the applicant also has an opportunity to test the officer's general reaction to his proposal and to see on what grounds it might fail. Moreover, if he can persuade the officer of the desirability of the scheme he may acquire an advocate who will support the application when the planning committee meets.

One further consideration, how planners see their professional role, has also attracted attention recently, even if empirical evidence linking the success or failure of particular development schemes to planners' attitudes has been difficult to acquire (see Underwood 1981). Nevertheless, given the discretionary nature of the system, the potential importance of this matter means that it cannot be dismissed lightly. Research in the USA suggests that only a minority of planners see their role as either fitting the 'technical role model', that is they see land-use planning as a rational activity in which they provide value-free advice to decision makers, or the 'political role model' in which they form their own, committed positions which they then wish to see implemented (Vasu 1979, Howe 1980, Howe & Kaufman 1979). Most fall into a mid-way position, adjusting their particular stances in the light of particular situations and as the climate of opinion over the purpose of planning changes.

Studies of the attitudes and characteristics of British planners indicate that most have middle-class backgrounds and limited experience of other social contexts (Knox & Cullen 1981). This leads Simmie to suggest that planners are, at heart, middle-class conservationists and supporters of the status quo, with the effect that the planning system *as practised* is a regressive rather than a progressive instrument of social policy (Simmie 1974, 1981). Knox and Cullen prefer to ascribe a 'managerial' approach to most planners in which officials seek to balance conflicting interests, to be pragmatic and to follow the procedural rules. This does not mean that planners are politically neutral. Most of them appear to hold 'left of centre' ideals, and are generally supportive of community rather than individual interests. They are not, therefore, very favourably disposed to developers and landowners. Nevertheless, it does seem that planners generally support establishment attitudes and their actions are usually cautious; furthermore, except where, for example, they have strong support from the planning committee, they rarely adopt a bold approach to controversial development proposals. In this day-to-day planning situation Knox and Cullen believe planners to be influential *vis-à-vis* the other actors in the development process, but in a broader, societal context in which a particular view of the role of planning is being espoused, as by central government today, they would expect planners to conform to the ruling 'ideology' and to be incapable of exerting much influence on it.

To sum up, planners generally think that it is difficult to initiate development themselves, despite the intentions embodied within the 1947 Town and Country Planning Act. Though development control is not a wholly negative power, it is essentially passive because the power cannot be exercised until the private sector or a public body wishes to carry out development (Ratcliffe 1976). In many cases, developers and planners both want to see a particular site developed even if each has a different idea of the form that the development should take. Where one of them does not wish development to occur, either because the scheme is not profitable or, because the development is contrary to stated policy, *no* development is likely, and at some point society has to decide whether inaction, as on many prominent inner city sites, is preferable either to developments that will be provided by the market or to the public sector taking the initiative and employing scarce public resources.

THE LANDOWNER
The role of the landowner in the development process centres on his decision to sell his land and the way he goes about this. There is one feature that particularly distinguishes the landowner from the other principal actors. Both the developer and the planner take part in the process because it is their occupation and they can be expected to gain in experience and understanding with time. The landowner, in contrast, may understand the process if he happens to be a speculator or an owner of a large site in the urban fringe which has been developed in a number of stages over a long period; but he may also be a farmer or factory owner who has little previous experience of the process. A greater range of behaviour can therefore be expected from landowners, even to the extent that a few may be unsuspecting participants who do not realise that they own land capable of development.

Motives of ownership The great majority of private developers attempt to maximise their profits from a development. The same assumption is usually applied to landowners, but this can be misleading where some landowners are involved in the development process through no conscious choice of their own. Their actions are significantly affected by their motives of ownership, and these need not be profit orientated. An owner, whose main motive is occupation, may sell for a wide variety of reasons, including the fact that the property is no longer suitable for its existing use. This may affect the time at which the land is released as much as the sale price accepted.

Some owners remain primarily concerned with the use value of their properties, use value being defined as the benefits, financial and non-financial, derived from the occupation of the property. It follows that an absentee landlord is more likely to view his property as an investment and be prepared to sell it than will an owner-occupier (see Kaiser *et al.* 1968). Nevertheless, at some stage in the development process all owners will be made aware of the exchange value of their properties as developers seek to purchase the land, often making offers at many times the original purchase price. Owners who hold their land as an investment may be of two types, those who purchase and those who have inherited their land. Those who purchase may be regarded as 'true investors'. These investors can also be subdivided into those who seek a 'nest egg' or some means of protecting their personal assets from the effects of inflation and those whose business it is to make a living from the gains in capital values of the properties in which they deal, i.e. speculating. The behaviour of 'inheritors' is likely to be more variable. In some cases their behaviour will be indistinguishable from that of the profit-maximising investor, in others it will be representative of someone whose ownership is accidental and in which they take little managerial interest.

To these two principal categories of motive, investment and occupation, may be added at least two more. One is the making of land available for others to use on a non-profit-making basis. Although such uses may have charitable status and so be exempt from tax, this is not always the case. Most private sports clubs, for example, do not operate to make a profit but the clubs are liable to tax, usually as companies, through the profit they obtain. A non-profit-making motive may be combined with either of the two principal motives, or even both, but a property which is both made available for others on a non-profit-making basis *and* held as an investment is rare. A further motive may be called 'control' and it arises where the principal reason for owning a parcel of land is to restrict or influence that land's use for the benefit of other land held in the same ownership. An example is provided by the owner who holds land solely to prevent its development and so safeguard the amenities enjoyed by his own house. Land may be owned by industrial concerns or public utilities adjacent to their existing premises to permit expansion even if there are no concrete plans to use this land. This is particularly important where the costs of moving are very high so that maximum flexibility can be obtained by holding extra land. This is often the case with power stations, for example, because the existing site is linked to a distribution network. Such land may, therefore, be held vacant for a considerable period (see Markowski 1978, also Ch. 8).

In the case of individual or family ownerships, motive may well change between generations and even during the lifetime of a single owner. The owner's attitude will be affected by the number of children he wishes to provide for, and as he grows older he may want to sell, but not to change, his place of residence. He may be prepared, as a way of reducing his work commitments but not his ownership rights, to lease the land short term to a neighbouring occupier whilst retaining occupation of the house. Smith (1967) argues that owners who are older, are in poor health or have retired are more likely to sell than those who are younger, in good health and in full-time employment, and this is confirmed by Brown *et al*. (1981). The motives of owners are also related to their general financial or business circumstances, over and above whether they occupy the property for business reasons or not. In particular, the wealthy owner has much more scope to manoeuvre his assets in order to achieve his goals (Denman & Prodano 1972). Manoeuvring assets involves a cost and a landowner in a poor financial position may have to sell certain of his assets to achieve the desired change or may not be able to afford the best professional advice. In the development context, owners with limited resources have less options and they may not be able to hold out for a higher price even if they want to. Testing this hypothesis is difficult in the absence of information on owners' consociate wealth, or that wealth not represented in the land holdings of the owner. Not only may the assets of wealthy people be held in very complex legal forms, often to mitigate tax liabilities, but these complex arrangements also make it difficult to assess their worth.

Finally, Brown *et al*. (1981) in their study of undeveloped land outside seven North American cities asked owners why they had bought their land and, if it had been inherited, why they had initially decided to retain the land. Unfortunately, the authors do not allow for the possibility of mixed motives in their classification, nor do they discuss whether owners' motives have changed. This would have been helpful as over 40% of the land parcels had been acquired by the owners in their sample before 1960 and only 25% since 1970. The authors present a simple categorisation of owners – users, investors and developers. The results show that users hold just over 70% of the land, although many of those who live on the land are residential owner–occupiers not farmers. The authors record that

> individuals who identify farming as their primary occupation own only 8% of parcels and 26% of total land area in the four US cities. The majority of landowners are instead employed in business, a profession, in real estate, or are retired. In Canada, however, farmers own nearly a quarter of all parcels and one-third of the fringe land held for personal or business use (Brown *et al*. 1981, p. 134).

Investors own 15% of the land and about two-thirds of this is held by individuals or families and only one-third by syndicates or corporations. Syndicates and corporations are very active in the land market and unlike individuals the particular properties in the survey did not represent their chief asset. Real estate agents and other professional people associated with the development process are the main individual investors. Among developers, who between them own about 8% of the total area, an important difference emerges between the Canadian and US samples. In the United States, individuals and families account for half the developers, but in Canada the proportion was only 20%, reflecting the more highly concentrated nature of the Canadian development industry. The composition of purchasers, as defined by motive, changes as development pressures grow (see Table 4.3; also Bryant 1982), but users remain the largest *holders* of land even where development pressures are regarded as intense and are only in a minority when those who purchased their land since 1968 are treated separately. It may also be deduced from Table 4.3 that developers land bank on a small scale well ahead of the date of expected development.

Landowners and the development process Historically, landowners and landowner-ship patterns have had a considerable influence on the spatial layout of development (Ward 1962, Mortimore 1969, Olsen 1973) and landowners have even imposed their wishes on the type of development to be constructed (Jenkins 1975). The scope for this second influence has been reduced considerably by the introduction of statutory planning. The ownership of land in large blocks can facilitate development just as the speculative letting of potential development land can have the reverse effect (Berkman 1956, Gayler 1970). Compulsory purchase powers now make the ownership structure a less important influence on development but it still can create difficulties, for example, if an allotment site with a mass of small ownerships is allocated for residential development.

The impact of landowners' actions on the development process can also vary considerably. Where a landowner obtains planning permission for development on his property and decides to sell without undue influence from developers or planners, the landowner will have contributed positively to the process. On the other hand, the landowner's contribution will be insignificant if he sells following an approach by a developer at a time when he is making no active attempt to sell the land himself. The contribution is also limited if planning permission is not obtained by the landowner prior to the sale of the property. If the landowner is able to obtain an outline planning consent before marketing the

Table 4.3 Owners' motives for acquiring land by development pressure (per cent of land area).

	United States		Canada	
	Intense (%)	Moderate/weak (%)	Intense (%)	Moderate/weak (%)
All Owners				
personal use	57.3	82.1	46.0	85.3
investment	30.6	14.1	20.3	9.5
development	12.1	3.7	33.8	5.3
Owners Acquiring Land since 1968				
personal use	31.9	69.0	20.0	74.5
investment	48.9	24.1	30.0	14.9
development	19.2	6.9	50.0	10.6

Source: Brown *et al*. (1981, p. 136).

property, its attractiveness to a developer increases for he knows it will take less time to obtain a full consent than where no prior consent has been granted. The importance of applications submitted by landowners is illustrated by the monitoring of such applications in the planning register by developers. Developers can then inform the landowner of their interest in his land before their competitors (Bather 1976).

Landowners are responsible for obtaining planning permission on a significant number of development sites. A survey carried out by the DOE found that more than one-third of the land on which an outline planning permission for residential development had been granted in 1975 was still owned by its original owners in 1977 (DOE 1978c). Even where the land was owned by a housebuilder (the definition used in the report for a non-landowner), it is likely that some of the outline planning permissions had been obtained by landowners who subsequently sold the land to a builder. In a study of an area south-west of Birmingham in the early 1970s, applicants for outline planning permission for residential development were approximately evenly divided between 'private applicants' and 'companies and firms', although the proportion submitted by the former group was greater during the housing boom of 1972 and 1973. The refusal rate, however, was much higher on the applications submitted by private applicants (JURUE 1977).

The landowner's role in the development process may range from an active one that has an important bearing on where and when development takes place, to a passive role where he is manipulated by other actors in the process. The manipulation is at its most extreme where land is compulsorily purchased and it can reasonably be assumed that in such circumstances the landowner plays no part in the process except to negotiate the most favourable compensation terms he can. The landowner's role in the development process revolves around the decision to sell, and, in particular, the circumstances under which the landowner can be expected to sell as soon as planning permission is obtained rather than delaying the sale and so holding up the process.

FINANCIAL INTERMEDIARIES

The supply of finance is of special importance to the development process because the production time is usually measured in years, and because the capital sums involved are often large. In addition, some of the same institutions that provide development finance are also interested in purchasing the finished development for investment purposes, especially where commercial and industrial property is concerned, and this aspect is discussed first.

Insurance companies have always held part of their investment portfolios as property assets. However, it is only comparatively recently that they began to purchase property outright rather than granting mortgage loans or holding shares in property-owning companies (Cadman 1984). Insurance companies were originally content to lend both long-term capital at fixed rates of interest secured on commercial property by mortgage and short-term capital for developers to undertake development schemes. During the post-war period the continual rise in property values has encouraged them to invest directly in commercial and industrial property instead of by fixed interest loan (PAG 1975, Massey & Catalano 1978, Wilson Committee Report 1980). As a result, they receive the benefit of a rising rental income and capital growth from their investment. The long-term investment horizons of insurance companies and pension funds (see below), and the need for investments to increase in value in real terms to meet payment obligations 20–40 years hence, have enhanced the attractiveness of property for direct investment and have reduced the advantages of holdings in mortgages because they show no capital growth.

The rapid increase in the number and size of pension funds during the same period has also emphasised the importance of this type of financial investor. This growth is illustrated in Table 4.4 which shows changes in the insurance companies' and pension funds' assets between 1956 and 1981 and the proportion of total assets the institutions hold in property. Generally speaking, it is only the larger companies and funds that have been constantly active in the property markets as the size of individual investments can run into many millions of pounds. Smaller institutions invest indirectly in property by holding units in a property unit trust and by purchasing the shares of property companies. The pension funds have generally been slower than the major insurance companies to involve themselves directly in property investment but they are now catching up rapidly, as Table 4.4 shows. This is mainly because their asset base has grown so quickly in recent years as a greater number of employees have been included in occupational pension schemes and, more especially, as occupational pensions have been improved in real terms. Further real growth in pension fund assets is expected for some time to come (Wilson Committee Report 1980).

The financial institutions are now major purchasers of new commercial and industrial property and their attitudes do influence the type of property built. This is particularly true with industrial property. Because the institutions require long-term investments they have demanded high quality industrial buildings. It has been argued that the specifications they demand are unnecessarily expensive for industrial occupiers and not always suited to their requirements. Even so, developers have tended to build to the financial institutions' specifications rather than those of industrial occupiers.[3] Prior to the 1970s the financial institutions were content to purchase completed property investments without involving themselves, to any great extent, in the development process.

Table 4.4 Assets of insurance companies and pension funds (in millions of pounds) 1956–1981.

	1956	1961	1966	1971	1976	1981
Insurance companies						
land and property	409 (7.9%)	714 (9.1%)	1 107 (9.4%)	2 193 (11.4%)	5 584 (18.6%)	15 941 (21.5%)
mortgages	594 (11.4%)	1019 (13.0%)	1 762 (14.9%)	2 449 (12.8%)	3 157 (10.5%)	4 000 (5.4%)
total assets	5206	7854	11 787	19 197	29 949	74 305
Pension funds						
land and property	n.a.		115 (2.1%)	777 (7.7%)	2 708 (13.1%)	9 475 (14.9%)
mortgages			297 (5.5%)	252 (2.5%)	478 (2.3%)	233 (0.4%)
total assets		n.a.	5 385	10 042	20 714	63 666

Source: Annual abstract of statistics.
n.a., not available.

Since then it has become common for them to agree to purchase a development before construction work has been finished and, often, before it has even started. In return they provide the development finance for the project. This reduces the developer's risk considerably. All he has to do is to ensure the scheme is built within the anticipated time scale and find an occupier for it, although a letting may have to be arranged before construction starts as a condition imposed by the institution for providing the development finance (Boddy 1979, Ratcliffe 1984).

The role of the financial intermediaries changed after the property crash of 1974–5 following the collapse of some of the secondary banks (Plender 1982). After the crash, the supply of prime commercial and industrial property developments virtually disappeared because no developer was prepared or able to undertake them. To replace the shortage the institutions began to act as developers themselves. This activity is still confined to the largest concerns, such as Norwich Union Insurance Group and the Electricity Supply Nominees, who are best able to bear the risk and have the greatest need to invest large sums in property because they receive the most income. The signs are that, in future, more institutions will start acting as developers to ensure for themselves a supply of good quality property investments in a market where prime properties are becoming increasingly difficult to find (see PAG 1980).

The role of the finance provider in residential development is different. In the private sector dwellings are built for owner–occupation not like factories and offices which are built mainly to let. There is, therefore, no residual income-producing investment for a financial institution after the property is occupied, except as mortgagees. Building societies are the principal source of mortgage finance for home purchase but they provide very little finance to developers. The clearing banks also entered the home mortgage market in a substantial way in 1981–2, but have since left the market with the fall in interest rates (Cheshire and Evans 1983). Occasionally a developer will have an arrangement with a building society for the provision of mortgage finance to purchasers of his houses but this is a comparatively rare occurrence. Although increasing, this is the closest that building societies come to a direct involvement in the supply of residential property.

One survey carried out in Britain that expressly studies residential developers and their sources of finance found that they obtained capital from the same sources that most companies use, namely from the clearing banks and from their own internally generated capital (Nicholls *et al.* 1980). This study was principally concerned with private sector residential development in the inner city and whether the financial intermediaries influenced the developers' site purchase decisions in that urban context. The results suggest that finance is infrequently provided on the basis of site-specific considerations but rather on the 'track record' of the developer and the collateral he can offer. The study concludes that sources of finance do not influence residential developers' site purchase decisions to any significant extent but they may affect the scale of his business activity, just as the level of economic activity generally is influenced by the amount of money clearing banks are 'permitted' to lend following the advice given by central government to the Bank of England. The effects are particularly marked during periods when government identifies development activity as an area to be squeezed for lending, or at least accorded a low priority, as it did for a while in the 1970s following the property crash (see Plender 1982).

The role of financial intermediaries in the development process therefore varies according to the type of property to be built. In the case of residential development it does not unduly influence the process but for commercial and industrial development these intermediaries play a more important role, taking some or all of the risk normally undertaken by the developer and, it should be stressed, this role tends to increase with the size of the development scheme. Up to the present time the number of schemes where financial intermediaries have undertaken a major role is comparatively small, particularly as most schemes are for residential development where their involvement is minimal. As a result the analysis that follows does not consider the financial intermediary's role in the 'key events' of the development process, but it is likely that, in the future, this analysis will require reappraisal.

Key events in the development process

The previous discussion shows that each actor is constrained by the actions of the others, and we would maintain that, in the literature, the British developer is too frequently regarded as in a controlling position in the development process. The constraints upon his actions are considerable even if in his public statements he over-states the powers of the other actors, as reflected, for example, in the House Builders' Federation's statements on the supply of land. To the private sector developer, the powers of the public sector planner look formidable. The planning officer dealing with development control matters, however, sees things quite differently. 'His' powers are constrained by elected representatives, statutory undertakers and other public bodies such as water authorities, the availability of public funds and central government policies. The result is that all the actors in the development process tend to under-estimate their own influence rather than the converse.

This leads us to present a description of the development process that reflects this view rather than one in which the importance of the developer is emphasised. Before a site can be developed it must be *identified* as building land. A study of housing land availability found that this occurs in two ways. It was hypothesised that 'over a period of time land listed as allocated will move forward to be granted planning permission, outstanding permissions not yet started will move forward to become under construction, and sites under construction will move forward to be completed' (DOE 1975b, p. 13), a flow with four stages:

allocated → outstanding → under → completion
              permissions   construction
              not started

In their survey of the stock of residential building land in Surrey for 1972 and 1973 the investigators established, however, that not all land entered at the first stage, namely allocation (see Table 4.5). Elements of the 1972 stock had moved to a different stage by 1973. Construction had started on 6844 units in 1973 where there had been an outstanding planning permission in 1972, but two new elements were also contained in the 1973 stock. Land for 10 570 units was newly

Table 4.5 The land stock in Surrey: 1972 and 1973 (dwelling units).

1972 stock	Component of stock		1973 stock
	1972 allocations–no progress	17 178	
	new allocations	10 570	
23 491	total allocations		27 748
	1972 outstanding permissions, still outstanding and not started	3 113	
	1972 allocations, now with outstanding permission	6 313	
	1972 non-allocated land, now with outstanding permission	9 552	
10 751	total outstanding permissions (not started)		18 978
	1972 under construction, still under construction	2 740	
	1972 outstanding permissions, now under construction	6 844	
7 116	total under construction		9 584
41 358	total allocations, outstanding permissions (not started) and under construction		56 310
	Completions		
	1972 under construction, now complete	4 376	
	1972 outstanding permissions, now complete	790	
	total completions		5 166

Source: Department of the Environment (1975) *Housing land availability in the south-east: a consultants' study*, HMSO.

allocated, and planning permission was granted for 9552 units on land that had not previously been allocated. There were, in fact, more consents granted on non-allocated land than on allocated land. Thus, developers and landowners were able to obtain planning consent on land that had not previously been *identified* as building land and this formed 50% of the stock of outstanding permissions.

This survey was carried out at a time when there was an unprecedented boom in house prices and residential building land values, and in a region where the supply of land is severely restricted by planning policies. Ths amount of land entering the stock at the outstanding permission stage is still surprising. The finding is supported by a survey carried out in the West Midlands of the land released for housing development between 1968 and 1973 (JURUE 1977). Data from this study is presented in a different but still revealing way (see Table 4.6). The table records the allocations of land on which both planning applications for residential development were submitted and where consent was granted. Of the land area released, 38% was not allocated for residential development prior to the submission of the application. The imbalance in the applications is still more

Table 4.6 Gross area of land (in hectares) subject to a planning application for residential development in part of the West Midlands, 1968–1973.

Year	Allocation of land on Development Plan (ha)		
	Housing	Non-housing	Total
Land on which planning application for residential development submitted			
1968–69	103.4	470.5	573.9
1969–70	130.2	201.1	331.3
1970–71	130.8	182.6	313.4
1971–72	110.2	313.9	424.1
1972–73	146.4	397.6	544.0
Totals	621.0	1,565.7	2,186.7
Percentages (%)	28.4	71.6	100.0
Land released for residential development			
1968–69	64.9	43.2	108.1
1969–70	36.8	22.9	59.7
1970–71	81.1	39.3	120.4
1971–72	63.5	51.1	114.6
1972–73	84.7	48.9	133.6
Totals	331.0	205.4	536.4
Percentages (%)	61.7	38.3	100.0
Success rate			
Success rate (%)	53.3	13.1	24.5

Source: JURUE (1977, p. 50).

marked as over 70% were submitted for sites which were not allocated for residential use, and consent was granted on only 53.3% of the sites actually allocated for residential use. Thus, even where land is allocated for the same use as that applied for, it does not necessarily follow that the site will easily pass through the stages of the development process, usually because of arguments over density and access (DOE 1975b).

Development land can be identified, therefore, in two ways and by any of the three principal actors. Either land can be allocated for development on a statutory or a non-statutory plan, or a planning permission may be granted. This apparently simple division is, in fact, complex. A house and garden within an urban area are probably designated as within a residential zone on a development plan, but this designation does not usually anticipate that development or re-development will take place at a higher density. Such sites do not generally appear on land availability schedules because most planners set a minimum site size of 0.4 ha in their search for land. However, the amount of development land likely to come forward on small sites has recently become an important issue (see Rydin 1983).

Land identified, when allocated for development, need not have been identified solely by the planners. When a review of land allocations in a district is carried out, the planners' attention may be drawn to particular sites because planning applications had been previously submitted by developers or land-owners. As a result, the site is allocated for an urban use. This was particularly noticeable during the period when county structure plans and local plans were being prepared. The situation at Wigston in Leicestershire provides a good example.

Wigston is a major suburb on the south side of Leicester. In the approved structure plan (Leicestershire County Council 1976) it was indicated that land to provide homes for 1500 people should be allocated there with its precise location to be defined in the local plan. A developer submitted applications on two sites of approximately 25 ha each on the south side of Wigston before the structure plan had been approved by the SOS. Both applications were refused by the district council and the refusals were upheld on appeal. However, when preparation of the local plan commenced both sites were shown as possible locations for residential development. The local plan (Oadby and Wigston District Council 1979) was eventually submitted to an inspector for his comments in 1979. By that time both sites had been excluded by the district council from their preferred options for development and instead the local plan allocated 15 ha on five separate sites on which it was estimated that 340 dwellings could be built. The inspector was critical of the limited amount of land allocated in the local plan and recommended that land for a further 200 houses be allocated. The district council reluctantly accepted this recommendation and allocated the additional land required by identifying one new site and enlarging two others, but still did not allocate either of the developer's sites.

During the preparation of the local plan a further application was submitted by the developer on the site known as Wigston East. This was again refused and an appeal was lodged with the SOS. His inspector held an inquiry a month before the local plan inquiry began and recommended that the appeal should be dismissed solely on the grounds that its merits could not be assessed accurately or comprehensively until the local plan was adopted and its proposals and policies finalised. The SOS delayed consideration of the appeal until the (other) inspector had made his report on the local plan which included the recommendation that land for a further 200 houses should be identified. Based on this report, the SOS concluded as follows:

> It is not considered that the proposals under appeal would seriously prejudice the Leicestershire Structure Plan provisions and in view of the deficiencies and consequent delays in the Wigston District Plan, it is concluded that the grounds of prematurity on which the Inspector based his recommendation are not strong enough to justify refusal of the application (DOE/APP/5307/A/76/11335, 1980).

He therefore allowed the appeal.

Although in this example the land was identified as a result of the developer's actions, the planners could have adopted his intentions and allocated the site in the local plan. If this had happened the identification of the site would still have been partially due to the developer drawing the attention of the planners to it, even though the site would have entered the land availability schedules from its allocation not from the grant of planning permission. Thus, where land is first identified by the grant of a planning consent, the developer or landowner who submits the application is responsible for its identification. Where land is newly allocated on a plan the planners will be at least partially responsible but, in some cases, may have been 'assisted' by the submission of an application by one of the other principal actors.

Simply identifying land as suitable for development is not usually sufficient to ensure that development will take place, although it can be in some circumstances, as is argued below. The key decision of the development process is frequently perceived as the developer's decision to purchase the land because, once acquisition has occurred, development is likely to follow (Craven & Pahl 1967). The landowner's reasons for selling his land, however, will often determine the timing of the sale and these reasons may be more important in influencing *when* development occurs than any decision of the developer. Where land is sold with the benefit of planning permission and it can be developed without the provision of major new services, it is highly likely that development will commence soon after the sale given the high cost of holding land and most developers' small land banks. Although the developer may postpone construction or sell the site to another developer, the most likely outcome is an early start on the project and, in these circumstances, the landowner's decision to sell is more crucial to determining the timing of development than the developer's decision to buy.

The planner may also initiate development but this is unusual. Where it occurs, however, the size of the development project tends to be large, so that the planner's role in initiating development must not be overlooked. Where land in the urban fringe is allocated for an urban use, the increase in land value that results encourages the owner to realise the gain by selling, with or without planning permission (see Ch. 5 below). If the developer who buys the land makes an early start on constructing a scheme, the planner's action in identifying development land has also initiated development because the other actors are effectively manipulated to implement the planner's wishes. It is very difficult to predict where planners may initiate development in this way, but where the land allocated is in the urban fringe, in one ownership, and there are no special servicing difficulties, development is quite likely to take place soon after the allocation is made.

Once planning permission has been granted it is likely that development will take place sooner rather than later, even if the length of time cannot be predicted with certainty. A national study of land with an outstanding residential planning consent in mid-1975 found that construction had started on 70% of the sites by mid-1977 and construction was expected to start on a further 14% of the sites by 1979 (DOE 1978c). Even though construction had started on at least 20% of these sites before mid-1975, because of errors in recording the stage each site had reached, this still represents an impressively quick flow through an important stage in the process. Only 8% of the land was unlikely to be developed for housing at any time, indicating that once planning permission is granted, development is likely to take place and sooner rather than later in most cases.

The two key events in the development process are therefore the *identification* of development land and the *initiation* of development upon it. Figure 4.1 sets out a descriptive model of the development process. This shows six routes by which undeveloped land may pass through four key 'nodes' before

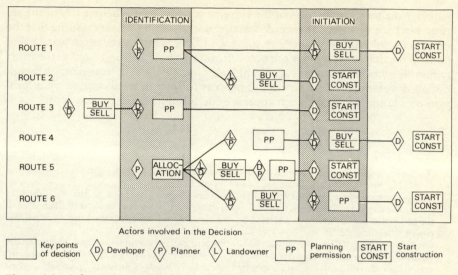

Figure 4.1 A descriptive model of the land development process.

development takes place. These nodes include the points where land is identified and where the development is initiated. The 'nodes' in the process are

(1) The allocation of land on a plan
(2) The sale of land to a developer
(3) The application and grant of planning permission either by the local authority or the SOS
(4) The commencement of construction.

Each of these nodes requires a decision by one or more of the principal actors in the process and, apart from allocation, each site must go through all the nodes.

This descriptive model is put forward as a simplified version of the development process that links the principal actors to the identification of development land and the initiation of development. The six routes shown in Figure 4.1 are not exclusive, nor is a dominant actor identified where two actors are involved in a nodal decision. The majority of development sites pass along one of the six routes.

This model has three advantages over those put forward by Lichfield and Drewett. These are as follows:

(a) It does not assume that all sites follow the same course through the development process.
(b) It recognises that the roles played by each actor can vary greatly in the development of land.
(c) It distinguishes the key stages through which each site must pass, namely identification and initiation.

All three points are important and must be recognised as such by policy makers seeking to alter the operation of the system. It is not clear whether any of the six routes in the model can be regarded as the 'norm'. Some writers assume that the process usually follows route 3 (e.g. Moor 1976), which is the most usual route in the American development process. Routes 1 and 2 are suggested as the most common by other writers (e.g. Shankland Cox 1972). It is clear that, although not all development land enters the process following its allocation on a local plan by planners, a large proportion is generally identified by this actor.

Notes

1 We have not specifically considered the estate agents' role in the development process either but see McNamara (1984) for a discussion of this aspect.
2 This is also true where the enforcement of planning controls is concerned. Section 87 of the 1971 Town and Country Planning Act, for example, indicates that enforcement is at the discretion of the local planning authority and should be effected only where it is 'expedient' to do so (see Jowell & Millichap 1983).
3 On 21 November 1983 Henry Stewart Conferences organised a seminar entitled 'Institutionally Acceptable Property' which it described as '. . . a major event covering the evaluation of commercial investment property, and is directed towards the needs of property principals, agents, surveyors, architects, pension fund advisors, insurance companies and lawyers'.

5 The landowner's investment strategy

Introduction

At the end of Chapter 1, a framework within which to examine the decisions of landowners was proposed and this framework is used here to structure a discussion on how landowners may be expected to behave. The framework identified the following three sets of related decisions:

(a) Financial decisions
(b) Operational decisions
(c) Management decisions.

The financial decisions the landowner has to make are crucial both for himself and for the development process because they determine when land is released to another actor. The discussion concentrates on the *timing* of the landowner's decision to sell, not on whether or not he should sell at all, because virtually every owner of development land sells at some time to realise the capital gain. The main exceptions are those owners who decide to develop the land themselves but, as is apparent in Chapter 6, such owners form a recognisable group who can be distinguished from the majority of land owners (see especially pp. 126–7 below). Attention is then turned to the operational strategy the landowner should adopt prior to the decision to sell, and the third section contains an analysis of how the land should be managed during the same period. In this chapter we build on the contextual information contained in Chapters 2 and 3 and the part the owner plays in the development process outlined in Chapter 4.

Much of the empirical work on the timing of the sale decision has been conducted in North America. There are few comparable studies for Great Britain. It is also worth noting that most of the empirical research was undertaken in the 1960s or the early 1970s against a background of rising land values and rapid, and relatively uncontrolled, urban growth by British standards. The effect of the British planning system on land values and the timing of development is not, therefore, reflected in these analyses. There is also one important contextual factor present in North America but absent in Britain. Over much of North America, land is taxed recurrently on its capital value so that the burden of taxation rises as the land's value increases and the prospect of development comes closer. In Britain, property taxes, i.e. rates, are based on rental values and reflect the current use value of the land, not its potential use value. Moreover, agricultural land and buildings are exempt from rating, so an owner of farmland in the urban fringe usually pays no rates except for his house and no rates are payable on the land until it is actually developed for an urban use. The situation is similar for an owner of vacant land in the inner city. Rateable values are assessed on the current use value of the land and no rates are levied on a derelict site. Where a building is empty, however, rates are payable except for industrial properties (see Rayner 1979). The absence of this direct holding cost means that owners of development sites in Britain are rarely forced to sell simply because they cannot afford to retain ownership, unlike some owners in North America where this consideration can be an important influence on the pattern of development (see, for example, Kenney 1965, Brown et al. 1981).

Much of the chapter focuses on landowners in the urban fringe rather than the inner city, simply because we know more about the former, and we preface our remarks with a brief discussion of what is known of the general attitudes of British owners of farmland. This is included because it will now be clear from earlier chapters that agricultural landowners on the urban fringe in Britain are party to at least the initial stages of the development process. Unlike the situation in North America, a change of ownership between the farmer and the developer or builder is quite rare. The absence of land dealers results from the more certain development process in Britain, because of planning controls, and the absence of property taxes on farmland leading to the premature sale of land before it is actually ripe for development.

Attitudes to farmland ownership in Britain

There is little detailed evidence on how rights to the ownership or occupation of farmland are held (see Ch. 1), or how farm businesses are structured (sole traders, partnerships, private companies, etc.; see Harrison 1975, Gasson 1983). In the past, and especially in the case of the large landed estate, landowners were regarded as owning land as much for its social and political significance as for its economic worth, even if the latter created the basis for the former (see Thompson 1971). The importance of this perspective has diminished during the 20th century with the economic decline and break-up of many large private estates (see Clemenson 1982), the growth of owner-occupation and the rise in agricultural land prices since 1950. The farming industry has become increasingly profit-conscious and while agricultural price supports have led to some improvements in farm incomes they have also been capitalised back into higher land prices (see Traill 1982). At the same time, inflation and a weak economy have encouraged insurance companies and pension funds to invest in farmland, these investors being very largely concerned with achieving growth in rental income and maintaining the real value of their land assets.

These largely tax-exempt investors represent a logical extension to changing attitudes among other owners of farmland. Rising land prices and more effective forms of capital taxation have encouraged both owner-occupiers and the remaining private landlords to pay increased attention to the asset value of their land; and as Newby et al. (1978) report, a large proportion of East Anglian farmers now articulate what the authors term 'capitalistic' or 'individualistic' ideologies of ownership. These ideologies emphasise the personal and financial benefits of ownership at the expense of the traditional notion of land stewardship.

The importance of this change in outlook is that landowners have become, even more than previously, aware of the high economic value of their land and the taxation liabilities that may arise from this; and, more particularly, owners on the urban fringe are even more alive to the capital gain they can derive from the development of their land. They may not know exactly what their land is worth at any precise moment, or what its development prospects are or what their tax liabilities following development might be, but the large sums involved mean that plenty of professional advice on these matters is readily available. Moreover, if they themselves have not had any direct experience of the urban fringe land market one of their neighbours probably has.

The decision to sell

The initial assumption throughout this chapter is that the owner is endeavouring to maximise his profit from his investment in land and it is upon this basis that a model is presented below. In practice, many owners do not conform to this model because of lack of knowledge or non-pecuniary motives. It is important, however, to establish how a profit-maximising landowner can be expected to behave and to compare actual behaviour with that predicted by the model. We do not analyse those circumstances where landowners should also consider developing the land themselves as this is largely dependent on their knowledge and experience as developers. Instead we analyse the optimum time at which landowners should sell.

Several models have been put forward to establish the course of action which landowners should adopt, assuming that they attempt to maximise the return from their investment in land. These models depend on the assumption that landowners compare the rate of return they enjoy, derived from both the current income they receive as well as the annual appreciation in capital value, with their opportunity cost of capital. When the rate of return produced by the land falls below the holder's opportunity cost of capital, the land should be sold and the capital re-invested to show a return equal to the owner's opportunity cost – always assuming that there is such an investment opportunity available. Other things being equal, owner-occupiers earning large agricultural incomes can be expected to hold their land longer than those whose land is of lower agricultural quality or lies idle (for empirical support for this assumption see Hart 1968, Berry 1978). The difference in timing will be inconsequential, however, where the level of recurrent income is small in relation to the size of the capital gain; but, in principle, owners of prime farmland might be expected to hold their land longer than owners of poor land, except for the fact that prime farmland is also often good building land as well.

Smith (1967) extends the basic model to incorporate the owner's expectations of future land prices. By discounting at the owner's opportunity cost rate of interest, the present value of the land to the owner is obtained, and the owner should sell if the market is ever prepared to offer more than this sum. The present value is therefore the owner's floor price, and it is reasonable to assume that the floor price will vary over time as the owner's circumstances alter, leading to changes in his personal opportunity cost of capital (Bahl 1968). Neutze (1973) has sought to explain a similar idea diagrammatically. In Figure 5.1, D_u represents the anticipated change in the market value of a property over

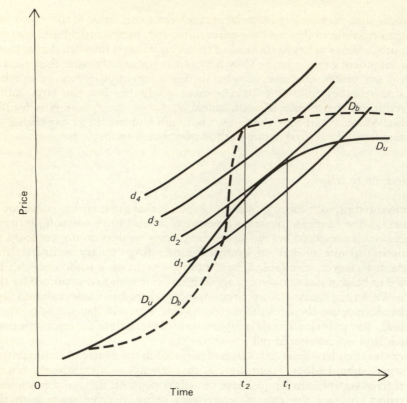

Figure 5.1 The time of maximum profit for selling development land.

time while d_1, d_2, d_3 and d_4 represent a series of 'discount curves' which each connect points with the same present value. The landowner should sell at the moment (t_1) when D_u touches the highest of these curves, thus achieving a sale at the point of the land's maximum present value. An assessment of the effect of using different opportunity cost rates of return may be carried out by constructing different series of 'discount curves'.

Neutze's approach lends itself to the British context where land values in the urban fringe do not rise gradually (see Ch. 3). Where values rise sharply in a very short space of time (along D_b), as at the receipt of outline planning permission for example, it is easy to see when the land's present value is maximised at the juncture of t_2 and d_4 (see Fig. 5.1). Selling at the point when planning permission is granted invariably maximises the return from the asset (see below) as the subsequent rate of increase in value as building land rarely, if ever, realises the same rate of return.

The landowner also has to consider the costs incurred by holding on to the land in order to sell at a profit at a later date. In Britain such costs are usually notional because a return can normally be obtained from the land in its existing use whether in the form of rent or as income from occupation. The holding cost is the difference between the interest received, if the land is sold and the capital re-invested, and current earnings from the land. If current earnings decline then the holding cost is increased and a sale is more likely. This is especially true if the decline in earnings is due in some way to the same factors which increase the development value of the land. Examples might include increasing urbanisation in the neighbourhood, making it more difficult to farm, or the existing built structure becoming obsolete with a change in user demand, as with the current lack of demand for multi-storey industrial buildings (see Dwyer 1976).

Descriptive models of landowner behaviour are likely to differ from this case on several counts (see pp. 101–3 and p. 107 below), but only two will be noted here. First it can be argued that this approach makes unrealistic demands on the evaluatory and anticipatory powers of the owner. Despite a high level of general awareness of market conditions, and the ease with which advice can be obtained, there is little evidence that farmers, an important group of owners in the urban fringe, consciously compare rates of return from alternative invest-ments (Scofield 1957), at least not until they actively begin to consider the sale of their land. This is because most farmers have not only an investment motive but also an occupational and business reason for owning their land and therefore moving out of one asset (their land) into another (cash) at a profit may not provide sufficient incentive to sell. Farmers, as an occupational group, are highly immobile and unless the sale of their land is linked to a wish to leave the industry then they have to face the consequences of buying back into farmland. The pecuniary and non-pecuniary costs of doing this are quite considerable.

Second, the models described assume that investors can anticipate future events with reasonable accuracy, such as the rate of urban growth and the future price of development land, and from these assessments determine the present and future worth of their land. Most of the empirical evidence suggests that owners over-estimate the future value of their land (e.g. Strong 1975), and this may reflect the fact that land prices have moved steadily upwards in the experience of most of today's owners. A general awareness of rising land prices, coupled with the knowledge of a few sales realising spectacular prices, encour-ages substantial increases in the reservation prices of most landowners. As a result, rising land prices do not necessarily lead to more land being offered for sale, at least not in the short term.

The analysis used below reflects the landowner's difficulties in assessing alternative investment opportunities by comparing their return with the return likely to be obtained in the future from the existing investment in development land. Land is rarely sold quickly at the best price (see below, p. 104) and it is unlikely that the ideal investment opportunity is available at exactly the same moment as the optimum time to sell the land. The investor who behaves normatively will obviously consider the most suitable alternative investment for his capital but there is likely to be at least a short period when the capital is held in a liquid form before it is transferred to a long-term asset, assuming this is thought to be the most appropriate form of investment. The important thing is for the landowner to maximise the return from the investment in land and then look at alternative investments rather than considering them at the same time.

Inner city land values are affected by different influences to those on the urban fringe. Demand for the land in a more profitable use is the key determinant of the land's value rather than whether planning permission is available for that use. This difference is reflected in the different financial profiles that are commonly associated with the development of urban fringe and city sites. This difference is illustrated by two worked examples based on the approximate level of values prevailing in the Leicester area between 1950 and 1982. The urban fringe case is investigated first.

TIMING OF THE DECISION TO SELL AN URBAN FRINGE SITE

This example assumes that 8 ha of agricultural land located close to the built-up area of Leicester were purchased in 1950 for £1600 (£200 per hectare), a price 25% in excess of the then agricultural value of £160 per hectare and so reflecting an element of hope value. For simplicity of calculation, it is also assumed that this land produced no income from its 'agricultural' use. Farm rents at that time would probably have been no more than £4 per hectare. In 1963 planning permission was granted for residential development on the whole site. The owner then had to decide whether to hold or to sell the land, and the sale prices and the internal rates of return the landowner would have received at various dates after 1963 are set out in Table 5.1.

In 1963, when planning permission was first granted, residential building land was valued at £12500 per hectare (column 3) so that the 8 ha could have been sold for £100000. As long as the owner was not a trader in land, *no* tax was payable at that time (see Ch. 2), and he would have obtained a yield equivalent to 38.1% per annum (column 6) on his initial investment of £1600 over the 13-year period. If the owner held the land until 1969, the value of the land for building would have risen to £180000 (£22500 per hectare). A sale at this figure would have given a gross annual yield of 28.2% per annum on the original 1950 investment of £1600 but, in 1969, the proceeds from the sale of development land would have been subject to betterment levy. This would have reduced the proceeds by nearly £70000 to £111200 (column 5). As a result, the net yield over the whole life of the investment is reduced to 25% per annum (column 7). Residential building values increased at an annual rate of 10.4% per annum between 1963 and 1969 (column 8) but, because of the tax, the return the owner would have received from holding on to the land during this period would have been only 1.8% per annum (column 9).

By 1972 building land prices had risen considerably to £75000 per hectare and the total value of the site to £600000. This produces a gross annual rate of return of 30.9% on the original investment, a higher yield than in 1969 because of the spectacular increase in land values over this period in the East Midlands (see Neuburger & Nicol 1976, p. 6). The advantages of a sale in 1972 were further increased by the abolition of betterment levy and the taxation of the proceeds by a capital gains tax only (see Table 5.1). As a result the net of tax yield on the original investment was 29.3% per annum and the marginal rate between 1969 and 1972 a staggering 60.5% per annum even though land values rose at 'only' 49.3% per annum.

By 1977 returns had fallen dramatically from their 1972 level, both as a result of a decline in land values and the introduction of development land tax. Building land values fell at a rate of 8.4% per annum and the marginal rate of return for holding the land between 1972 and 1977 was −28.3% per annum. Since 1977, land values have risen again in the area at an average annual rate of 14.9% and in 1982 the land was worth approximately £800000. By 1982 the tax regime was also less onerous, with DLT levied at 60% instead of 66⅔% and 80% (see Ch. 2) with an annual exemption of £50000 instead of £10000. The net

Table 5.1 The change in value and rate of capital appreciation of an urban fringe site in the Leicester area, 1950–1982 (no allowance is made for inflation).

Year	Values per hectare				Internal rates of return per annum			
	Agricultural land (£)	Residential building land (£)	Sale/(purchase) price (£)	Net of tax sales proceeds (£)	Gross annual (%)	Net annual (%)	Gross marginal (%)*	Net marginal (%)*
(1)	(2)	(3)	(4)	(5)	(6)	(7)	(8)	(9)
1950	160	—	(1 600)	—	—	—	—	—
1963	625	12 500	100 000	100 000	38.1	38.1	38.1	38.1
1969	500	22 000	180 000	111 200	28.2	25.0	10.4	1.8
1972	1250	75 000	600 000	459 600	30.9	29.3	49.3	60.5
1977	2500	50 000	400 000	132 000	22.7	17.8	−8.4	−28.3
1982	4000	100 000	800 000	378 800	21.4	18.6	14.9	23.4

* Columns 8 and 9 give the marginal rates of return, gross and net of tax, achieved between each consecutive date.

marginal return for holding the land from 1977 to 1982 was 23.4% per annum and a sale in 1982 would have shown an annual rate of 18.6% after tax on the original investment of £1600 as against a return of 17.8% if the land had been sold in 1977.

The highest annual yield on the original investment would have been achieved by selling in 1963 when the rate was 38.1%. This rate of growth is never exceeded in any subsequent period in terms of either the gross sale price or the net of tax sale price. In general, the longer the land is held, the lower the yield. Only between 1969 and 1972 does the marginal rate of return exceed 38.1% but this period of boom in the property market was exceptional. However, the effect on the rates of return of the different tax regimes is also important to this example. A sale in 1972 was better than one in 1969 and a sale in 1982 better than one in 1977. In the short run it always paid the landowner to wait for a more favourable tax regime.

There are dangers in seeking to draw general lessons from particular examples. The results are specific to changes over the whole of the period from 1950 to 1982, and to the sub-periods used, and to the Leicester area. The pattern of values, however, is not untypical for the country as a whole (see Ch. 3). The example suggests a strategy that owners of urban fringe sites should adopt if they wish to maximise the annual yield from their investment. The owner should seek planning permission at the earliest opportunity and sell immediately this is obtained unless there is a likelihood that the rate of tax on the proceeds will be decreased in the near future. The owner, before taking a decision, should also consider whether changes in the other contextual factors will affect the issue. Land values may be expected to rise, there may be a threat of compulsory acquisition or there may be a total lack of alternative investment opportunities. These are usually of much less significance, however, and in most circumstances the return is maximised by the sale following on quickly from the grant of planning permission. The only period when such a strategy would not have maximised the gross annual yield was between 1969 and 1972 when land values rose sharply. The figures emphasise, however, that changes in the rate of taxation are much more important in determining the optimum time to sell a greenfield site than changes in the level of land values, once planning permission has been obtained.

The example permits examination of the circumstances of tax-exempt bodies, such as charities. It does not, however, allow for the varying tax liabilities of owners because of their other assets or the varying ability of owners to mitigate their tax liabilities in various ways, such as joint ownership. Neither does the example take into account inflation. The average annual rate of inflation was approximately 7.5% between 1950 and 1982, significantly reducing the real rate of annual return, especially during the last decade.

TIMING OF THE DECISION TO SELL AN URBAN SITE
The owner of an urban site does not have a comparable strategy to adopt as changes in the value of an urban site do not follow a clear pattern. An example is set out in Table 5.2. It is assumed that a multi-storey warehouse of 3000 m² located close to the CBD of Leicester was purchased in 1950 for £20 000. The warehouse was let in 1950 for a term of 14 years without review at a rental of £1500 per annum. Planning permission was granted in 1964 for an office

Table 5.2 The change in value and rate of capital appreciation of an urban site in the Leicester area, 1950–1982 (no allowance is made for inflation).

Year	Income from current use (£ per annum)	Current use value (£)	Development value (£)	Net of tax sales price (£)	Internal rates of return per annum			
					Gross annual (%)	Net annual (%)	Gross marginal (%)*	Net marginal (%)*
(1)	(2)	(3)	(4)	(5)	(6)	(7)	(8)	(9)
1950	1500	20 000	Nil	—	—	—	—	—
1964	2250	22 500	35 000	35 000	10.2	10.2	10.2	10.2
1969	3000	30 000	85 000	64 900	12.6	11.6	24.1	18.3
1972	3000	30 000	275 000	209 150	16.0	14.9	50.4	51.0
1977	7500	64 000	Nil	60 200	10.3	10.2	−23.2	−19.6
1982	Nil	60 000	Nil	57 400	10.1	10.0	6.4	7.2

* As footnote to Table 5.1.

building with a gross external area of 3000 m^2 and a net internal area of 2700 m^2 allowing 10% of the gross area for staircases, circulation space, walls, etc.[1] It is further assumed that the building will take 18 months to construct and let.

The changes in the value of the property, both gross and net of capital taxes, are set out in columns 3 to 5 of Table 5.2 for the period from purchase in 1950 to 1982. The values of the property in its current use as a warehouse are shown in column 3 and income received from that use in column 2. The rent increases in 1964 on the expiry of the original 14 years lease and short leases are granted thereafter leading to further regular increases in income until 1980. By 1980 the property is unlettable in its existing state so that it no longer produces an income. The development values of the property are shown in column 4. Although this increases to £275 000 in 1972, the poor demand for offices in Leicester since the mid-1970s, coupled with an excess supply, has meant that new office development is unprofitable because the building cost would exceed the value of the new building. Thus, in 1977 and 1982, the market is not prepared to offer more than the current use value because the prospect of office values increasing significantly is remote. Columns 6 and 7 show the internal rate of return produced by the investment if held from 1950, with and without allowance for the tax payable on the sale of the investment. Columns 8 and 9 give the marginal rates of return, gross and net of tax, achieved between each consecutive sale date. The internal rates of return reflect the income produced by the property but no allowance is made for any tax on income.

The internal rate of return from the investment in gross and in net terms shows less variation over the life of the investment than for the urban fringe site (see Table 5.1). The gross yield rises from 10.2% per annum in 1964 to a peak yield of 16% in 1972. The yield net of tax shows a similar pattern but at a lower level. The major influence on the internal rate of return of this urban site, whether measured gross or net, is the level of land values. The annual rates of return from 1950 (columns 6 and 7) rise and fall with the movements in land values, and it is these unpredictable movements that determine the optimum time to sell. Changes in the tax regime have little influence although the introduction of DLT in 1976 would have reduced the net sales price substantially if there had been any development value to tax!

The owner of an urban site does not have the comparatively simple point of reference that obtaining planning permission provides to the owner of land in the urban fringe. The value of an urban site is as likely to rise faster after planning permission has been granted as before. A landowner's decision to sell must, therefore, be primarily determined by his own assessment of future land values, and owners may simplify their decision by waiting until prices rise above a certain predetermined level (their 'reservation price'). The only other major consideration is the rate of DLT on the sale proceeds.

As in the case of the urban fringe site, the return produced by an urban site is mainly in the form of capital appreciation. However, on an urban site and occasionally on a greenfield site with an intensive agricultural use, an important part of the return may be derived either from rental or earned income from the existing use. In the example described in Table 5.2, the contribution of rental income to the rate of return is greatest between 1950 and 1964 because this period does not see such a rapid growth in capital value. This is demonstrated by the fact that a gross marginal rate of return of 48% per annum would have been achieved between 1969 and 1972 even if the site had been held vacant for that period. Income from an urban site may fall not because the owner deliberately holds the site vacant, but as a result of the increasing obsolescence of the building, which in turn reduces its rental value, or because of the unwillingness of a tenant to accept responsibility for repairs as a building ages. This consideration may also affect the optimum time at which to sell.

In determining when to sell, therefore, owners of inner city and urban fringe sites have to consider the same contextual factors. The weight they should place on each differs, although the level of taxation is important for both of them. The owner of urban fringe land is primarily concerned with getting planning permission. The owner of the inner city site is more concerned with the demand for, and therefore the value of, his plot.

DESCRIPTIVE MODELS OF THE DECISION TO SELL

Surveys of why landowners choose to sell their land, and why they opt to do so at a particular time, regularly reveal a much wider range of motives for holding land than simply its investment value and a wish to maximise it. Non-planning and personal factors often affect the timing of the sale of individual parcels of land. Personal factors include the stage in the life-cycle of the owner (e.g. the wish to retire), family commitments, and the need to raise capital to expand the business or to meet tax demands. In these respects the owner may not be in as strong a negotiating position *vis-à-vis* developers as is sometimes suggested (Clawson 1971, Clawson & Hall 1973). These considerations may lead to land being offered for sale on a depressed market and owners being obliged to accept lower prices than they would have done if they could have sold the land at a time of their choosing. On the other hand, non-pecuniary considerations, such as a long family association with a particular property, may raise the owner's reservation price considerably, especially if he is also the occupier, and lead him to hold on to the property much longer than someone who only has a pecuniary interest in it (see Smith 1967).

A recent survey of more than 700 owners of undeveloped land around six metropolitan centres in the United States and Canada (Atlanta, Boston, Buffalo, Calgary, Sacramento and Toronto) reveals a great deal about the owners of urban fringe land and their properties, about their previous sale decisions and their sale intentions (Brown *et al.* 1981). It shows that certain owners, especially private individuals, farmers and those of middle-age, retain a strong attachment to their property and are often not interested in selling their land. Their attitudes contrast strongly with those who neither occupy nor use their properties, public companies, and owners who are either young or close to retirement. While personal considerations become less important to the decision to sell as development becomes increasingly imminent (see also Kaiser *et al.* 1968), the authors rightly draw attention to the continued importance of family and life-cycle circumstances, even in areas of intense development pressure which are defined as locations within which development may be expected in the next ten years. The study also indicates the importance of local taxation in forcing land on to the market in areas where development pressure is intense (see Table 5.3).

In the rather different circumstances of Britain, a classification of the kind recorded in Table 5.4 is to be preferred. Most sales provide the vendor with a

Table 5.3 Reasons for considering the sale of land in the USA. Table refers to the percentage of owners in the United States sample who are considering selling their land. The sample size is 44 for intense development pressures and 54 for moderate/weak pressures. Column totals may exceed 100.0% since more than one response was allowed.

| | | Development pressures | |
Factor	Total	Intense	Moderate/weak
family or life–cycle factors	36.4%	34.9%	40.4%
good offer or area ripe for development	19.6	27.3	14.8
tax factors	16.8	31.8	5.7
better investment elsewhere	14.7	13.6	16.7

Source: Brown *et al*. (1981).

Table 5.4 A classification of the reasons for selling development land based on British experience.

	Category	Elaboration
1	financial gain	sale determined by financial factors alone, e.g. because the price is too good to refuse or because there is a more attractive investment for the owner's capital
2	need for cash	a sale which the owner has been forced into because of a pressing need for cash
3	property obsolescence	a sale to move out of premises which are old and/or expensive to maintain, or which are no longer suitable for their present use due to technological changes, or have become unsuitable from a change in the neighbourhood rather than the premises themselves
4	personal	a sale for non-pecuniary reasons which are personal to the owner, e.g. a wish to retire or live in a different location, or move forced by illness, or often, following the owner's death

financial gain, but the gain may neither be the primary reason for the sale nor explain the timing. Individual sales regularly combine two or more of these reasons. Some sales are affected by changes in neighbouring land uses (category 3). These changes range from the owner of a large house standing in extensive grounds deciding to sell because similar properties in the neighbourhood have been demolished and the sites re-developed with smaller dwellings thus altering the character, to a farmer selling land adjacent to a housing estate whose occupants seriously impede his farming activities. Category 3 also includes the sale of land that is surplus to requirements on properties that are old, expensive to maintain and unsuited to existing production methods. Asset stripping clearly falls into category 1, but the sale of a property belonging to a business operating from several locations that is in overall financial difficulty, not necessarily because of the unprofitability of the site concerned, would be classified as a category 2 type sale – the need for cash. It is important to emphasise that just because an owner wants to sell his property at the highest possible price this does not make financial gain the primary reason for selling. The concern at this point is with the underlying reason for putting the land on the market, not the method of selling which is considered as part of the landowner's operational strategy. The classification in Table 5.4 deliberately excludes the approach of an intent purchaser as a reason for the sale of land. The approach itself only encourages an owner to consider whether to sell or not, unless the approach is made by a body possessing powers of compulsory purchase which makes it clear to the owner that it would invoke those powers if they cannot reach an amicable agreement.

The decision to sell — operational strategy

The previous discussion of the timing of the decision to sell has concentrated on the elements that each landowner should consider in deciding when to sell. Although most landowners cannot influence even local land values because they do not have sufficient monopoly power, they can influence the value of their own land by, for example, obtaining planning permission. It is in this context that each owner should have an operational strategy. As was made clear in Chapter 2, the granting of planning permission depends on a wide range of considerations. Among other matters, the discussion indicated that there is considerable scope for the private sector to put forward land as suitable for development even though the development of that land is contrary to local planning policy. It is in the financial interest of urban fringe landowners to get planning permission at the earliest opportunity and this should be the principal objective of their operational strategies.

Landowners seeking to maximise their profits should play an active part in the development process and try to obtain planning consent by submitting their own applications, including being prepared to take them to appeal if necessary. They can, of course, wait for an approach by a developer who will probably have much more experience of the development process. If the developer is seriously interested in the site, he will be prepared to take an option or conditional contract on it which may well require him to appeal against the local authority's planning refusal as well as pay the fees for the planning application (see Ch. 4). The landowner, however, will not get the best price for his site by this method because the developer will want a significant profit margin for risking his money on the costs of the application and the appeal. If the landowner has the resources to mount an appeal himself, and is prepared to lose the money if the appeal is unsuccessful, then he is much better advised to proceed on his own with the aid of professional assistance. Then, when he is successful, he is free to sell the land to the highest bidder.

An owner of an inner city site is less concerned with obtaining planning permission because market demand for the land is a more important consideration. However, his operational strategy should also include obtaining planning permission before offering the land for sale if he is to maximise his return. A developer will pay more for a site with planning permission as it makes the purchase a less risky venture. He knows what can be built on the site, and more or less within what time-scale, and will bid on that basis. Where consent has not been granted, a developer will have to make his own enquiries to determine what may be permitted and will make due allowance for the fact that consent may not be granted, may take time to obtain and be costly to acquire.

Obtaining a *full* planning consent before the land is offered for sale, to reduce delay in the development process still further, is not likely to increase the market value of the land. The developer will, almost certainly, want to submit his own detailed planning application for the site. The landowner should, therefore, obtain *outline* planning consent that specifies the density of development. This simplifies the issues to be finalised as reserved matters and reduces delay (DOE 1975b). Moreover, density is of prime importance in enabling a developer to know how much to offer for a site. It can be argued that a developer is more likely to obtain a higher density than a landowner because of his greater expertise and, as a result, establishing this figure should be left to the developer. In practice, this rarely happens, especially if the owner has employed a planning consultant.

Once planning permission has been granted, the next step in the operational strategy is for the land to be offered for sale by a method that permits competitive bidding and is likely to realise the highest price. Development land is usually in limited supply in the more favoured locations and a higher price can often be realised by selling at auction or by tender rather than quoting a sale price. At an auction, potential purchasers can hear the other bids even if they do not know who are making them or whether they are even genuine. At a sale by tender, the potential purchasers neither know who else is in the market nor the level of their bids, and sales by tender sometimes result in the purchaser offering a price much higher than the next bid. Developers prefer to avoid such situations, particularly tenders, and will only buy land this way when their other means of acquiring land (see p. 69) are not providing them with a sufficient supply of land on which to build. The limited evidence available suggests that land sold at auction realises prices higher than at private treaty, particularly when land prices are rising (Munton 1975). However, the bargaining position of the owner is weakened considerably if land offered at auction fails to reach its reserve price and has to be withdrawn. The owner needs to display an acute awareness of the state of the local property market in deciding how to market his land. It is clear, though, that the best price is unlikely to be obtained by accepting the first offer received. The property should be fully exposed to the market to achieve the best price.

The owner's management strategy

The third aspect of the landowner's investment strategy concerns his land management strategy, i.e. what to do with the land while waiting for the appropriate moment to sell.

A significant quantity of land awaiting development or re-development lies vacant or generally under-used in inner city areas and on the edges of towns and cities. Many reasons have been put forward to explain this phenomenon and several researchers have drawn attention to the uncertainties surrounding aspects of the development process. In particular, they say that while owners may be confident that their land will be developed, they are often unsure *when* this will occur, and this uncertainty makes them reluctant to refurbish buildings or to put further capital into existing enterprises. This is a response to circumstances largely beyond the owner's control. An alternative explanation is that leaving land and keeping buildings vacant should be seen as part of the owner's profit-maximising strategy. Land is left idle and untidy in the belief that this will hasten the procurement of planning permission, and the temporary loss of income will be more than offset by the earlier receipt of a substantial capital gain.

These arguments have received most attention in the context of the urban fringe where the value of land declines sharply with distance away from the urban edge as the development potential of the land falls (see Ch. 3). At the same time the proportion of its total value that is attributable to its agricultural worth rises, both absolutely and proportionately, to a point where the land's value is determined by agricultural considerations alone (Sinclair 1967; see Fig. 5.2). In other words, as the development of the land becomes both more certain and more imminent not only does its development value rise, but also its agricultural value is depressed by the prospect of development. It follows that those farming enterprises that require the greatest amounts of fixed capital and the longest return periods on that capital, and which Sinclair assumes make the most intensive use of the land, are the most likely to be abandoned. On this basis, Sinclair postulates a series of agricultural land-use rings of increasing farming intensity away from the urban edge, with land adjacent to the city having little or no agricultural value (Sinclair 1967, pp. 79–81). The explanatory power of this model depends crucially on the assumption that the anticipation of urban encroachment is the exclusive, or at least the dominant, factor determining the occupiers' investment and enterprise choice decisions.

Sinclair developed his ideas in the mid-1960s on the basis of his North American experience where planning controls over suburban development were weak. Boal has tried to reinterpret his model in a context of much more clearly defined planning policies (Boal 1970). Specifically, he sought to predict the effect on land values of introducing a green belt around Belfast (see Fig. 5.2). Boal argued that the effect would be to raise the development potential of any undeveloped land remaining between the green belt and the urban edge whilst increasing the security of farming within the green belt. This would raise the

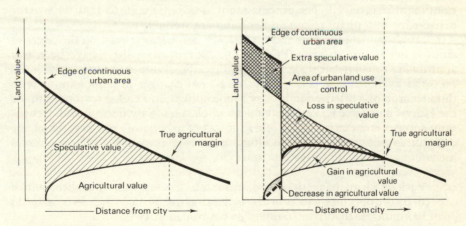

Figure 5.2 Land values at the urban edge, with and without urban restraint policies.

agricultural value of the land in the green belt, whilst at the same time reducing its development potential and encouraging its retention in full agricultural use. The development potential of land within the green belt would not be eliminated entirely unless the green belt was maintained effectively and the owners of land within it were persuaded that its boundaries were not going to be altered in the future (see Ch. 7).

A similar line of reasoning under-pins policies put forward to protect prime farmland from urban encroachment. There are many such schemes in North America (for a review see Furuseth & Pierce 1982), but most are regarded as only partially effective because of the ease with which zoning ordnances may be altered and the inadequate compensation offered to owners who agree not to develop their land (Carman 1977, Esseks 1978). Moreover, protecting agricultural land from development does not ensure that it will be farmed. In Britain, DOE and MAFF agree that land of high agricultural quality (Grades I, II and possibly IIIa under the MAFF's Agricultural Land Classification Scheme) should not be developed if at all possible (DOE 1976, 1979a), although Gilg found little evidence that applications relating to good land were refused more frequently than those relating to poor land (Gilg 1975).

In seeking to operationalise Sinclair's model, Bryant has defined farmers' behaviour in profit-maximising terms under conditions of uncertainty (Bryant 1974). Farmers' investment decisions were seen to depend on an assessment of comparative rates of return from alternative production systems, as affected by interest rates, and by what he termed 'time-left-for-agriculture'. Subsequently, he relaxed the assumption of profit maximisation in order to account for observed variations in farmers' behaviour in the Paris region (Bryant 1981). He acknowledged, for example, that farmers' expectations over the speed of urban growth vary and, more importantly, that farmers make quite different but equally rational responses to the economic consequences of urban encroachment. These responses depended in part on the kind of farming business being operated. Some farmers sought an early sale of their land with the intention of investing the proceeds in a larger farm elsewhere, while others made additional farming investments in order to capitalise on the new market opportunities created by suburban development. Bryant also maintained that farmers' reactions to urban growth became increasingly consistent the closer they were to the urban edge and the more certain development seemed.

That substantial idle areas and extensively farmed areas exist on the edges of cities is not in doubt (see OECD 1979). Nevertheless, there have been few attempts to test Sinclair's arguments rigorously, although partial analyses are reported by Mattingly (1972), who measured changes in labour input with distance from the urban edge, and by Munton (see Ch. 7). One reason for this is the lack of detailed data on land values and changes in ownership and occupation; another is the existence of other sources of uncertainty or stress which are difficult to isolate from that resulting from land conversion. These sources include:

(a)   Various forms of urban intrusion such as trespass and vandalism which affect the occupier's ability to farm the land (see MAFF 1973, 1976, ACAH 1978, Coleman 1976, Countryside Commission 1981)

(b)   The secondary effects of urban development, such as the subdivision and severance of farms and industrial pollution (see Bell *et al.* 1978, Bryant 1982)

(c) Local taxation leading to the premature abandonment of farmland (see Furuseth & Pierce 1982).

For these reasons it is difficult to synthesise the empirical evidence, much of which has been collected by a variety of methods and for widely differing reasons. If, however, attention is focused on land *close* to the urban edge, where development is a reasonable short or even long-term possibility, then the following tentative conclusions can be drawn. First, analyses of aggregate land-use and farming data do confirm the general supposition that farmland is less intensively used the closer one moves to the urban edge (see, for example, Berry 1979, Thomson 1981). The severity and spatial extent of the aggregate effect is, as would be expected, influenced by the level of uncertainty surrounding the development. Planning controls and attempts to protect prime farmland do direct and do reduce the spatial extent of the impact but rarely, if ever, eliminate it altogether (Coleman 1977, Munton 1983). Furthermore, variations in the natural environment and historical circumstances both between and within conurbations significantly affect the impact of urban encroachment on farming patterns (Moran 1979, Bryant & Greaves 1978), sometimes to the point where no clear type of urban fringe farming can be discerned. Second, the land-use rings postulated by Sinclair rarely seem to exist. Instead, the pattern of response to urban encroachment varies considerably between farmers. The main reasons for this are similar to those used earlier to explain variability among owners in their timing of the decision to sell. In particular, the model incorrectly assumes that all owners are profit maximisers and that they can accurately assess the rate of urban growth. It also fails to take into account differences in land tenure.

It is important to appreciate the different interests held in land and how these may be reflected in the objectives that landlords, owner-occupiers and tenants may have. Public utilities, for example, which own significant areas of farmed land on the urban edge, will always be required to meet their statutory obligations, and even to satisfy their budgetary targets, before acceding to the land management needs of their tenants. Developers and mineral companies will rarely invest in fixed improvements to their farmland and, where possible, will lease the land short term and without security for their tenants. Other landlords, and owner-occupiers, will have a range of motives. In Britain at least, there is one important group of occupiers who may well attempt to farm their land intensively irrespective of the prospect of development. These are tenants on secure leases. For although a tenant on such a lease can be given notice to quit if his landlord obtains planning permission for development, he has to be compensated for the improvements he has made to the land. More importantly, in Britain today the compensation he receives for the loss of his tenancy will in no way give him the means to buy a comparable farm and today new tenancies are few and far between (see Northfield Committee Report 1979, pp. 41–50). His whole livelihood is at risk, unlike the owner-occupier who will receive the proceeds from the sale and can purchase replacement land. The tenant may, therefore, seek to demonstrate his farming efficiency, and the hardship that could arise from dispossession, at a planning inquiry in an attempt to forestall his landlord's attempt to gain planning permission (Munton 1984).

The intensity of farming activity falls close to the urban edge, but acquiring evidence on the extent to which this is a deliberate management strategy aimed at hastening the development of the land, rather than an understandable reluctance to invest in a difficult and uncertain farming situation, is difficult. Owners are loathe to admit to speculation. Moreover, the evidence lacks consistency. The evidence varies between conurbations depending largely upon the effectiveness of planning controls, whether the land is subject to local taxation and whether it is of high agricultural quality. Individual owners may also take differing views about whether further improvements in the land are justified. As a result, major differences in land management can occur on adjacent properties, and these differences may be the result of land tenure. A significant proportion of urban fringe farmland in Great Britain is occupied by secure tenants (see Ch. 7) and in the short term they will largely determine the way the land is farmed. In the long term, the landlord will be the primary determinant of use as he will not necessarily agree to any further investment in fixed improvements of the land.

An investment model

The preceding discussion has illustrated the range of complex and often uncertain circumstances which affect the landowner's investment decisions. Nevertheless, it is possible to identify the main elements of a strategy the landowner should adopt if he wishes to maximise the return from his investment in land. The main elements are made up as follows:

MOTIVE
(a)   The landowner should purchase land as an investment with the intention of re-selling it for a profit at a later date.
(b)   The landowner's decision to sell should depend solely on financial criteria.

KNOWLEDGE
(a)   The landowner should have been aware of the development potential of his land from the date of purchase.
(b)   The landowner should possess a broad understanding of the contextual factors relevant to his property and how these are changing. In particular, he needs to have an accurate perception of the land's development prospects and its current value.

TIMING OF SALE
The following strategy should be adopted by an owner of a greenfield site in order to maximise his rate of return:

(a)   He should actively seek planning permission at the earliest opportunity whether the land has been identified on the relevant development plan for a change of use or not.
(b)   On receipt of planning permission, sell the land immediately to a developer, unless one, or a combination, of the following considerations *strongly* suggest otherwise:[2]

(i)   A favourable change in the rate of tax on the proceeds from the sale of development land is expected in the near future.
(ii)   A significant increase in the value of development land can be confidently expected in the short term, i.e. 12–18 months.
(iii)   There is no possibility that the land will be compulsorily purchased and there is a lack of alternative investment opportunities (unlikely).
(iv)   There will be a rapid growth in income from the land's current use (unlikely).

The following factors should be considered by the owner of an *urban site* when deciding the moment at which to sell:

(a)   The likelihood, and rate, of the future increase in land values
(b)   A change in the rate of tax on the proceeds of the sale of development land.
(c)   The availability of alternative investment opportunities
(d)   A change in compulsory purchase policy
(e)   The amount of income produced by the land in its current use, both now and in the future, and the owner's liability for expenditure on repairs.

METHOD OF LAND SALE
(a)   If possible and sensible, the owner should seek to play a full part in the acquisition of planning permission in order to avoid sharing all or part of his gain with, for example, a developer.[3]
(b)   The land should be sold with the benefit of outline planning consent, obtained on appeal if necessary, that specifies the density of development.
(c)   The land should be sold by a method that requires potential purchasers to submit their highest offer, for example, through its sale by auction or tender.

MANAGEMENT
(a)   On an *urban site* the aim must be to minimise outgoings, e.g. rates, avoid refurbishment costs that do not increase the value of the site for its prospective use, and take advantage of any income earning opportunities from temporary uses such as parking or open storage as long as vacant possession can still be obtained quickly.
(b)   On a *greenfield site* the owner should proceed as follows:

(i)   Endeavour to ensure that the planning status of the land is not changed in such a way as to make development more difficult, e.g. its incorporation into a green belt or its re-designation as open space on the revision of a local plan
(ii)   In the case of let farmland, where the occupier usually has considerable security of tenure under the Agricultural Holdings Legislation, not re-let tenancies other than on insecure, short-term licences (usually 364 days or less) that can be speedily revoked
(iii)   Not invest in improvements to the land of no value to the developer and, where this is thought relevant, be prepared to run down the use of the land, exchanging the loss of current income for an earlier receipt of planning permission.

Within the confines of current legislation, the above model aims to maximise the financial gain of the individual landowner. For several reasons many owners fail to adopt such an approach to the development of their land, even where they know about its potential. first, much property is inherited rather than bought as an investment, and as a result many owners exhibit a range of motives for continuing ownership, including occupation, use and emotional attachment. Its sale may be forced upon them, and not necessarily at a time of their own choosing, by family commitments, age, tax demands or the need to raise capital. Second, because of the inevitable uncertainties surrounding the development of a particular property, no *one* course of action can be firmly prescribed for its owner by this model, as perfectly sensible but differing assessments of how to maximise financial returns can be made which result in different strategies. finally, the discussion has, so far, treated properties as if they were indivisible. In many cases, and especially in the case of farms on the urban fringe, properties are divisible and are even marketed on that basis. This can permit the owner to maximise a range of motives and to do so over a period of time.

The case studies

The analysis developed in both this chapter and in Chapters 2, 3 and 4 is now used in looking at the behaviour of landowners through three case studies. These are as follows:

(a)   Owners of development land in and around Leicester (Ch. 6)
(b)   Owners and occupiers of land in the Metropolitan Green Belt around London (Ch. 7)
(c)   Owners of inner city land (Ch. 8).

Chapters 6 and 7 are based on the results of substantial surveys carried out by the authors separately. The material for Chapter 8 is drawn from a large number of sources supplemented with information obtained by the authors from Land Registers for certain London Boroughs and for Tyneside.

The policy contexts for the three case studies are very different. The sites examined in the Leicester study were all ones where both the planning authority wished development to take place and development could be carried out profitably. In the Metropolitan Green Belt, development is contrary to planning policy but the financial rewards to the landowner are enormous if planning permission can be obtained for, say, residential development. In the inner city the problem is mainly one of finding profitable uses for vacant sites. The planner is prepared to grant consent but the developer does not want to develop there.

Landowners' financial, operational and managerial decisions are considered in these three locations. The Leicester study concentrates on the financial and operational aspects while more emphasis is placed on managerial decisions in Chapters 7 and 8. The lessons learnt from these surveys are then drawn together in Chapter 9.

Notes

1   The distinction is drawn between gross external floor area and net internal floor area because valuers assess building costs on the gross external floor area and the rental value from the net internal floor area.
2   Although these factors themselves may be capitalised into the land's price if potential purchasers are also aware of them.
3   The only consideration here is whether there is a realistic chance of success in relation to the cost of the application, especially if the application requires the employment of specialist advice and where an appeal to the DOE will almost certainly be required (see Ch. 7).

6 *Leicester – an expanding city*

This chapter is based on a detailed survey made during 1977 of landowners in the Leicester area who either held, or had sold in the recent past, a parcel of development land. The objects of the study were to investigate the role of the landowner in the development process and to find out how much land was being withheld from the market as a result of the Community Land Scheme and the taxation of development gains at a rate of up to 80% – the policies in force at the time (see Ch. 2). It was the first study of its type in Britain and landowners' attitudes have not been investigated in such detail since. Landowners are difficult to study in Britain because there are no public records of land ownership (see Ch. 1). Studying owners of development land is still harder because each site has to be distinguished from development plans and other planning documents before work on tracing the owner can commence. To minimise this problem, the study was confined to one area – Greater Leicester – and information obtained about as many sites in that area as possible.

In this chapter emphasis is laid on two aspects of the landowner's decision model – deciding when to sell and what part to play in the development process. The consequences of these decisions on both the supply of development land and on the development process are investigated. A comparison is also made between the normative model of landowner behaviour set out in the previous chapter and the behaviour revealed by the owners in the survey.

The policy context

Leicestershire is regarded as one of the best examples in England of a city region, with Leicester situated at the centre of its sphere of influence (Hall *et al.* 1973). The county had a population of 788 589 in 1971 and a population of 835 647 in 1981 and is growing at a rate well in excess of the national average for England and Wales. The area from which the sample of landowners is taken is shown in Figure 6.1 and is the area defined as Greater Leicester in the county structure plan (Leicestershire County Council 1976).

Since 1945 the development of Leicester has progressed in a manner similar to many other provincial cities. Expansion during the 1950s and early 1960s took place on the fringe of the city, although mainly outside the city boundary as envisaged by the Leicester city development plan of 1952 (City of Leicester 1956). This period saw the creation of a continuous urban area extending from Glen Parva and Wigston in the south, to Braunstone and Glenfield in the west, Scraptoft and Thurnby in the east and Thurmaston to the north. Much of this development was unplanned in the proper sense because, although the county development plan (Leicestershire County Council 1959), first published in 1951, included a commitment to prepare town maps for a number of settlements on the periphery of Leicester, none were actually presented for statutory approval.

During the 1960s the county produced a series of village plans that allocated

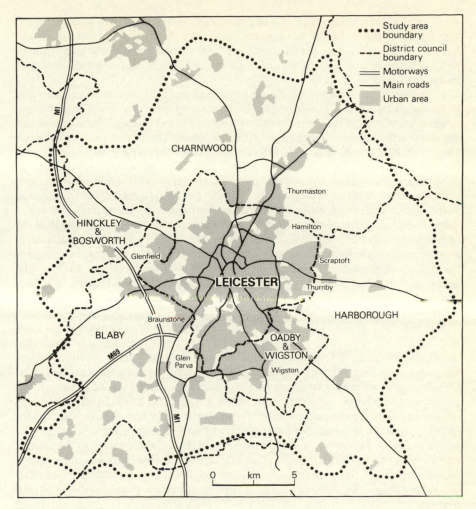

Figure 6.1 The Greater Leicester area.

large areas for residential development and between the late 1960s and late 1970s major schemes took place in villages away from the main built-up area of Leciester. Following approval of the structure plan in 1976, planning strategy has reverted to concentrating growth around Leicester although two events have occurred since then which make the structure plan a less relevant guide for development control. First, the National Coal Board's decision to exploit the Vale of Belvoir coalfield near Melton Mowbray is not anticipated in the structure plan; and second, the county has been unable to carry through a policy of developing Hamilton. This is the only large area of undeveloped land remaining within the city boundary, and in the structure plan it was proposed that the area should house 19 500 people as well as catering for industrial development. Although little objection was raised to this scheme at the public enquiry at which the structure plan was examined (Bridges & Vielba 1976), considerable local opposition was encountered when a local plan was prepared. As a result, there has been a severe shortage of housing land in central Leicestershire and a number of sites have been released on appeal even though their development does not accord with the policies of the structure plan (see Herington 1982).

Commercial and industrial development in the area has not been actively encouraged by central government. Leicester was always subject to industrial development certificate control until its suspension in January 1982 and was also subject to office development permit (ODP) control for a short period in the late 1960s. ODP control had little effect though as office space in the centre of Leicester increased by 91% between 1960 and 1975 (Strachan 1977). Some of this space still remains empty over ten years after it was built and in some cases can currently (1984) be rented at less than £15 per square metre, which is lower than current rents for modern industrial accommodation. In contrast, there has been a notable shortage of good industrial accommodation during most of the post-war period (see Fagg 1973). During the late 1970s Leicester's reputation as a prosperous manufacturing centre became dented and the city has not escaped the effects of the latest recession with an unemployment rate at 11.7%, just below the national average (February 1984). New industrial space is still in demand though, especially if the site has good access to the M1 and M69 motorways on the west side of Leicester.

The planning policies for Leicestershire adopted by local government have not sought to restrict development unduly, rather to direct it to preferred locations. These locations have varied in the post-war period from suburban sites adjoining Leicester to peripheral villages, and now back to suburban sites. Development within the inner city is also encouraged as the City of Leicester is a programme authority under the Inner Urban Areas Act 1978. In effect, owners of land in the urban fringe have some prospect that their sites will be released for development while owners of inner city sites know that development is likely to be encouraged. However, it should be stressed that *all* the owners in the sample had a real prospect of obtaining a planning consent if their land was in the urban fringe and, for most inner city owners, development was a viable prospect that would produce a site value in excess of current use value, even if only by a small margin.

The sample

The sample consists of 139 properties in either the urban fringe or within the built-up area for which information was obtained both about the owner and the site, and about the factors influencing the owner's behaviour. These sites were split approximately equally in number between those that had been sold or were currently on the market, including those subject to an option agreement (45%); and those retained by their owner (55%). According to the planning policies in force at the time, development was likely to be permitted, if not immediately at least in the near future, on all the properties in the survey and this stands in contrast to the properties considered in Chapter 7 where the policy context is rigidly opposed to development.

Details of the properties and their owners were derived in three ways. First,

47% of the sites were ascertained from the structure plan and other planning policy documents. The owners of these sites were then traced through the statutory register of planning decisions which each district council is required to keep (see McAuslan 1975) or by asking neighbouring occupiers. If it transpired that the land had been sold recently to a developer, an attempt was made to trace the previous owner or his agent.

Second, to ensure that the study included some small sites, use was made of data held by Leicester City Council and Leicestershire County Council. The city had recently identified all undeveloped parcels of land of less than 0.8 ha within their area and a sample was taken from these. The county keeps records of unimplemented planning permissions for small schemes and a sample was also taken of these. Although a number of the properties obtained in this way were not pursued because development was not likely to be a practical possibility in the foreseeable future, 24% of the sites in the sample are small sites derived from these sources. In all, both for the small sites and for sites on development plans, an approach was made to 128 owners and a successful interview was obtained with 78% of them.

Third, local estate agents were approached and encouraged to provide details regarding sales of development land with which they had been involved and of development properties which they were currently marketing. In the main, they proved most co-operative and generally had sufficient knowledge of their client owners to provide the required information. Details for 29% of the sample were obtained in this way, almost all of which related to owners who had sold rather than those still retaining their land.

The sites do not form one block of land either on the edge of Leicester or in the inner city but are located throughout the area delineated in Figure 6.1. Although it would be easier in some ways to take one specific block of land in the urban fringe, it is unlikely that it would contain sufficient parcels of land where there is a real prospect of obtaining planning permission in the foreseeable future and *at the time of the study*. It would be fascinating to monitor land ownership and development changes in such an area over a long period of time but this would require a study of at least ten years, which, so far, has not been carried out in Britain (but see Milgram 1967 for an example of an American study of this type). The approach used here of obtaining details about as many development sites as possible in one urban area, including its urban fringe, is the only alternative where the research is to be carried out over a period of one to two years (see Goodchild 1978b for further details).

Landowner and property characteristics

PROPERTY CHARACTERISTICS

The sample included 68 greenfield properties in the urban fringe ranging from small plots used for horticulture to extensive agricultural estates. All were allocated in a development plan for an urban use. The other 71 sites were within the urban area and fell into two groups. There were 31 re-development sites mostly located close to the CBD, where the land was more valuable for a commercial use than in its existing state, usually an industrial complex. Forty sites were 'infill' sites whose development would not involve the demolition of

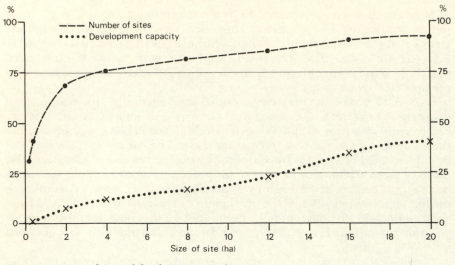

Figure 6.2   Size of site and development capacity.

existing buildings, only an increase in the density of development. Many of
these sites were parts of gardens of suburban houses. All types of site from the
cycle of re-development, therefore, were represented in the sample (see Ch. 4).

The sites ranged in size from small garden plots of approximately 0.02 ha to
one site of over 150 ha. The vast majority were comparatively small (42% were
less than 0.4 ha in extent) with most of the development capacity being
concentrated on a handful of large sites. This phenomenon has been noted
elsewhere. In JURUE's study of the West Midlands 2% of the sites with
planning permission for residential development contained 45% of the total
number of housing units for which consent had been given (JURUE 1977), and
in Leicester approximately 60% of the development capacity was contained on
8% of the sites which each had an area of 20 ha or more (see Fig. 6.2). By
contrast, nearly 70% of the sites had an area of less than 2 ha but contributed
only 7.5% of the development capacity. Thus it is the behaviour of those
holding the large sites that is important for assessing the impact of the owner on
the development process.

For analytical purposes, the 139 sites are classified into five types of property.
These are:

(a)   Agricultural land that is owner-occupied
(b)   Agricultural land not occupied by its owner (hereafter referred to as 'let'
      agricultural land)
(c)   Residential property
(d)   Commercial and industrial land
(e)   Vacant land.

The five types are chosen because it is relatively easy to classify a site into the
appropriate category and within each type the properties tend to have similar
attributes relevant to both landowner behaviour and to the development

Table 6.1 Usual attributes of the five types of property.

Property characteristics	Agricultural land		Residential property	Commercial and industrial property	Vacant land
	(a) Owner-occupied	(b) Not owner-occupied			
size of site	Large (>2 ha)	Large (>2 ha)	Small (<0.2 ha)	Small (<0.4 ha)	★
type of site	Greenfield	Greenfield	Infill	Re-development	★
developed use	Residential	Residential	Residential	Commercial/ industrial	Commercial/ industrial
whole/part of property unit	Part	Whole	Part	Whole	Whole
whole/part of development unit	Part	★	Whole	Whole	Whole
Percentage among the sample with three or more of these attributes	96%	97%	83%	100%	83%†

★ No usual attribute for this property characteristic.
† Percentage among the sample with two or more of these attributes.

process. These characteristics are set out in Table 6.1 and consist of size, type of site (greenfield, infill, etc.), developed use, and whether they consist of a whole or just part of a property unit and whole or part of a development site. The first three of these characteristics require little explanation other than to point out that vacant land is rarely suitable for residential development (see Ch. 8). The last two are important because they influence landowner behaviour. Where part of an owner's property forms a development site, the effect of its sale on the part that is left is an important consideration, particularly if the owner occupies that part. Where an owner's site can be developed on its own without the need to combine it with land in other ownership, it is more likely that the owner will influence the development process because his decision to sell can permit development to take place immediately.

LANDOWNER CHARACTERISTICS
Hypotheses can be formulated about both the characteristics of the owners for each of the five property types and about their behaviour. The owners of vacant land, 'let' agricultural land that is not owner-occupied and, to a lesser extent, commercial and industrial properties, are likely to have a greater knowledge of property matters through their occupation and/or experience with property transactions than are owners of the two other types of property. Most commercial and industrial properties and residential properties are occupied by their owner so that occupation is an important motive for both the owners of these types of property and for owner-occupiers of agricultural land. Vacant land and 'let' agricultural land are likely to be owned by 'investors'. This suggests, therefore, that there are four types of landowner, three of whom are owner-occupiers of agricultural land, residential property, and commercial and industrial land, with the fourth being an investor.

The survey indicates, however, that five types of landowner can be distinguished, not four, and these are (a) farmers, (b) residential owner-occupiers, (c) commercial and industrial concerns, (d) owners by inheritance, (e) professional landowners/speculators. The three types of owner-occupier are as described but there are two types of investor, not one. The professional landowner is the 'true' investor in land because he both buys and sells land with the intention of making a profit. Part of this profit may be obtained by developing the land as well so that it is not always possible to distinguish the professional landowner from the developer (see also pp. 126–7 below). 'Owners by inheritance' are those long-term landowners whose motives are not purely financial even though they do not occupy the land, and widely differing behaviour is apparent among this group.

The types of owner are distinguished by a specific set of attributes for nine types of characteristics and these characteristics are set out in detail in Table 6.2. They are

(a)   Occupancy status, i.e. whether the land is owner-occupied, let or held vacant
(b)   Occupation of the owner, i.e. whether a developer, estate agent, farmer, etc.
(c)   Whether the owner had purchased land at any time with the object of re-selling it at a later date for a profit

Table 6.2 Types of landowner and their characteristics.

Landowner characteristics	Farmers	Owners by inheritance	Residential owner-occupiers	Industrial and commercial concerns	Professional landowners
(a) Occupancy status	owner-occupier	land let	owner-occupier	owner-occupier	held vacant
(b) Occupation	farmer	non-property related occupation nor farmer	non-property related occupation	non-property related occupation	developer
(c) Purchased land speculatively at some time	no	no	no	no	yes
(d) Consociate wealth	not a 'millionaire'	not a 'millionaire', inheritance, control or charitable	not a 'millionaire'	'millionaire'	'millionaire'
(e) Motive of ownership	occupation or 'occupation and investment'		occupation	occupation or 'occupation and investment'	investment
(f) Legal personality	individual or joint owner	not a company	individual or joint owner	company	company
(g) Income from the property	over 10% of total income	yes	none	over 10% of total income	negligible if any
(h) Length of ownership	over 5 years	over 5 years	over 5 years	over 5 years	less than 6 years
(i) Method of acquisition	purchase	not purchase	*	purchase	purchase
Percentage among the sample with six or more of the attributes	90%	85%	76%	81%	82%

* No usual attribute for this characteristic.

Table 6.3 Type of Landowner by Type of Property.

Type of landowner	Agricultural land		Residential property	Commercial and industrial property	Vacant land	Total (no. of sites)
	(a) Owner-occupied	(b) Not owner-occupied				
farmers	16	3	2	—	—	21
owners by inheritance	—	14	6	2	4	26
residential owner-occupiers	5	2	30	1	1	39
commercial and industrial concerns	1	1	—	15	6	23
professional landowners	1	9	4	2	12	28
Total	23	29	42	20	23	137
Percentage	17	21	31	15	17	100

Percentage figures may not sum to 100 due to rounding (see also other tables in Ch. 6).

(d) Consociate wealth, i.e. the amount of other assets owned, expressed simply in terms of whether the owner is likely to be a millionaire or not
(e) Motive of ownership, i.e. occupation, investment, etc. (see pp. 77–8 above)
(f) Legal personality, i.e. owned by an individual, a company, a trust, charity, etc. (see Turner & Forse 1976 for further details)
(g) The proportion of the owner's total income that he receives from the property in its current use
(h) Duration of the present ownership
(i) The method of acquisition, i.e. purchase, inheritance or gift.

All the landowners in the sample had at least five of the attributes associated with one type of owner and most had six or more so that it was possible to classify each with some certainty.

The distribution of the five types of landowner among the five types of property is set out in Table 6.3 and, not surprisingly, each type of owner is associated with one particular property type. The majority of farmers, residential owner-occupiers, commercial and industrial concerns and owners by inheritance hold owner-occupied agricultural land, residential property, commercial and industrial property and 'let' agricultural land respectively. However, each type of landowner is found with at least two other types of property and professional landowners are least strongly associated with any particular type of property. They are the main owners of vacant land but are also a major owner of let agricultural land, even if much of this is kept vacant rather than actually let to a tenant. As a result, 'let' agricultural land is the one type of property where no single landowner type holds a majority of the sites. These five types of landowner are now used to analyse the behaviour of the different groups.

The decision to sell

The four basic reasons why a landowner decides to sell his land are set out in Chapter 5 above (see, in particular p. 102 above). They are as follows:

(a) A sale to achieve a financial gain
(b) A sale because of a need for cash, i.e. a forced sale
(c) A sale because the property has become unsuitable for its current use
(d) A sale for reasons personal to the landowner.

Table 6.4 lists the distribution of landowner's reasons, or likely reasons, for selling development land both by the type of property held and by the type of landowner. It should be borne in mind that over half the sample had *not* sold their land at the time of the interview and the classification for these owners is based on responses to a number of questions designed to ascertain the circumstances in which they would sell and the reasons why they had considered a sale in the past, assuming that this was the case. To emphasise this point the words 'sold' and 'selling' are used in inverted commas wherever owners' reasons for selling are discussed and no distinction is made between those who had actually sold and those retaining their land.

Table 6.4 Reasons for 'selling' development land by (a) type of property and (b) type of landowner.

Reasons for 'selling' development land	Financial gain	Need for cash	Property obsolete	Personal	Financial combination	Total (no. of sites)
(a) *Type of property*						
agricultural land						
(i) owner-occupied	14	—	2	5	2	23
(ii) not owner-occupied	15	1	1	4	8	29
residential property	7	2	3	25	5	42
commercial/industrial property	9	1	1	2	7	20
vacant land	11	1	—	4	7	23
Total	56	5	7	40	29	137*
Percentage	41	4	5	29	21	100
(b) *Type of landowner*						
farmer	13	—	2	4	2	21
owner by inheritance	12	2	1	2	10	27
residential owner-occupier	5	2	2	28	2	39
commercial and industrial concerns	9	—	1	4	10	24
professional landowner	17	1	1	3	6	28
Total	56	5	7	41	30	139
Percentage	40	4	5	29	22	100

*Two sites could not be readily classified and have been excluded from this part of the analysis.

It can be seen from Table 6.4 that 40% of the owners 'sold' for purely financial reasons. In other words, these owners sold or would sell because they found that the price which the market would offer for their land was sufficiently high to make a sale worthwhile to them. Very few owners (9%) had 'sold' either solely because of a need for cash or solely because the property was unsuitable for its current use. The latter reason, however, was often included with financial factors as a reason for 'selling' and is classified as 'financial combination'. It is noticeable that the highest proportion 'selling' for this reason is among commercial and industrial concerns. When their premises no longer meet modern standards they will endeavour to relocate but they may be unable to finance such a move unless the sale price from the property contains a significant amount of development value. This gives the owner a chance to buy modern premises and have sufficient monies to cover the cost of the move as well. The existence of the development value is, therefore, a critical or at least a very important consideration affecting the sale.

Twenty-nine per cent of the owners 'sold' for personal reasons; for example, following the death of the immediate owner a sale was made by his or her executors. Although there are examples of each landowner type 'selling' for this reason, the residential owner-occupier is the only type of owner where this reason is important (72% of residential owner-occupiers sold or were likely to sell for personal reasons). The distinction between residential owner-occupiers and other types of landowner is drawn even more sharply if the categories 'financial gain' and 'financial combination' are combined and compared with the other three. Eighty-two per cent of residential owner-occupiers had sold or were likely to sell for a reason unrelated to the land market. The equivalent percentages for farmers, owners by inheritance, commercial and industrial concerns and professional landowners are 29%, 26%, 21% and 19% respectively. Thus, apart from residential owner-occupiers, landowners are generally motivated by profit when deciding to sell, although professional landowners are the only group who both buy and sell for this reason.

Taxation and the decision to sell

The effect of a special tax on the supply of development land is debated furiously every time a new tax is proposed, and one of the objectives of the study in Leicester was to find out how much land was being withheld by owners because of DLT. At the time of survey in 1977, DLT had been in operation for less than a year and was levied at a top rate of 80%. Most owners of development land have to pay some tax on selling and will try to ensure that their tax liability is as small as possible. However, tax affects the timing of the decision to sell only when an owner decides either to sell because he believes the level of tax is favourable at the time or to retain the land and postpone the sale until the tax regime is less onerous. The distribution of owners for whom the level of taxation was an important consideration in deciding when to sell is shown in Table 6.5 for both the five types of property and the five types of landowner. In 24% of cases, the timing of the decision to sell was affected, or likely to be affected, by DLT while in a further 4% other taxes, usually CTT, were influential. These proportions are not particularly large but they merit further investigation.

Table 6.5 The influence of taxation, and especially DLT, on the decision to sell development land by type of property.

Type of property	Affected by DLT	Affected by other taxes	Not affected by taxation	Don't know	Total (no. of sites)
agricultural land					
(i) owner-occupied	8	1	14	—	23
(ii) not owner-occupied	12	2	14	1	29
residential property	4	—	38	—	42
commercial/industrial					
property	5	2	13	—	20
vacant land	4	1	16	2	23
total	33	6	95	3	137
percentage	24	4	69	2	100

From Table 6.5 it can be seen that owners of agricultural land are more likely to be influenced by DLT than owners of other types of property. This conforms with the model presented in Chapter 5 to the extent that the impact of DLT tends to be greatest on greenfield properties because the development value is large in relation to the current use value. On urban sites, the *total* value may be higher but the development value forms a much smaller proportion because of the more intensive (and valuable) current use of the property (see the example in Ch. 5). Residential owner-occupiers are the least affected (10%) both because their property is usually exempt and because financial gain is of less concern to them. Professional landowners, ironically, are the next least affected by DLT because, in many cases, they have recently purchased the land and the acquisition price gives them a high base value so that little, if any, tax is payable.

DLT impinges most on greenfield sites and on the large sites. The owners of 35% of greenfield sites, where land was passing from a rural to an urban use for the first time, were affected by DLT in their decision. This is a significantly higher proportion than for owners of urban sites (12.5%), whether infill or re-development. In general, the larger the parcel of development land, the greater is its value, and the larger the site, the more likely is its owner to be influenced by DLT. For parcels of 2 ha and over, 42% were affected by DLT and, if other taxes are included, this proportion is increased to approximately half. Owners of small sites may avoid DLT simply because the amount of development value realised is insufficient to produce an assessment. In 1977, an owner could receive £10 000 of development value before being subject to DLT. This important exemption has now been raised to £75 000 per annum (see Ch. 2) but this amount soon disappears with a site of even 2 ha. An owner of agricultural land in Leicester selling such a site with planning permission for residential development in 1977 would have paid approximately half the proceeds of £100 000 in tax. It is not surprising, therefore, that owners were reluctant to sell at that time if they thought there was a prospect of DLT being reduced in the future.

A series of questions was put to the landowners in the sample with the object of ascertaining both their knowledge of DLT and their expectations and attitudes towards the tax. Of those with sufficient knowledge to have an opinion (46% were excluded on this account), 89% thought that the rate for DLT was too high and 66% thought that it would be reduced in the future. The reasons given for the anticipated reduction in the tax rate were slightly unexpected. At the time, the Conservative opposition was pledged to reduce DLT to 50–60% (Rossi 1977). A change of government, however, was not seen as the only reason for a change. A reduction in the supply of development land as a result of the tax, it was argued, would force the government, *regardless of party*, to reduce DLT.

Nineteen (25%) of the 76 holders of the development land in the sample were unlikely to offer their sites for sale whilst DLT was in force at 80%. Twelve of these owners had a sufficient understanding of DLT to know its likely impact on their net of tax proceeds while the remaining seven owners did not possess sufficient knowledge to make this assessment or their information was inaccurate, and this lack of knowledge led them generally to over-estimate the amount of tax that would be payable on sale. With one exception, these seven owners all held sites of less than 2 ha. The importance to the development process of the owners of large sites is emphasised by this example as the 19 holders who were not likely to offer their land for sale, because of DLT, held approximately 300 ha of develoment land between them and this represented about 60% of the development capacity owned by all 76 holders in the sample.

Three of these 19 holders intended to develop the land themselves. DLT is still payable when a development project commences so that these 'landowners' may have postponed the start of development if they considered that there was a possibility of the rate of DLT being reduced in the future. If, however, these three sites are removed from the schedule of land withheld because of the tax and transferred to those unaffected, which is probably optimistic, more than 50% of the development capacity among the holders of the sample was still unlikely to be offered for sale while DLT remained at a top rate of 80%.

The evidence is therefore clear. A large proportion of the development capacity was withheld from the market in Leicester while DLT was levied at a rate of up to 80%. Although this view was widely held at the time by those involved in the land market (see, for example, the results of the FT/RICS poll – *Financial Times* 1978) and a similar view was expressed during the lives of the development charge and of Betterment Levy (see Ch. 2), this is the first time evidence, which is not anecdotal, has been obtained in support of this contention.

The landowner and the development process

This section looks at the extent to which landowners involved themselves in the planning process and the effect of this involvement in the identification of development land and in the initiation of development (see Ch. 4).

A synopsis of the planning history for the development sites is set out in Table 6.6. A planning application had been submitted on 93 (68%) of the sites and a consent had been obtained in 69 cases (50%). On only 24 sites had there been

Table 6.6 The distribution of planning applications and planning permissions among the five types of property.

Type of property	Planning history				
	Planning consent only	Planning consent and refusals	Planning refusals only	No planning applications	Total (no. of sites)
agricultural land owner-occupied	3	6	8	6	23
agricultural land not owner-occupied	7	3	8	11	29
residential property	16	4	5	17	42
commercial and industrial property	12	1	2	5	20
vacant land	12	5	1	5	23
total	50	19	24	44	137
percentage	36	14	18	32	100

planning refusals. These refusals were concentrated on the agricultural properties, the rate of refusal on the three types of urban property being comparatively low. Both planning consents and refusals had been received on some of the sites and more than one planning application had been submitted on 54 sites and more than five applications on eight sites.

The majority of the planning applications were decided by local planning authorities but an appeal had been lodged on 12 sites. The appeals were undertaken by seven landowners and by five developers holding either an option or a conditional contract to purchase the site. Four of the appeals were upheld, two of which were undertaken by landowners. In both of these cases, once consent was obtained, the development site was sold by the landowner. One other landowner who had undertaken an appeal sold his property despite receiving a planning refusal. None of the other three landowners had sold after receiving a planning refusal on appeal. In the cases where a developer held an option and the appeal was dismissed, the options had not been exercised although they had been renewed by the developer who presumably thought there was a possibility that planning permission would be granted at some time.

The reasons landowners gave for submitting planning applications are worth noting. Fifty-five per cent of the applications were submitted to 'realise the development value' of the site or, in other words, so that the land could be sold with the benefit of planning permission. The remainder had been submitted either because the owner wanted to develop for his own use (9%) or to develop the land speculatively for profit (36%). The applications submitted for this last reason were all made by professional landowners; there was no question of any other type of landowner becoming a 'developer'. This is emphasised by the intentions of those holding land at the time of the survey. Fifteen (83%) of the 18 professional landowners thought that there was some likelihood of developing

Table 6.7 The strategy adopted by owners of urban fringe sites by which to sell development land (sellers and holders).

Strategy	Sub-total	Total (no. of sites)
Sellers		
(a) Land sold with the benefit of planning permission:		
(i) obtained at the earliest opportunity	10	
(ii) not obtained at the earliest opportunity	6	
Total: land sold with permission		16 (24%)
(b) Land sold without the benefit of planning permission:		
(i) where an application had been submitted	7	
(ii) where no application had been submitted	9	
Total: land sold without permission		16 (24%)
Total: sellers	32	32 (47%)
Holders		
(a) Land to be sold with the benefit of planning permission:		
(i) where planning permission already granted	6	
(ii) where an application submitted but refused	11	
(iii) where no application submitted	6	
Total: land to be sold with permission		23 (34%)
(b) Land to be sold without the benefit of planning permission:		
(i) where planning permission already granted	2	
(ii) where planning application refused	5	
(iii) where no application submitted	6	
Total: land to be sold without permission		13 (19%)
Total: Holders	36	36 (53%)
Total: sellers and holders		68 (100%)

the land themselves in contrast with only 10% of the other types of landowner. The distinction, therefore, between landowners and developers is usually clear cut, except in the case of professional landowners. Many of the sites held by owners of this type were part of a developer's long-term land bank. Others were held more speculatively in that the owner would sell or develop himself depending on market circumstances. Other types of landowner rarely contemplated developing their land themselves unless it was for their own use because development lay outside their competence.

The data show that there had been a considerable amount of activity in terms of planning applications on the 139 sites. The purpose of that activity needs to be considered in a little more detail as planning permission is important to the investment strategy of urban fringe site owners (see Table 6.7). Thirty-one per cent of those that had sold behaved 'normatively' in that they had obtained planning permission at the earliest opportunity. It is more difficult to judge the

Table 6.8 The distribution of owners who had offered, or intended to offer, their land for sale with the benefit of planning permission by type of landowner.

| Types of Landowner | Consent obtained | Planning permission before sale | | Total |
		Consent not obtained	'Other' and don't knows	
farmers	17	3	1	21
owners by inheritance	19	5	3	27
residential owner-occupiers	15	12	12	39
commercial and industrial concerns	15	5	4	24
professional landowners	24	1	3	28
Total	90	26	23	139
percentage	65	19	17	100

position for holders because even though six had obtained a consent none were obtained at the earliest opportunity. Seventeen holders, however, had applied for planning permission but had received only refusals and were, therefore, *trying* to get a consent as early as possible. They too are regarded as behaving in accordance with the investment model. Thirty-seven per cent of the urban fringe site owners, however, decided not to sell because planning permission had been refused, in contrast to only 16% of the owners of urban sites, showing, as suggested by the model, that consent is of greater importance to the investment strategy of owners of greenfield sites.

Selling land with the benefit of planning permission, whether it is an urban fringe or an inner city site, is to be anticipated because the owner obtains a higher price (see Ch. 5). The owners who had sold, or intended to sell, their land with the benefit of planning consent are shown in Table 6.8. At least two-thirds of the sample intended to do this but it is noticeable that the proportion (86%) is much higher for professional landowners than for some other categories of owner. The lowest proportion is for residential owner-occupiers (38%) and provides further evidence of the divergence of this group's behaviour from that antici-pated by the model. Owners are also expected to appeal against the refusal of planning consent (see Ch. 5, p. 103). Appeals had been lodged on only 12 of the sites, but 42% of the owners were prepared to make an appeal to the SOS if this proved necessary in spite of the costs that could be involved. Most were not put to the test because consent was granted. Again, professional landowners (at 61%) were more likely to lodge an appeal than other owners, while residential owner-occupiers were the least likely (21%).

Landowners' influence on the development process

The identification of development land and the initiation of development on it are distinguished in Chapter 4 as the key events that must occur before development can take place (see in particular pp. 88–9). The actors responsible for identifying sites and initiating development among the Leicester sample give results in marked contrast to those in the previous sections of this chapter. Whereas each type of landowner is associated with a pattern of behaviour in their decision to sell, it is the characteristics of the property that are more likely to determine the influence of that behaviour on the development process.

There is one circumstance where the landowner clearly contributes nothing to the process and this is where he sells following an approach by a prospective purchaser. Twenty owners (14%) fall into this category and they own urban fringe sites usually in excess of 2 ha which are not capable of being developed on their own. The owners are either farmers or owners by inheritance but never professional landowners. It is known that developers work hard to obtain building land which is generally in short supply (see Ch. 4) so that it is not surprising that they concentrate their efforts on seeking out large sites because contacting the owner and negotiating with him can take the same amount of time regardless of the site's size. Properties that cannot be developed on their own are rarely pooled by neighbours and offered for sale as a developable unit.

IDENTIFYING DEVELOPMENT LAND

A site is identified as development land either by its allocation on a development plan or by planning permission being granted on land not previously allocated. The planner is usually responsible for identification where land is allocated while the landowner or developer is responsible where a site is identified through a planning consent (see Ch. 4). The distribution of actors responsible for identifying the development sites in the sample are subdivided by the nature and type of development site, and by the size of site (see Table 6.9). Twenty-seven per cent of the sites were, or were likely to be, identified by a combination of actors which included the landowner. Thus, landowners were responsible, either wholly or partially, for identifying almost half the total number of sites in the sample. In contrast, developers, on their own, were responsible for identifying only 10% of the sites. The planner was responsible for identifying 23% of the development sites without assistance from other actors. A 'non-landowner combination' of actors was responsible for identifying a further 13% of the sites and this combination usually consisted of the planner and developer. Consumers and adjoining owners were very occasionally responsible for identifying development land either on their own or in combination with other actors, usually the planner.

There is a clear pattern in the type of sites that the various actors identify. Landowners identify many of the small sites within the urban area, particularly infill sites that can be developed individually. The planners identify the large agricultural sites in the urban fringe which are held in more than one ownership. The sites that developers identify are of no particular size but tend to be re-development sites or vacant land. Developers also concentrate on identifying sites that can be developed as a whole. The developer has most to lose if, having assembled a site from a number of ownerships, his planning application is refused. He will have incurred time, effort and expense (even if only options are taken out on the land) but have nothing to show for it. The landowner, however, has little to lose but everything to gain if an application is successful.

Table 6.9 The distribution of actors responsible for the identification of development land by various site characteristics.

	Landowner	Landowner combination	Developer	Planner	Non-landowner combination	Others	Total (no. of sites)
Nature of site							
urban fringe	9	13	5	30	10	1	68
infill	20	8	3	1	3	5	40
re-development	8	11	6	1	5	–	31
Size of site							
<0.4 ha	20	14	6	4	9	5	58
0.4–2.0 ha	10	11	4	9	3	1	38
>2.0 ha	7	7	4	19	6	–	43
Whole/part site							
whole site	30	20	11	12	7	3	83
part site	3	10	3	17	8	3	44
don't know	4	2	–	3	3	–	12
Total	37	32	14	32	18	6	139
percentage	27	23	10	23	13	4	100

As a consequence, developers are prepared to assemble a site from land in more than one ownership only when that site has been allocated for development and the risk of not obtaining a planning consent is minimal.

The actions of landowners in selling their properties, or an interest in them, results, therefore, in a large number of sites being identified as development land; but the importance of the role played by landowners is exaggerated when the analysis is based solely on the *number* of sites. If the analysis is conducted on an areal basis the results are very different. The development sites that were identified or were likely to be identified by landowners, either alone or in combination with other actors, only made up approximately 20% of the development capacity contained in the sample. The planners, because they had identified the largest sites, were responsible for identifying approximately 60% of the development capacity, while the remaining 20% had been identified or was likely to be identified by developers, 'non-landowner combinations' and other actors. The proportion of development capacity identified by landowners alone is about 9% while developers are responsible for identifying 8%. Thus private sector actors were responsible for identifying, wholly or partially, about 40% of the development capacity contained by the sites in the sample, and 77% of the sites.

The figure of 40% can be contrasted with data obtained from two other surveys. The JURUE survey found that 38% of the land released for housing development in their study area was not allocated for residential use on an approved development plan (JURUE 1977). The DOE's study of the south-east found that 'less than half the land actually becoming available for development has progressed through the process from land previously considered as available in *planning terms*' (DOE 1975b, p. 19).

Although slightly different criteria have been adopted here, the private sector actors appear to have identified a marginally smaller proportion of the development capacity in the Leicester area than shown by the other two studies. This is due to the following:

(a) The pressure for new development in the Leicester area was probably not as great, nor the planning policies as restrictive, when compared with circumstances in either the south-east of England or the West Midlands.

(b) The other two studies were conducted in the early 1970s during a period of exceptional demand for building land when the private sector actors were especially keen to identify development land.

(c) A large amount of land had recently been identified in the Leicester area by the planners through the approval of the Leicestershire structure plan.

The more extensive role played by the planners in identifying land in the Leicester area, when compared with those played in the West Midlands and the south-east, is further emphasised by the fact that approximately 90% of the development capacity contained in the sample sites was allocated on a development plan as suitable for a use for which it had been or was likely to be developed. However, this stems largely from the selection of the sites in the survey. The sample sites were chosen principally because they *were* allocated for development to ensure that there were no sites where the prospect of development was remote. Since 1977 development has taken place in Leicester on land that was not allocated for an urban use at the time of the survey and the sample probably contains too few of these examples (see Herington 1982).

INITIATION OF DEVELOPMENT

Any of the three principal actors in the development process can be responsible for initiating development, but the developer is more likely to be responsible for this event than the landowner or planner because the key decision in the development process is generally regarded as the developer's decision to buy a parcel of land (see Ch. 4). There are circumstances, however, where the landowner's decision to sell is more influential in at least determining *when* a site is developed. These situations are as follows:

(a) Where land is sold with the benefit of planning permission
(b) Where the decision to sell is not influenced by the other actors in the development process, i.e. an approach by a developer
(c) Where development can and is likely to commence soon after the land is sold.

It is not always easy to judge how quickly development will commence once land has been purchased by a developer. One factor to be considered is the availability of services. Services need not be available even if outline planning permission has been granted so that development cannot take place until these are provided either by statutory undertakers or by the developer. Once land has been purchased by a developer, he may choose to hold it in his land bank simply because it does not suit his schedule of work to proceed immediately. He may also decide to acquire adjoining parcels of land to enlarge the development site. In either case, the landowner's decision to sell will not initiate development. Owners of land that cannot be developed on its own are very unlikely to initiate development, except where they can postpone their decision to sell and prevent development taking place on the remainder of the site until it suits them. It should be remembered, however, that a DOE survey carried out in 1977 found that development had commenced on 70% of the land for which there had been an outstanding planning consent two years earlier (DOE 1978c). As landowners are often responsible for obtaining planning permission before selling, their decision can be influential in determining when a development scheme takes place.

Table 6.10 shows the distribution of the actors responsible for initiating development on the sites in the survey. Landowners were regarded as solely responsible for initiating development by their decision to sell on 19% of the sites, while their decision to sell was partially responsible for this event on a further 29% of the sites. Thus, the landowners contributed to, or were likely to contribute to, the initiation of development on approximately 48% of the sites in the sample. Developers were considered responsible for initiating development on 28% of the sites with a further 19% initiated by a combination of actors that excluded the landowner and was usually formed by planners and developers.

The sites that landowners identify as development land are very similar to those on which they initiate development. These are small urban sites, particularly infill sites, which can be developed singly. Many are found on residential

Table 6.10 The distribution of actors responsible for the initiation of development by various site characteristics.

	Landowner	Landowner combination	Developer	Non-landowner combination	Others (inc. planners)	Total (no. of sites)
Nature of site						
urban fringe	10	14	21	18	5	68
infill	13	16	7	4	–	40
re-development	4	11	11	5	–	31
Size of site						
<0.4 ha	13	26	10	9	–	58
0.4–2.0 ha	13	7	13	4	1	38
>2.0 ha	1	8	16	14	4	43
Whole/part site						
whole site	26	24	26	7	–	83
part site	–	10	10	19	5	44
don't know	1	7	3	1	–	12
Total	27	41	39	27	5	139
percentage	19	29	28	19	4	100

properties and are typically plots for small houses. It is not surprising that residential owner-occupiers are often responsible for initiating development by their decision to sell because they tend to sell for personal reasons and not in response to market forces.

Developers play an important role in initiating development on all types of site but their role is particularly important on vacant land. Such sites often have problems and there is no guarantee that development will start simply because the property is sold. This is reflected by the fact that professional landowners had not initiated, or were unlikely to initiate, development as *landowners*. Most intended to build on the land themselves and so would initiate development as a developer. Where they intended to sell, it was highly likely that the new owner would continue to hold the land vacant.

Planners are responsible, albeit partially, for initiating a large amount of development (Table 6.10). This is reinforced if the contribution of each actor is analysed in terms of the amount of land instead of treating each site as an equal unit. The development on four of the six sites with an area of 30 ha and over was likely to be initiated by the developer and the planner in combination and approaching 60% of the total development capacity was likely to be, or had been, initiated by non-landowner combinations principally formed by these two actors. On these sites, the planners' decisions to allocate particular parcels of land for development resulted in a developer acquiring the land and the necessary services being provided either by the local authority, a statutory undertaker or the developer himself under a Section 52 Agreement. Although the planner was not in direct control of the process throughout, the initial decision to allocate started a chain reaction which, in a reasonably short timespan, led to the desired result. This is, of course, on urban fringe sites where the development pressures are greatest. The same is not true for inner city sites.

Landowners' decisions to sell were solely responsible for initiating development on 19% of the sites in the sample but these sites contained only approximately 3% of the total development capacity. The sites on which the landowners were partially responsible for initiating development make up 29% of the sites by number but only approximately 11% in terms of area. Thus, the landowner's decision to sell had been responsible or was likely to be responsible for initiating development on less than 15% of the development capacity contained by the sample.

The importance of the landowner in the development process tends to be, therefore, in inverse proportion to the size of the site owned. In general, the smaller the site the more crucial are the landowner's actions to determining when a site is developed. In the largest development schemes, the landowner's role is insignificant and these are the schemes of greatest importance. Just as the landowner's role is inversely proportional to the size of the site, so the planner's is directly opposite. The larger the scheme, the more likely it is that a public sector decision is crucial to the project (see further discussion in Ch. 9).

Speculation and the investment model

The final section of this chapter reverts to a comparison of the behaviour observed among the sample of owners and the investment model set out in Chapter 5. This comparison is achieved through giving each site owner a 'speculator score' by attributing points, up to a maximum of 100, to the owner on the basis of the decisions he took and the degree to which they accord with the model. The more important decisions, such as the reasons for acquiring the site and for selling, are weighted more heavily than some operational aspects such as whether the property was sold by auction or by tender, but points were awarded for all aspects of the normative model (see Goodchild 1978b for further details). It is not claimed that there is much observable difference between the behaviour of owners with scores of 40 and 50, but a score of over 80 does indicate a landowner whose actions conform with most aspects of the investment model, while a score of less than 20 indicates a landowner not especially motivated by financial gain.

The individual scores among the sample range from three residential owner-occupiers with zero to two professional landowners with scores of 97 out of 100. The mean score was 45.8 and the distribution of values amongst the owners is normally distributed around the mean.[1] The scores for each of the five types of landowner are shown in Figure 6.3. Three general positions are apparent. Professional landowners and residential owner-occupiers stand out as distinct groups whilst the three other types of landowner occupy an intermediate position. The behaviour of the professional landowner conforms fairly closely to the model particularly among the 12 that have a score of 80 or over. The professional landowners with scores of less than 60 (eight in all) consist mainly

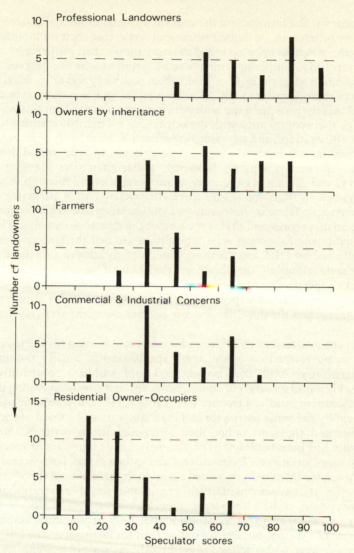

Figure 6.3 Frequency distribution of speculator scores among the five types of landowner.

of those who had either sold their businesses, including their land banks, or intended to develop the land themselves and could not envisage disposing of the land in any other way. The 'owners by inheritance' show a greater range in their scores than any other type of landowner. At one extreme, a number conform quite closely to the normative model of behaviour, principally because they were often wealthy and had investment as their motive of ownership. At the other end of the scale, the behaviour of some 'owners by inheritance' was similar to that associated with residential owner-occupiers and it may be no coincidence that the owners by inheritance with the lowest speculator scores frequently held residential property.

In contrast, the farmers and the commercial and industrial concerns showed relatively little variation in their behaviour, reflecting their willingness to sell as long as the purchase price exceeded the use value of their property by a sufficient margin to allow a superior property to be acquired with the proceeds. To both types of landowner the level of land values was a key factor in determining the timing of their decision to sell. Most residential owner-occupiers in the sample realised that they owned a site with development potential but this was often the extent of their conformity with the normative model. Most such owners with scores of 40 or more, and who were influenced or were likely to be influenced by contextual factors in the timing of their decision to sell, owned development sites that formed a separate property, rather than sites forming part of a property, and often had experience of property matters through their work.

In general, a high speculator score is associated with particular *landowner* characteristics. There is, however, one *site* characteristic which correlates with the speculator scores and that is the size of the development site. This may be explained in the following way. Those who owned the largest sites were the most affected by DLT and the most concerned to achieve a financial gain. The larger the development site, therefore, the harder it became for a landowner not to act like a speculator attempting to maximise the return from the asset. Careful analysis of the individual speculator scores suggests that this change in attitude takes place when the development site reaches the comparatively small size of 0.4 ha.

Speculation is an emotive term and it is not uncommon for the troubles of the world to be blamed on speculators. Speculation is usually thought of as a short-term affair with land bought and sold within a comparatively short period. The rapid turnover of land is, however, not common among the owners of development land in Leicester (see Table 6.11). Only 26% of the sites had been held by the same owner for less than six years and a third of these owners had inherited the land rather than purchased it. In contrast, 60% of the properties had been held in the same ownership for ten years or more and 47% for 20 years or more. Even among the professional landowners it is not uncommon for them to have owned a particular piece of land for over five years. In Leicester, the ownership of development land, whether in the urban fringe or inner city, tends to be a long-term affair.

It also seems reasonable to conclude that only professional landowners act largely as speculators, buying *and* selling land for financial reasons. If, however, speculation were to be defined more broadly as simply holding and using an asset in the hope that its value will increase, or not selling that asset except at a price which exceeds a specific sum regardless of the reason as to why the owner acquired the asset, then the extent of speculative activity is considerable. Most landowners in the sample sold, or were likely to sell, for reasons that include the achievement of a financial gain. Only 38% of the sample sold, or were likely to sell, for personal or other non-investment reasons. Moreover, the importance to the development process of these owners is much less than this when the size of the development sites they hold is taken into account. Less than 15% of the development capacity of the sample was sold, or was likely to be sold, for reasons that did not include obtaining a financial gain. But is speculation, in this broad sense, necessarily bad?

It may be argued that the landowner makes a positive contribution to the

Table 6.11 Duration for which land had been held by type of landowner.

Duration	Farmer	Owner by inheritance	Residential owner-occupier	Commercial and industrial concerns	Professional landowner	Total	
<6 years	4	5	9	2	16	36	(26%)
6–20 years	6	4	13	4	9	36	(26%)
>20 years	11	18	16	18	3	66	(48%)
Total	21	27	38★	24	28	138	
percentage	15	20	28	17	20		(100%)

★One site could not be dated.

development process by identifying development land, principally small urban sites. Where a development site exists on residential property, it is not unreasonable to regard the landowner as the principal actor in the development process because his decision to sell frequently initiates development as well as resulting in the identification of development land; and if the development process benefits from landowners making sites available at about the time when development can first take place, landowners' actions do not conflict with the development process.

Conflicts can arise. It has been contended that a major cause of delay in land progressing through the planning stages of the development process from the submission of an outline planning application to the start of construction is 'change of ownership' (DOE 1975b, 1978c). On the other hand, if landowners do not sell development land until planning permission has been granted this helps developers to the extent that it reduces their risk; and on the assumption that no development can take place until the landowner has decided to sell, and that an outline planning application is unlikely to be submitted without the owner first considering the possibility of selling, a change in ownership during the planning stages delays development only if it takes longer to transfer the land after an outline consent has been obtained than before, and/or the planning process operates less effectively where the applicant changes during the course of the site's progress through the planning stages.

The principal conflict arises where a landowner does not want to sell land that is required for development. This happens quite frequently on urban sites where the development value does not exceed the current use value of the land. It also occurs where owners are withholding land because they expect that the rate of tax on the proceeds from the sale of development land will be reduced in the future, or they do not regard the net of tax proceeds from the sale as sufficient inducement to sell. But this kind of 'speculation' is not the only reason why land is withheld from the market. Those sites which have been on a land availability schedule the longest are usually owned by persons who are not looking for a financial gain. This aspect of the development process is not revealed, by, for example, the two EIU studies (DOE 1975b, 1978c) because they were concerned only with land that had actually received planning permission, not with land that was just allocated for development.

This is an important point. Whenever a landowner is withholding land it is unlikely that he will submit a planning application. Thus, the imposition of a tax, such as DLT, not only leads to conflict between landowners and the development process, because they do not want to sell, it also discourages landowners from submitting planning applications which may result in the identification of development land, further decreasing the positive contribution that they can make to the process. The evidence from the survey shows that the supply of development land was reduced partly because owners expected the rate of DLT to be reduced and partly because the net of tax proceeds did not provide a sufficient inducement to sell.

Finally, landowners may be in conflict with planners because they want development to take place on their land, land which is not considered appropriate by the planners. Disagreement also occurs when the planners have allocated an owner's land for development but do not wish to grant consent until further plans are prepared or until infrastructure has been provided. This conflict, however, is unavoidable in a system that allows landowners to submit planning applications from which they will obtain a financial benefit if consent is granted and where that consent is not readily granted by the planners. Yet the same action by landowners, of submitting planning applications, sometimes leads to the identification of development land and the landowner making a positive contribution to the development process. Just because the landowner is often in conflict with the planner it does not necessarily follow that the former is in conflict with the development process.

Conclusion

The principal findings from the study in Leicester can be briefly summarised as follows:

(a)   There are at least five types of landowner each with their own pattern of behaviour.

(b)   The behaviour of professional landowners conforms quite closely with the normative model set out in Chapter 5, although most landowners sell for financial reasons to obtain a capital gain. The only group who rarely sell for this reason are residential owner-occupiers.

(c)   Landowners, through their decision to sell, are responsible both for identifying a significant amount of development land and for initiating development on it, and their importance to the development process is inversely proportional to the size of site they own.

(d)   Landowners are influenced by the taxes imposed on them and in the Leicester area 60% of the development capacity was being withheld from the market in 1977 while DLT was levied at a marginal rate of up to 80%.

Some of the policy implications from these findings are discussed in Chapter 9.

Note

1 The mean and standard deviation for each group are as follows:

	Number	Mean	Standard Deviation
professional landowners	28	72	16.5
owners by inheritance	27	53	21.4
farmers	21	44	13.3
commercial and industrial concerns	24	45	14.1
residential owner-occupiers	39	24	16.5

7 Landowners and the development of land in the Metropolitan Green Belt

Introduction

In spite of continuous pressure for development, restraint on the development of land within the Metropolitan Green Belt (MGB) has, for the most part, been firmly imposed for the last 30 years. Throughout the post-war period, southeast England has experienced economic growth and population increase. The region's population rose from 15.216 million in 1951 to 17.027 million in 1981, and at the same time has been re-distributed, people moving, first, largely from London to the Outer Metropolitan Area, and then from London to the rest of the region (SEJPT 1970, 1976, Standing Conference 1983a). Nevertheless, acquiring planning permission for residential development within the MGB has normally proved a difficult and protracted procedure, usually requiring a successful appeal decision following refusal by the local planning authority. The financial rewards for the successful landowner have, however, been substantial, continuing to encourage land speculation among those owning land close to the urban edge.

Two of the three main decision areas discussed in Chapter 5 receive particular attention in this case study. They are the involvement of the owner in the development process, and especially the relations the owner establishes with the developer, and the land management decisions of the owner prior to acquiring planning permission. As argued in Chapter 5 (see p. 98), there is no reason to believe that the owner should not seek planning permission at the earliest possibility in the MGB, as elsewhere, with one important qualification. Despite the demand for development in green belts, planning permission is not easily obtained (see JURUE 1974, 1977) and depends largely on the particular characteristics of the site (see Smith 1983). Under these circumstances owners have to think carefully about the financial consequences of failure. The high cost of appeals for example, has to be traded-off against the financial rewards of success. It follows that if land is bought in the expectation that it will have to be held for some time before there is a reasonable chance of its development, its purchase price will be heavily discounted to reflect both this delay and the risk that planning permission may never be given.

In order to examine these issues in detail, several surveys were conducted as part of a broader study of London's Green Belt (see Munton 1983). The first of these surveys consisted of interviews with district valuers, conducted with the assistance of the Chief Valuer's Office, and carried out because of the lack of published information on land values and the structure of property markets within the MGB. In the second survey, 13 developers known to have built houses on green belt land were interviewed in order to establish what property

Figure 7.1 The Metropolitan Green Belt, 1976 and 1984.

interests they held within the MGB and how they worked alongside landowners in trying to bring green belt land forward for development. In the third study, 185 farmers, both owner-occupiers and tenants, in three separate locations within the inner half of the MGB (see Fig. 7.1), were interviewed in order to obtain information on the attempts that had been made to acquire planning permission on the land they occupied and to discuss with them the manner in which they farmed and maintained their land.[1]

Before these issues can be examined in detail, it is necessary to sketch out important matters of background, including the nature of green belt policy, the rate of urban development in the MGB and what is known of the pattern of ownership in London's Green Belt.

The MGB: planning policy, development and land ownership

PLANNING POLICY

In the absence of any other effective means of controlling urban growth, a substantial area of land (about 20 000 ha) was purchased by local authorities in the inter-war period with the intention of creating a green belt. This land was subsequently incorporated into a much larger statutory green belt in the 1950s following the approval of the initial development plans for the London County Council and surrounding counties (see Fig. 7.1). Since that time local planning authorities have sought to extend the area of restraint in order to restrict the growth of towns beyond the outer boundary of the original green belt, and there followed a period of confusion during the 1970s when various categories of statutory and non-statutory green belt were in existence. This confusion was brought to an end in the early 1980s with the approval of structure plans by the SOS (DOE). He insisted that the Green Belt did not need to be more than 20–25 km wide, except for some extensions along axes of especially severe development pressure (see Fig. 7.1), with the result that the MGB now covers an area of 4300 km^2. This area is approximately 50% greater than that agreed to in the 1950s but is considerably less than the 5800 km^2 of green belt proposed by the local planning authorities in their structure plans (see Munton 1983, Ch. 2).

The aims of green belt restraint were laid down more than 25 years ago in Circulars 42/55 and 50/57 (MHLG 1955, 1957), and they still form the basis of government policy (see DOE 1984b). Green belts are regarded as strategic planning instruments designed to check the outward growth of an urban area, to prevent the coalescence of neighbouring towns, or to preserve the special character of a town. In the case of the MGB, the first of these aims remains the most important, although the second has assumed greater significance as the MGB has been extended. These aims are largely realised through the operation of the development control system. Paragraph 5 of Circular 42/55 reads

> inside a green belt approval should not be given, except in very special circumstances, for the construction of new buildings or for the change of use of existing buildings for purposes other than for agriculture, sport, cemeteries, institutions standing in extensive grounds, and other uses appropriate to a rural area (MHLG 1955);

but the key point to emphasise is that central government regards green belt restraint as a strategic planning instrument capable of shaping the pattern of urban growth at regional and sub-regional scales, while local authorities treat the green belt as an additional development control tool with which to limit development and to protect local amenities.

Government policy on the purpose of green belts has remained virtually unchanged since 1955. Until recently, most controversy has centred on matters of implementation rather than questions of principle. On the two occasions central government has sought the release of land in the MGB in order to meet some of London's housing needs (MHLG 1963, DOE 1973c), little *additional* land was identified, partly because of the opposition of local authorities (Munton 1983, pp. 64–7). A greater degree of uncertainty over the future of green belts was introduced in 1983 with the publication of two draft circulars on the supply of housing land and green belts (DOE 1983b, 1983c) and the proposal by a consortium of volume house-builders to construct a number of 'villages' in green belts. The green belt draft circular encouraged local authorities to exclude land from green belt restraint that might be needed for future development. The draft circular on green belts became the subject of popular outcry, not only because it appeared to weaken green belt restraint but also – unlike central government's previous attempts to amend green belt policy – did not specify the amount of land central government would like to see released. To make matters worse, many of those opposed to the draft circular's proposals believed them to reflect the pressure brought on central government by the house-building industry which, were the draft circular to become official policy, would result in developers making large profits from their speculative land holdings (see below), as well as from the increased supply of land in areas where the demand for housing remains strong.

In the light of the furore the DOE was obliged to withdraw both draft circulars and to replace them with revised versions before publication of the final circulars (DOE 1984a, b). The final draft on green belt more explicitly confirms the government's commitment to the long-term retention of green belts than does the initial draft, as well as re-affirming the government's opposition to frequent changes in green belt boundaries to accommodate urban growth. Nevertheless, it still leaves the door ajar to allow for minor adjustments to green belt boundaries to accommodate urban growth. This is a sensible position inasmuch as both central government and some local authorities have begun to reconsider their approach to green belt restraint in the light of continuing levels of high unemployment. The MGB area remains one to which it is still possible to attract new private industrial investment without the need for substantial financial inducements from the public purse. With both unemployment and the space requirements per person employed in manufacturing industry still rising, Elson (1983) reports that more relaxed planning criteria are now being used for assessing those planning applications that will generate new jobs in at least one local authority (Dacorum, Hertfordshire) in the MGB. For local political reasons, however, these more relaxed criteria are still cast in a general policy context which emphasises the need to maintain restraint. The final wording of the green belt circular has also taken note of the recommendations made by the Select Committee on the Environment of the House of Commons whose own enquiry into green belt and the supply of housing land was published in June 1984 (House of Commons 1984). In particular, the circular places an additional function on green belt restraint, namely assisting with urban regeneration, and emphasises the contribution that secure or permanent green belt boundaries can make to the agricultural, amenity and recreational value of green belts by reducing uncertainty over the development prospects of green belt land adjacent to urban areas.

RATE OF URBAN DEVELOPMENT WITHIN THE MGB
The rate of urban development in the MGB is clearly a sensitive matter. Central government has never assumed that there would be no growth. The MGB is bound to attract certain kinds of development that cannot be accommodated within the urban area, the most notable example of which is the M25 motorway.

Measuring the rate of urban growth leads to numerous problems, not least in deciding what to measure and how to account for the changing and imprecise definitions of the MGB's extent. Nevertheless, several land-use surveys using different definitions and covering different periods all lead to broadly the same conclusions (see Thomas 1970, Standing Conference 1976, DOE 1978b). These conclusions are as follows:

(a)   Throughout its statutory existence, development has occurred within the MGB, albeit at a slow pace.
(b)   The rate of growth of urban land uses has been much greater near to London than further away, especially just to the east and west of the capital, and while retaining a degree of openness, much of the MGB close to London is now urban in character.

More recent evidence does not invalidate these findings. If land being taken for the M25 motorway is excluded from the calculations – it will take about 1900 ha – then it would seem that the rate of development has not increased since the mid-1970s. Most development is the direct result of public sector investment and is not primarily an outcome of successful appeals decisions. (Standing Conference 1983b; see Table 7.1). The results in Table 7.1 need to be interpreted cautiously as it is not clear whether the residential units include 'approved' development, such as those for agricultural dwellings. But assuming an average of 30 dwellings per hectare, then new housing was constructed on only about 145 ha of the MGB (0·03% of the total area) over the three-year period. The proportion of development arising from appeals decisions is also quite modest, except for industrial and storage projects where central government may, on occasion, be according precedence to its industrial strategy (DOE 1977b) over green belt policy. Local authorities might maintain, however, that they have allowed some development against their better judgements as they anticipated losing the decision on appeal; and it is the regular occurrence of this particular possibility that is of central concern to local authorities were the circular on green belts to be interpreted as a weakening of central government's resolve to

Table 7.1 Development within the MGB between spring 1979 and spring 1982* (excluding the GLC area).

Type of development	1979/80	1980/81	1981/82	Total	Percentage given on appeal†
Residential (units)	1 698	994	1 677	4 369	19.3
industry/warehousing					
storage (ha)	13.37	31.10	8.63	53.1	38.3
offices (m²)	14 929	41 195	8 539	64 663	5.5
shops (m²)	8 814	10 484	4 704	24 002	19.8

Source: SCLSERP (1983b). NB the definitions of green belt vary slightly between authorities.
    * The periods returned by each county vary slightly from calendar year figures for Surrey to mid-year figures for Berkshire and Hertfordshire.
    † Appeal figures not returned by Buckinghamshire other than for residential units.

Table 7.2 Pattern of farm occupation: farm sample in the MGB.

Category	Total area (ha)	Percentage
Owner-occupation		
respondent owned	2 984	20.1
joint ownership	979	6.6
family farming company	286	1.9
trust	1 168	7.9
sub-total	5 417	36.5
Full tenancies from		
private landlords	2 664	17.9
companies	784	5.3
public landlords	2 348	15.9
charities, traditional institutions	2 746	18.5
sub-total	8 522	57.6
Rented on short-term agreement	871	5.9
Total	14 810	100.0

Source: Munton (1983, p. 117).

Table 7.3 Sites in public ownership surplus to current requirements in the statutory green belt and within the GLC, mid-1983.

Owner	Number of Sites	Area (ha)
local authority	59	236.3
British Rail	5	15.9
regional health authority	4	81.4
water authority	2	31.1
Ministry of Defence	6	43.9
Department of the Environment	1	11.7
Total	77	420.3

Source: Land registers.

maintain restraint. If the MGB is taken as a whole, the overall pattern is one of slow development and difficulty for the landowner or developer in getting planning permission. Nevertheless, locally, close to the edge of London or free-standing towns embedded within the MGB, development occurs sufficiently frequently to encourage land speculation, especially when land prices are rising.

LAND OWNERSHIP IN THE MGB
Information on ownership is patchy. More is known about land in public or

institutional hands than in private ownership. In the late 1960s, Thomas estimated that at least 12.9% of the statutory green belt at that time was in public or institutional ownership (Thomas 1970, pp. 113–18), and in 1976 Standing Conference[2] published a map from which it may be estimated that 12–15% of the MGB was held by public owners alone (Standing Conference 1976, see also Ferguson & Munton 1979). It is doubtful whether private individuals own more than 80% of today's MGB, and the proportion is undoubtedly smaller than this close to London. This is a low figure by national standards (about 90% of farmland is in private ownership) and is the result of the land acquisition programme of local authorities for green belt purposes noted previously, the sizeable amount of land held as public open space and statutory smallholdings, and the large area owned by public utilities.

A little more detail may be added from other sources. The proportion of let farmland is high by national standards (Thomson 1981). Data from the Agricultural Census indicate that about 42% of all farmland in England and Wales is tenanted, but the proportion is in excess of 70% in some local authorities near to London (e.g. Croydon, Havering, Hertsmere, Spelthorne – see Munton 1983). The figures in Table 7.2, based on the farm survey conducted in the MGB, suggest that let land may constitute in excess of 60% of the total farmed area in the inner half of the MGB. They also confirm the importance of public and institutional landowners, which together own one-third of the total area, and public companies which let over 1000 ha (some of which is leased on short-term agreements), including 311 ha held by mineral companies and 152 ha by builders and developers. Most of the land in public ownership is owned by local authorities (see also Countryside Commission 1981, Williams 1979), a finding that has been indirectly confirmed by a scrutiny of the Land Registers for the London boroughs (see Ch. 8). An analysis of the entries in the Registers revealed at least 77 publicly-owned vacant sites lying within the boundary of the GLC and inside the MGB. The great majority of the sites are close to the urban edge, and three-quarters were in the hands of local authorities (see Table 7.3).

The MGB land market

The MGB land market consists of several overlapping markets. The same parcel of land may attract a wide range of prospective purchasers including farmers, hobby farmers, developers and mineral companies. Their motives for purchase will be different, they will make varying assessments of the worth of the land to them, and they may well not be committed to the existing use of the land. In these circumstances, vendors are often encouraged to lot their properties when offering them for sale so as to widen the range of prospective purchasers, each of whom may be interested in buying a part of the property but not necessarily in purchasing the whole of it (MAFF 1982).

Information on land prices and level of market activity is not available for London's green belt. In the case of private-sector housing land, for example, the closest approximation to its price is provided by data for the Outer Metropolitan Area (see Fig. 3.1), where prices are normally 65–100% above those for England and Wales as a whole. Likewise, there is a similar difficulty with using the information on farmland sales contained in the MAFF/Inland Revenue

Agricultural Land Price Series. Data are only available for the whole of south-east England, where prices are usually 5–15% above the mean for the whole of England.

To obtain data that were specific to the MGB and which would allow an analysis of markets other than those for agricultural and building land, a survey was conducted of district valuers within the MGB area. District valuers were asked to put sales of green belt land, where they had experience of these, into one of five categories – namely, agricultural land, 'long'- and 'short'-term hope value land, mineral land and building land for the years 1969, 1971, 1973, 1975 and 1977. As data on individual transactions could not be made available for reasons of confidentiality, to obtain an idea of changing land values, the district valuers were asked to put a high and low valuation on seven 'typical' properties for the same years. The properties and their characteristics are described in detail elsewhere (Munton 1983) but may be broadly defined as two farm properties, a piece of pasture land, a hobby farm, one site with 'long-term' hope value, one site with 'short-term' hope value and one consisting of building land with outline planning permission. Land with 'long-term' hope value might be developed during the next five to ten years while that with 'short-term' hope value holds out the firm prospect of planning permission for residential development over the following two to five years. Not all the valuers (16 in all) had sufficient experience with each kind of property to give a high and low valuation for each year (70 valuations in all for each valuers), and some did not have sufficient staff to collate all the necessary data. Nevertheless, 640 valuations out of a possible 1120 were provided and 60% of the district valuers gave detailed, quantitative answers based on their records to questions on changing levels of market activity.

In describing market activity within the MGB (see Table 7.4), the replies have been weighted to allow for non-response. It will be immediately evident that the great majority of sales concern farmland, with mineral land sales in second place. Allocating sales to the 'hope' value categories was not always easy, especially in the case of 'long-term' hope land sales where extraneous influences affecting the price of a particular property may have been present but were unknown to the district valuer. Nevertheless, even allowing for possible mis-classification, it is clear that at least some speculative land market activity occurs pretty well continuously; but there is little evidence from this sample that such activity increased dramatically during the property boom of 1971–3, although the data record the greater level of purchasing of 'long-term' hope land in 1973 and a decline in the level of speculation generally in 1975. Likewise, in each year, there are between 20 and 45 sales of land for urban development averaging approximately 100 ha in extent. This figure is not out of line with those presented earlier, indicating the slow but persistent growth of urban land in the MGB. If the valuations to be presented below are related to this turnover of development land and land regarded as having development potential, then at the height of the property boom in 1973 as much as £22.5 million could have changed hands for such land in the MGB. This figure must be regarded as no more than an informed guess, as it depends on *valuations* of particular types of property and not on actual sales data.

Valuers were asked to give a high and low valuation for each property at each date. These two figures were averaged in each case and these averages used to

Table 7.4 Sales of land in the MGB, 1969–1977 (weighted returns).

	1969			1971			1973			1975			1977		
	No.	ha	percentage*	No.	ha	percentage	No.	ha	percentage	No.	ha	percentage	No.	ha	percentage
agricultural land	55	1639	72.3	107	2453	90.3	90	2505	70.0	107	2908	94.9	170	4462	75.7
'hope' value, long term	8	16	0.7	8	130	4.8	18	348	9.7	—	—	—	10	173	2.9
'hope' value, short term	5	203	9.0	2	2	0.1	5	10	0.3	5	18	0.6	3	3	0.1
mineral land	23	320	14.1	8	33	1.3	20	595	16.6	5	40	1.3	5	1138	19.3
development land	20	88	3.9	28	98	3.6	45	120	3.4	20	98	3.2	28	115	2.0
Total	111	2266	100.0	153	2716	100.0	178	3578	100.0	137	3064	100.0	216	5891	100.0

Source: Survey of district valuers.
*All percentages are of the total land in the MGB sold in the year in question.

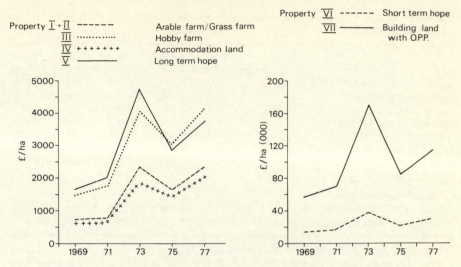

Figure 7.2 Land values in the Metropolitan Green Belt, 1969–1977, by type of property.

derive the mean values (in pounds per hectare) displayed graphically in Figure 7.2. In the first half of Figure 7.2 the values for the pasture land (Property IV), the hobby farm (Property III), the 'long-term' hope land (Property V) and the two full-time farms (Properties I and II) are described. Valuations for the latter have been combined because they were almost identical. Throughout the period, all the valuations moved in a similar way in response to market changes. Valuation of the hobby farm was heavily influenced by the value placed on the house and the hobby farm's value per hectare exceeded that of the 'long-term' hope value property in 1975 and 1977. The values placed on the other two properties ('short-term' hope and building land – Properties VI and VII) exhibit a similar temporal pattern, their values doubling between 1971 and 1973. However, the absolute difference per hectare between the valuations for these two properties increased from £53 980 per hectare to £132 960 per hectare between 1971 and 1973.

The substantial increase in the land's value as development becomes an increasing possibility is illustrated dramatically in Table 7.5. The top row of the table records an average valuation for the main farm properties by year, indexed on the second row at 100. Between 1969 and 1973 land with 'short-term' hope value was worth about 20 times its agricultural value, between seven and ten times its 'long-term' hope value but only about one-quarter of its value as building land with outline planning permission. After 1973 the value of building land falls and by 1977 it had not recovered to the same extent as farmland values, although the relative values of the three 'development land' markets remained similar to each other in spite of changing market conditions. In the years up to 1973, building land is valued at a staggering 80–95 times its agricultural value, falling to a mere 50 times in 1975 and 1977. The immense discount (75%) on 'short-term' hope land, when its value is compared to that of building land, emphasises the high cost of borrowed money during the 1970s and the risk of failing to acquire planning permission, even in situations where a successful

Table 7.5   Relative property valuations: agricultural land and building land, MGB, 1969–1977 (no adjustment for inflation).

	1969	1971	1973	1975	1977
agricultural land (£/ha)*	703	742	2 169	1 574	2 256
agricultural land (index)	100	100	100	100	100
hobby farm (index)	207	237	187	192	182
'long-term hope' land (index)	234	271	218	182	166
'short-term hope' land (index)	2 034	2 165	1 936	1 402	1 326
building land (index)	8 063	9 520	7 892	5 248	5 121
building land (£/ha)	56 700	70 670	171 240	85 470	115 570
absolute difference (gross) between agricultural and building land prices (£h/a)	55 997	69 928	169 071	83 896	113 314
difference net of tax (£/ha)†	33 626	49 130	118 530	40 352	36 843

* Based on the average valuation (£/ha) for properties I, II and IV.

† Assumes an agricultural land price of £600/ha in 1965, that a sale of 2 ha is involved and there were no improvements made to the land. No allowance is made for inflation or for consociate wealth. For changes in the tax regime see Chapter 2, p. 28.

application could reasonably be expected in the next few years. The net of tax figures, based on a set of simple assumptions and the tax regimes in operation at the relevant dates (see Ch. 2), indicate the substantial net gain a landowner could hope to realise, and the continuing incentive the owner has to speculate. They also reveal the substantial variation in net return the owner would receive over a mere eight-year period as a result of a volatile market and frequent changes in tax liability.

The landowner's operational strategy

How in these circumstances does the landowner go about seeking planning permission? It was suggested in Chapter 5 that the landowner would be more likely to maximise his return, provided he obtains professional advice, by submitting his own application to the local planning authority as the developer would require an interest in the property in exchange for his time, expertise and resources in seeking planning permission on the owner's behalf. On the other hand, landowners readily testify to the difficulty of getting planning permission in the MGB and, in these circumstances, it can pay the landowner to involve a developer in all the stages in the development of his land. Both can provide a service to the other; but equally both are prepared to operate independently. Landowners submit planning applications on their own account and some developers purchase the freehold to land. Evidence on the kinds of procedures adopted in the MGB was obtained from the interviews with occupiers and developers.

The 185 occupiers interviewed farmed 14 810 ha, all within the MGB. Of this land, 14.6% (2162 ha) lay in fields adjacent to residential development and, given the general difficulty of acquiring planning permission, this area provides one estimate of the amount of land within the sample that stands an outside chance of development. In practice, the amount likely to be developed in the foreseeable future would be much less. Some of the land would require additional servicing (main sewers, etc.), and some consists of large fields part of which lie a considerable distance from the urban edge. The 2162 ha were divided between 88 occupiers, only 47 of whom were owner-occupiers. Almost all the 47 owner-occupiers admitted to having either enquired about the development prospects of their land from their local planning office or had submitted a planning application between 1970 and 1977. Twelve had submitted more than one application. Most of the applications were for staightforward housing development, offered little by way of planning gain, and were, without exception, refused. In such circumstances landowners may be attracted by the offers made to them by developers. Between 1970 and 1977, 78 of the 88 occupiers (including many tenants) had been approached informally by developers or their landlords to discuss various development schemes. In 31 cases, detailed schemes were drawn up and applications submitted. Occupiers were reluctant to reveal details of these arrangements but it became clear that in the vast majority of cases development did not occur. A better idea of the kinds of arrangement that were reached between owners and developers was obtained from the more general discussions held with the developers.

The land assembly policies of the 13 developers who consented to an interview varied significantly, depending largely on whether they had the resources to stand the risk of speculative purchase and, even then, whether it was the company's policy to tie up capital in this way. As a result of their cash-flow difficulties in the mid-1970s most had become reluctant to buy the freehold to land in the MGB. Existing land banks often consisted in part of the assets acquired from other developers who went out of business in the mid-1970s and had been purchased at a highly discounted price. By the end of the 1970s developers preferred to take out an option on a piece of land or to enter into a conditional contract rather than purchase the freehold, and by this time options were also rarely open-dated or available for long periods. Landowners had become aware of the long-term upward trend in land prices, or at least assumed that this was the case, and they therefore sought contracts with developers that were conditional on acquiring planning permission quickly, that were finalised soon after planning permission had been given (usually 28 days), and that would ensure them a given proportion of the development value of the land at the time of sale. Developers were often unwilling to reveal the prices they paid for land. Prices did not always relate to a 'going rate', or even to a precise calculation of what they thought they could afford to pay and still make a profit. The price agreed was often specific to the financial circumstances of those doing the bargaining at the time.

Of the 13 firms in the survey, three claimed never to have bought an interest in any land in London's green belt, except where it had been sold with outline planning permission already granted. Of the six firms owning significant areas of freehold land in the MGB five were prepared to give details. Between them, they owned 17 sites covering 230 ha, scattered around the inner edge of the MGB adjacent to existing development. None of the companies had been successful in getting planning permission for any of these sites during the 1970s. Twelve of the sites, extending to 177 ha, were purchased at low historic cost in the 1960s and the companies concerned were under no short-term financial pressures to release them; but their long-term intentions were clear. No site in agricultural use was let on a full agricultural tenancy. Much of the land (140 ha) was let on short-term agreements for horse grazing while a further 60 ha or so were admitted to be lying vacant.

Nine firms had options on land or conditional contracts with owners. Over 100 separate options had been arranged between 1970 and 1977, but only 23 had been exercised. Most had lapsed by 1978, but at that time five of the developers also held conditional contracts on a further 32 sites. It is impossible to put an accurate figure on the area of land covered by the various options and conditional contracts described because of the differing details disclosed by the respondents. The six firms providing figures would admit to an area of at least 185 ha. The three other major firms concerned would only reveal the number of arrangements to which they were party and, on the assumption that the average area covered by these was similar to those for which the area was known, the total area under consideration would be more than doubled to approximately 400 ha.

By the end of the 1970s, most developers no longer regarded land in the MGB as a worthwhile speculative risk. Planning applications were being processed slowly, the DOE was largely supportive of local authorities when applications went to appeal, and, where development was allowed, permission was often accompanied by numerous planning conditions. Nevertheless, the major developers were continuing to monitor land policies in structure and local plans, to assess the impact of the M25 motorway on land release, and to treat land in the MGB on its merits. High prices would be paid for land with planning permission but, unlike the early 1970s, not for land with 'hope' value. Risk, the companies maintained, was being assessed in a different way to ten years earlier, although there is no particular evidence to support this view (see Table 7.5) in the records of district valuers.

The landowner's management policy

In presenting the investment model in Chapter 5 (p. 109). under the section on the owner's management strategy for greenfield sites three matters were identified. First, it was argued that owners would seek to ensure that their land was not covered by a planning designation, such as green belt, within which there was a presumption against development. Second, if owners did not occupy their land they would only grant leases that could be terminated speedily. Third, owners would not invest in fixed improvements to their land and that it might even pay them to run down the use of their land deliberately as one means of trying to persuade the local authority to give them planning permission.

The detailed study of occupiers can throw little light on the first of these matters as all the farms lay within the MGB as statutorily defined and were not affected by the debates during the 1970s on the extent to which the MGB should be enlarged. The preparation of district plans was also at an early stage and a final decision on whether county or district planning authorities should decide the precise delineation of greenbelt boundaries had not been taken. Subsequently, the SOS decided that this should be a responsibility of district authorities (DOE 1979b, p. 4), and examinations in public into district plans have become a battleground between the development industry and landowners on the one hand and local planners and residents on the other. The battle may well be intensifed by the wording contained in the recent circular which says,

> if Green Belt boundaries are drawn excessively tightly around existing built-up areas it may not be possible to maintain the degree of permanence that Green Belts should have. This would devalue the concept of the Green Belt and also reduce the value of local plans in making proper provision for necessary development in the future (DOE 1984b, para. 3).

Past experience of the MGB suggests, however, that development pressures are rarely satisfied by the release of modest quantities of green belt land (and the circular implies no more than this) and this experience, in combination with the planners' inability to define precisely how much development land might be 'necessary' in the future, means that the issue of permanence will not be resolved as easily as the circular might be taken to imply.

Nevertheless, given the balance of political forces at work, it still seems likely that only land adjacent to existing residential areas in the MGB will stand any chance of being developed in the foreseeable future. It is possible, then, to compare the tenurial status and management characteristics of this land with the other green belt land contained in the farm sample in order to examine the second element of the owner's management strategy. Three categories of tenure relevant to this discussion were identified, namely owner–occupation, land let on full, secure tenancies under the Agricultural Holdings legislation, and land leased short term either on leases of less than 365 days duration or on licence (only two cases) for a maximum period of five years. Since 1976, land let on full agricultural tenancies has under normal circumstances given the occupier security of tenure for three generations from that date, although legislation currently before Parliament will reduce this to the life of the original tenant.

The results of the survey are shown in Table 7.6. The proportion of owner-occupied land is lower right on the urban edge than on the farms as a whole. This may be explained, at least in part, by the substantial programme of land purchase by local authorities of land close to London for green belt

Table 7.6   Land adjacent to residential development: form of tenure (sample of 185 occupiers: area 14 810 ha).

Form of tenure	Land next to residential development		All other land		Total	
	ha	%	ha	%	ha	%
owner-occupation	727	32.6	4 690	37.3	5 417	36.5
secure leases	1 220	54.6	7 302	58.1	8 522	57.6
short-term leases	286	12.8	585	4.7	871	5.9
Total	2 233	100.0	12 571	100.0	14 810	100.0

purposes. At the same time, there is a substantially higher proportion of land let short term on the urban edge (12.8%) than elsewhere (4.7%). It is important to recognise that while planning permission for development can form the basis of a valid notice to quit from landlord to tenant on any kind of agricultural or commercial lease, landlords prefer to avoid the additional complications of having to settle with their tenants who are on secure leases, who might oppose them at public inquiry and who might be keeping the land in an excellent farmed condition (Munton 1984).

The third element of the management strategy suggests that the owner would not invest in the long-term maintenance and improvement of the land in its current use. The owner might not bother to farm the land at all or he might farm it in such a way as to extract from it the greatest short-term agricultural benefit he could at the least cost to himself. A common practice is to lease the land short term for horse grazing. Given the high demand for 'pony paddocks' this form of temporary use can realise high rents whilst at the same time may lead to the land having an untidy or unkempt appearance.

Standards of agricultural land maintenance were assessed for almost all (95·3%) the land in the sample and the procedure for defining these standards is described in detail elsewhere (see Munton 1983). Three categories were established. These can be characterised as land that was being well or adequately maintained for continued agricultural use (Category I), land indicating a deterioration in maintenance standards (Category II), and land lying derelict or semi-derelict (Category III). The results are at Table 7.7. From the top row of the table it can be seen that about two-thirds of the area was at least adequately maintained, about 30% showed clear signs of deterioration and 5.5% lay derelict or semi-derelict. On average, standards of maintenance are much lower in fields adjacent to residential development than in the sample as a whole, with nearly 20% of this land being allocated to Category III. It is also possible to compare standards of maintenance between land with different forms of tenure on the urban edge (see Table 7.7). There is some evidence to suggest that owner-occupied land is less well maintained than land let on a full tenancy. Although the sample is small, and it is not detailed in Table 7.7, land leased from charities, institutions and private landlords seems to be maintained better than that leased from companies and public bodies, especially in terms of a lower proportion of land falling into Category III. In the case of land let from public landlords, which constituted almost a quarter of the total on the urban edge, compared to 15.9% of the land in the sample as a whole, there were higher (relatively) maintenance standards on land leased from local authorities than from statutory bodies whose primary commitment is not to the needs of agriculture. Finally, the figures for land let short term speak for themselves.

At face value, these data endorse most of the assumptions noted in Chapter 5 upon which the owner should base his management strategy. But two further points need to be made. First, the pattern of land maintenance is no more than generally supportive of the assumptions. There are, plainly, many cases where land was better maintained than might be expected. This reflects the mixed motives of owner-occupiers towards the future use of their land and the difficulty of acquiring planning permission; and, where developers take out options or conditional contracts on some of the land, the occupier may not feel it essential to run down the condition of his land. It is the developer's problem to

Table 7.7 Standards of land maintenance by location and tenure.

	\multicolumn{2}{c}{I}		II		III		Total	
	ha	%	ha	%	ha	%	ha	%
all land	9 131	64.7	4 200	29.8	782	5.5	14 113	100.0
land next to residential development	727	35.0	926	45.1	407	19.8	2 060	100.0
all remaining land	8 404	69.7	3 274	27.2	375	3.1	12 053	100.0
land next to residential development that is								
(a) owner-occupied	211	35.3	292	48.9	94	15.7	597	100.0
(b) let on a full secure tenancy	505	42.1	532	44.3	163	13.6	1 200	100.0
(c) let short-term	11	4.2	102	38.8	150	57.0	263	100.0

Source: Field survey.

get planning permission, even if the owner benefits financially from this as well. Second, the data are only *indicative* of motive, and there is the danger of implying, perhaps incorrectly, the owner's motives from the condition of the land. Discussions with the occupiers when they were interviewed suggested that the interpretation being made here is largely accurate, but it is also true to say that trespass and other forms of urban intrusion from neighbouring housing estates undermine the confidence and resilience of the occupier in his efforts to farm well. Land speculation may *result* from these difficulties, as much as being the *cause* of poor land maintenance.

Conclusion

This particular case study has focused on the operational and land management aspects of the investment strategy as laid down in Chapter 5. Development pressures remain strong in the MGB, but the area of restraint has been largely maintained. This means that whilst a small amount of land is being constantly developed, the timing of any particular development is even more uncertain than around most other urban areas. Moreover, development prospects depend significantly on matters beyond the landowner's control. In particular, these matters include public investment, as in new roads for example, which may be used to persuade the local planning authority or the DOE at appeal that, locally, the former green belt function of a particular site has been nullified by the investment. They also include short-term amendments to government policy on housing land supply in south-east England. When supply is seen as inadequate this will make success at appeal more likely. The wording of the new circular on green belt might just allow this to happen if the economy expands and development pressures resulting from the completion of the M25 motorway accumulate.

The evidence also draws attention to the enormous financial gain, net of tax, the landowner in the MGB can realise. The gain is measurably greater than that for the Outer Metropolitan Area as a whole and ensures continuing speculative activity among landowners, with or without the assistance of developers, even if much of the activity fails to bear fruit. Developers, for their part, learned some painful lessons during the 1970s and today are much less prepared than previously to buy the freehold to land in the MGB. There can be no doubt, however, that developers hold an interest in a significant quantity of land close to the inner boundary of the MGB, some of it acquired at a knock-down price in the mid-1970s from those builders and developers that went bankrupt. Any uncertainty over how firmly central government will uphold the present boundaries of the MGB will ensure an increase in speculative activity. This activity will further lower the standards of maintenance on some land, although some land is already in a derelict condition, whilst other land will continue to be farmed well. It will be interesting to see, for example, how those public owners charged with disposing of land surplus to their requirements will act. Of the 77 sites listed in Table 7.3 which lie within the MGB and the boundary of the GLC, over 50 are largely or wholly vacant, and many of the remainder are used only for temporary grazing. The pressure to allocate at least some of this land to new employment generating activities – and similar land in adjacent authorities – may become irresistible when the M25 motorway is completed and if unemployment levels stubbornly refuse to fall.

Notes

1   Full details on the conduct of these surveys are to be found in Munton (1983).
2   Standing Conference is short for Standing Conference on London and South East Regional Planning (SCLSERP).

8   The inner city: market failure or planning problem?

Introduction

In the last two chapters attention has centred on areas in which there is a significant demand for development land and in which landowners stood to realise a substantial capital gain from the sale of their land. In Leicester, local planners were keen to see that development took place and had some success in directing development to the land they had identified. Within the Metropolitan Green Belt, the demand for development land was also clearly evident but local planners and the DOE vigorously opposed development and, again, generally prevailed. In the inner city, from which we exclude the CBD and its associated office and retailing functions, planners are keen to see the re-development of land but the generally low demand for land creates difficulties. Land often lies un-used or even derelict and in the latter condition especially can be more costly to redevelop than to build on greenfield sites. The main issue is, therefore, one of land values and the ability of public policies to create a level of values sufficient either to encourage owners, many of whom are in the public sector, to market their land or to get private investors and developers to buy the land.

For 20 and more years after the Second World War, planning policy was directed towards decentralisation of people and jobs from the congested inner city areas. Decentralisation was to provide migrants with better living and working conditions and local authorities, within inner city areas, with the scope to clear slum housing and to engage in comprehensive re-development. But the very success of decentralisation has led to new problems. Some observers complain at the amount of farmland lost to urban growth when land lies vacant within the city and others note the poor quality of much public housing on the edges of urban areas. Others again report that the inner city continues to contain a disproportionate number of people experiencing low material standards of living; unemployment is high and the vitality of many inner city communities remains low.

Not all inner city areas accurately reflect this picture, and there is a danger that the social and economic problems of the inner city are assumed to be unique to it. They are not (see Hall 1981b, Ch. 1). Nevertheless, in terms of the development process inner city areas may be characterised as follows. First, by comparison with the urban fringe, the demand to develop or re-develop land is relatively low, and in places non-existent.[1] Second, many of the sites available for re-development require considerable rehabilitation, making them more costly to develop than greenfield sites; and the income from temporary uses, such as car-parking, can combine with low holding costs to generate a higher economic rent than the developer is prepared to bid. Third, much of the land available for re-development is owned by public bodies and they are not always responsive to market signals. They may have little incentive to sell if they cannot benefit significantly from the sale proceeds, and bodies and institutions that have used public monies to acquire or to develop property are not always permitted to retain more than a small proportion of the proceeds (Hallett 1977). Fourth, until recently some inner city local authorities have not been favourably disposed towards private-sector development, especially where this development was seen as in conflict with the council's own industrial and housing programmes. Although the climate of opinion in local authorities is now changing rapidly as a result of the continuing recession and the particular orientation of government policy, partnership initiatives between the public and private sectors were slow to get under way until the early 1980s.

The first three of these characteristics emphasise the importance of land values to the development process and the responsiveness of landowners to market opportunities while the fourth feature draws attention to the difficulties a private developer or owner could face in seeking planning permission. Owners' investment strategies will depend very largely therefore on whether the market value of their land exceeds its current use value. In so far as government policy is directed towards raising land values in the inner city, and thereby encouraging the re-development of land, three strands of policy should be noted. One concerns the creation of a better informed market among both owners and developers and may be linked to the publication of Land Registers (see below). Another consists of a set of pump-priming initiatives, such as derelict land grants and urban development grants, aimed at rehabilitating land at public expense in order to stimulate the private re-development of sites for which the grants are available. But the matter does not stop here. As the White Paper *Policy for the inner cities* warns (DOE 1977c, p. 28), the price offered by developers is also affected by the confidence they have in the economic future of the inner city. Confidence is especially important to such investors as pension funds which would more naturally restrict their investment to properties in prime locations with a high standard of amenity and long-standing public investment in the local infrastructure (Cadman 1979) – neither of which are apparent in some inner city areas.

In spite of a long-standing concern for the resuscitation of the inner city, detailed knowledge of the process of re-development, the operation of the land market and the part played in them by the owner is still restricted. Most of the published research is a by-product of studies of vacant land. These studies provide a fair knowledge of the extent of such land, its ownership and its physical characteristics; and the publication of the new Land Registers adds valuable detail. But beyond this there are only two published enquiries that examine the relationship between the ownership of inner city development land and the development process. One is based in the London Borough of Tower Hamlets (Thames Television 1980) and the other in Nottingham (Nicholls *et al.* 1980), and these are examined in detail at the end of the chapter.

The inner city: definition, character and policy context

Government initiatives for the inner city have been introduced with bewildering frequency since the mid-1960s. There is insufficient space to do more than note the major changes made to policy and the economic, social and environmental circumstances to which they have been directed. All these matters are discussed at much greater length elsewhere (see Lawless 1981, Hall 1981b, Moor 1983, Regional Studies Association 1983).

There is no satisfactory definition of the inner city 'problem', or any agreed means of deciding whether it is getting 'worse'. Aspects of the problem vary between urban areas and none are unique to the inner city. All that may be said with confidence is that inner city areas contain a disproportionately large number of the unemployed, of low-income earners, and of families living in sub-standard housing within unattractive environments. But not all those living in inner city areas are poor, not all inner city areas contain inadequate housing and, in absolute terms, many more poor people live elsewhere than in the inner city (Hall 1981b).

All inner city areas have experienced a sharp fall in their resident populations since 1951. More importantly, whatever their past social conditions, cities were once seen as offering a step up the ladder for those moving into them (Hall 1981b, p. 114), but for the last 30 years the reverse has been true with many of those able to flee the city doing so. Decline in the number of jobs in the inner city is probably more recent, dating from the late 1950s, but becoming especially marked since the mid-1960s. The degree to which the decline can be attributed to the characteristics of the inner cities and their industries *per se* – the lack of opportunities for business to expand, high rates levied on obsolete premises, an industrial structure overly dependent on declining sectors of manufacturing industry, and so on – remains a matter of dispute (see Lawless 1981, pp. 9–18; Regional Studies Association 1983). Without doubt, national economic decline is partly responsible for the economic difficulties of the inner city and measures to resuscitate the economies of inner city areas must be viewed within a national or even an international economic context.

Until the 1970s most inner city local authorities either assumed that incentives to promote their local economies were beyond their brief and resources, or that incentives were unnecessary. Certainly, authorities seemed ill-prepared to cope with the social consequences of the industrial decline and re-structuring that has taken place and many have continued to focus their attention on traditional areas of activity, such as comprehensive redevelopment schemes and environmental improvement. Until 1977, central government initiatives also centred on social questions and in particular the elimination of deprivation. These issues deserved the consideration given to them but they diverted attention away from the key question. How could the economies of inner cities be made more dynamic? For without a local source of wealth creation there would be reduced multiplier effects from personal spending and a smaller local tax base.

The central importance of economic matters to government policy was only made explicit in 1978 with the publication of the Inner Urban Areas Act which followed the White Paper *Policy for the inner cities* (DOE 1977c; see also DOE 1977b). Under the terms of the Act, the Urban Programme was to be expanded primarily through the introduction of local–central government 'partnership areas' in seven of the inner urban areas with the most severe economic problems, and 'programme areas' in a further 15 districts with slightly less serious economic difficulties. Since 1978 another eight 'programme' authorities and 16 'designated' districts have been added to the Urban Programme. The Act was welcomed but its effectiveness has been questioned. Government finance for the inner city has been substantially increased and more heavily concentrated in areas of greatest need, and spending has increased from £30 million in 1976/7 to £348 million in 1983/4. Nevertheless, the earmarked monies amount to less than 2% of the value of the rate support grant, and in the case of Liverpool (one of the partnership areas), for example, they added only 5% to the local authority's budget in 1980/1 (Hall 1981b, p. 95). Furthermore, in the early years of the Act, only about a quarter of the extra monies were being allocated to more traditional areas of social spending (Lawless 1981, pp. 99–103, Nabarro 1980).

On its return to office in 1979, the Conservative government reinforced the policy of encouraging economic activity in the inner city by retaining the partnership scheme but placed greater emphasis on other more direct incentives for private enterprise (for a description see Howes 1983). In late 1979, for example, two Urban Development Corporations were introduced into the London and Liverpool docks. These had the powers to assemble land, to grant planning permission on their own land and to provide services and housing. The Corporations were supplemented in 1980 by seven enterprise zones (by 1983 there were 20), or small areas of up to 200 ha in extent within which there were to be much less stringent planning controls as well as major tax incentives for firms prepared to locate there, including exemption from rates and DLT and 100% capital allowances over a ten-year period. Early results from the monitoring of enterprise zones demonstrate that they did create some new jobs but the most important gains were indirect – better site and property development and an improved level of co-operation between the public and private sectors (Roger Tym & Partners 1983). These indirect benefits were not of much value to the locally unemployed. Finally, in 1983 the government introduced urban development grants, the purpose of which was to provide a limited amount of public money to create financial circumstances on particular inner city sites that would attract private investment (see Mallinson & Gilbert 1983), an approach similar to that adopted for derelict land grants (see below).

Central government has also accepted the view that not only do the environments of inner city areas need to be improved for their own sakes, but also that vacant and derelict land has a blighting effect, discouraging private investment. This view follows the publication of several studies which measured the extent of vacant land (e.g. Civic Trust 1977, Bruton & Gore 1980). These and other studies all come to broadly the same factual conclusions, even if their evaluations of them are different. Their conclusions are that the area of vacant land is substantial (estimated at 10–12% in the east end of London, central Liverpool and Glasgow – see Thames Television 1980); most of this land is owned by public bodies (83% in central Birmingham – BICP 1981, but see Nicholson 1984); within the public sector, local authorities are the largest single owners (Liverpool City Council owned more than 75% of all vacant land in one area of the city – Wilson & Wormsley 1977); and many of the vacant sites are small and of less than 0.4 ha in extent.

What has been missing from most studies is any idea of the duration of vacancy, as some vacancy is both desirable and inevitable in areas of active re-development. Some evidence is produced by Markowski in his study of the London boroughs of Wandsworth and Barking. Within these boroughs 23% and 37% respectively of the area of vacant land had been in that condition for at least ten years and 74% and 68% for at least five years (Markowski 1978). These comparatively long periods have, Nicholson (1984) argues, encouraged a 'stock' rather than a 'flow' perspective on vacant land, drawing attention away from the causes of vacancy and the processes of re-development. Re-development is bound to be slow in the current economic environment but it is not non-existent; and since Markowski conducted his research government has introduced a number of measures to tackle the problem of vacancy. For example, the derelict land grants system has been extended in order to reduce the costs involved in preparing sites for re-development. Under the Local Government Act 1972, grants for the reclamation of derelict land were only payable to local authorities, but in 1980 the government made the grants available to 'any person' prepared to reclaim land. Furthermore, from the end of 1981 preferential treatment has been given to joint schemes by local authorities and private developers, the idea being to couple public expenditure on reclamation with the private financing of subsequent development. The funding of land reclamation schemes is complicated with the rate of grant depending on location. Nevertheless, in 1983, 46 joint schemes in England were allocated £32 million to which it is confidently expected that about £196 million will be added by the private sector (Thompson and Edmondson 1984).

THE NEW LAND REGISTERS

In an important departure from established practice, a system of partial land registration was introduced in England and Wales in 1981 under Part X of the Local Government, Planning and Land Act 1980. The Act gave the SOS (DOE) the power to order the registration of all land held by public owners that was surplus to their operational needs and to direct any owner of registered land to dispose of its interest in it. Up until the summer of 1984 the power of direction had not been used.[2] The registers, one for each local authority, were to be made freely available for public inspection. The intention behind the land registers was to bring home to public owners the development potential of their surplus land. Ministers claimed that the registers would act as a spur to development and as a means of reinforcing 'normal discipline' in the management of public property (DOE 1981c); and, as much of the vacant land was believed to lie in the inner city, re-development would improve the quality of the built environment in inner city areas and reduce pressures to build on greenfield sites.

As a pilot scheme, the SOS requested the registration of land in 35 local authorities and these registers were published in 1981. In December 1981 the scheme was extended to the rest of the country and 365 registers were available by November 1982. The registers include all sites of more than 0.4 ha in which a public body has the freehold interest (or a leasehold with more than seven years to run) that are surplus to current operational needs and will not be included in a development programme within the next two years. An example of an entry is given in Figure 8.1. The level of detail varies from register to register and from owner to owner. Most land lies vacant, although some sites are used informally for recreation or for other temporary uses. The registers neither list all vacant sites (some may be incorporated in a development programme in the near future, sites in private ownership and of less than 0.4 ha are omitted), nor do they give any idea of the full extent of public ownership. Nevertheless, they do provide a figure of the amount of land in public hands that is available for development or re-development (see Stungo 1984).

EAST GREENWICH GAS WORKS

Department of the Environment

Local Government, Planning
and Land Act 1980 Part X

REGISTER OF PUBLIC BODIES' LAND

Land (including buildings) held by   British Gas Corporation, South Eastern Region.

and situated within or adjoining the London Borough Council of   Greenwich.

---

1. **Site details** – *Note 1*
   (a) Address or location (with national grid reference, if available and OSF number, if necessary)

   Parts of East Greenwich Works, Blackwall Lane, Greenwich.

   (b) Approximate area   150.51   acres (60.911   hectares)

---

2. **Interest held in site** – *Note 2*   Freehold

   If there are tenancies please tick and list briefly overleaf ☑

---

3. **Current Use (including any temporary or periodic uses)** – *Note 3*

   Former Gasworks with major demolition programme in progress. ((4) on plan).
   Parts of site still in operational use and some cleared areas (1) (2) and (5) leased for open storage use.

---

4. **Previous or known permitted use** – *Note 4*

   Part Gas purposes since 1880. (1, 2 and 4)
   Part formerly used by British Steel. (2).

---

5. **Development Plan Notation** – *Note 5*   Draft Local Plan indicates site as being industrial but agreement entered with
   Greater London Council and London Borough of Greenwich acknowledges future B.G.C. requirement for Gas Manufacturing
   Station.

---

6. **Site Characteristics (brief, factual description only)** – *Note 6*

   Areas of level land adjoining and near the River Thames.
   Part former Gasworks.
   Probable ground contamination, underground structures and sub-soil movement due to low load bearing capacity.

   If reverse of form or separate sheet used, please tick ☐

---

7. **Reason for retaining the land or indication of disposal intentions** – *Note 7*

   Land retained as strategic site against future operational requirement for new Synthetic Gas Manufacturing Plant.
   This is acknowledged by an agreement entered into by the London Borough of Greenwich, Greater London Council and the
   Corporation dated 16th September, 1980.
   Interim uses being made of parts of cleared site until required for construction.

Person to contact for more detailed information   J. D. Lowman. Estates Manager.

Address: British Gas Corporation, South Eastern Region, Estates Department, "Segas House", Katharine Street, Croydon.
CR9 1JU.

Telephone No.   688.4466. Ext. 371.   Date   9th December, 1982.

DOE 14068

---

overleaf

Area 1 – 21 lettings for Road Hauliers and open
          storage use expiring in 1990.

Area 2 – Licence to Metropolitan Police.

Area 5 – Lease to London Borough of Greenwich
          expiring 1994.

Figure 8.1 An
example of an entry in a
land register: the case of
East Greenwich gas
works, London.
(Crown Copyright
reserved.)

CHARACTERISTICS OF THE REGISTERED SITES

As at January 1st 1983,[3] 11 600 sites were listed in the registers, extending to more than 43 000 ha, 59% of which was owned by local authorities and 27% by nationalised industries and statutory bodies (Howes 1984). From publication to 1 June 1983, about 3400 ha or 1100 sites had been removed from various registers. Two-thirds of the land had been sold to developers and one-third brought into use by existing owners.

Two examples will illustrate the nature of the information contained in the Registers. *First*, the entries in the 33 registers for the Boroughs and City of London were analysed during the summer of 1983 (see Fig. 8.2). London has been divided into two to compare the inner and outer parts of the capital. Inner London was defined as the area of the Inner London Education Authority plus Newham as this borough includes much of the land controlled by the London Docklands Development Corporation (LDDC). Inner London has 31.4% of the entries and 30.8% of the vacant land but only 19% of the area of the GLC. Yet were Newham to be excluded from Inner London, the inner area would only contain 18% of the registered land in the GLC on 16.5% of the area of the capital (see Table 8.1).

There are, however, significant differences in the pattern of ownership between the two halves of London. In terms of area, Inner London has four major types of owner – the Boroughs (who hold 23.6% of the total), British Gas (22.1%), the British Railways Board (20.0%) and the LDDC/PLA (Port of London Authority) (18.7%). Although owning over 40% of the area between them, the LDDC/PLA and British Gas only have an interest in 11% of the sites. The GLC, on the other hand, owns 26.4% of the sites but only 10.0% of the land; and over half these sites are in Tower Hamlets alone. Land held by the PLA is almost all in Newham, the borough in which Beckton Gas Works is located. This obsolete gas works accounts for the majority of the land held by British Gas and as a consequence 267.1 ha or 40.6% of the total land for Inner London lies in Newham. In Outer London, the largest area of registered land lies in the Borough of Bromley (156.5 ha or 10.6% of the outer London total), closely followed by Barking (154.0 ha) and Croydon (142.7 ha). The Boroughs have interests in more than half the sites, the British Railways Board owns nearly one-fifth of the land and the holdings of the Property Services Agency (PSA) and the Regional Health Authorities (RHAs) are much greater than in Inner London. The overall average size of site (2.95 ha) changes little between Inner and Outer London.

The *second* example is taken from Tyneside. Tyneside is defined as the four authorities of Gateshead, North and South Tyneside and Newcastle-upon-Tyne. In October 1983, these authorities contained 280 registered sites covering 1196.4 ha or nearly twice the area for the whole of Inner London. The ownership pattern is described in Table 8.2. Over half the area is owned by the district authorities and a further 18.6% by the Tyne and Wear County Council. About 30% is held equally between the British Railways Board, the public utilities, and the Port of Tyne Authority (PTA) and British Shipbuilders (BS).

The sites are widely distributed. Using the maps accompanying each register it is possible to allocate sites to one of three categories – urban edge, the inner city and other sites outside the inner city but embedded within the built-up area. The definition of the inner city is the same as that used in the Tyne and Wear

Table 8.1 Entries in the land registers for the area of the Greater London Council, mid–1983: comparison between inner and outer London by type of owner.

	Owner*										
	Boroughs	GLC	BRB	PSA	RHAs	BG	RWAs	CEGB	PLA/LDDC	Other	Total
Inner London†‡											
area (ha)	155.1	65.7	131.8	9.3	6.9	145.4	4.6	11.7	123.5	3.9	658.0
no. sites	63	60	59	7	3	7	1	5	18	4	227
percentage of total area in registers	23.6	10.0	20.0	1.4	1.1	22.1	0.7	1.8	18.7	0.6	100.0
Outer London											
area (ha)	741.0	44.9	278.2	143.5	105.9	70.5	56.0	34.8	—	1.2	1476.1
no. sites	285	14	144	13	9	14	9	7	—	1	496
percentage of total area in registers	50.2	3.0	18.8	9.7	7.2	4.8	3.8	2.4	—	0.1	100.0
Total GLC area											
area (ha)	896.1	110.6	410.0	152.8	112.8	215.9	60.6	46.5	123.5	5.1	2134.1
no. sites	348	74	203	20	12	21	10	12	18	5	723
percentage of total area in registers	42.0	5.2	19.2	7.2	5.3	10.1	2.8	2.2	5.8	0.2	100.0

Source: Land registers.

* *Abbreviations*: BRB (British Railways Board); PSA (Property Services Agency – effectively government departments); RHAs (regional health authorities); BG (British Gas Corporation); RWAs (regional water authorities); CEGB (Central Electricity Generating Board); PLA (Port of London Authority); LDDC (London Docklands Development Corporation).

† Defined as the London Borough of Newham plus the London Boroughs of the Inner London Education Authority (i.e. Camden, City of London, Greenwich, Hackney, Hammersmith and Fulham, Islington, Kensington and Chelsea, Lambeth, Southwark, Tower Hamlets, Wandsworth, Westminster).

‡ All figures rounded to the first decimal place.

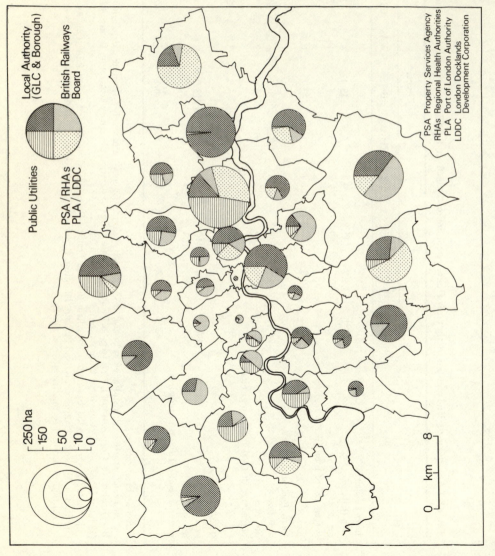

Figure 8.2 Registered land within the GLC by type of owner, 1983. (*Source*: Land registers.)

Table 8.2   Land registered as surplus to current operational needs on Tyneside by type of owner, October 1983.

	District	County Council	BRB	Public utilities	PTA/ BS	RHAs	PSA	Other	Total
				Owner*					
area (ha)†	434.8	341.3	118.5	110.3	131.4	19.2	21.2	23.4	1200.1
percentage of total area	36.2	28.4	9.9	9.2	11.0	1.6	1.8	1.9	100.0
number of sites	152	52	28	11	20	7	6	4	280
percentage of sites	54.3	18.6	10.0	3.9	7.1	2.5	2.1	1.4	100.0
mean size of site (ha)	2.9	6.6	4.2	10.0	6.6	2.8	3.5	5.9	4.3

Source: Land registers.
   * *Abbreviations*: BRB (British Railways Board); PTA (Port of Tyne Authority); BS (British Shipbuilders); RHAs (regional health authorities); PSA (Property Services Agency).
   † All figures rounded to the first decimal place.

structure plan (Tyne and Wear County Council 1979) and is largely coincident with the area of the Inner Area Partnerships of Newcastle and Gateshead and the extended Urban Programme of North and South Tyneside (see Fig. 8.3). Sites on the urban edge are less numerous than in the inner city but much larger, while infill sites in the rest of the urban area are small (Table 8.3). In the inner city, the mean size of site (3.5 ha) conceals a skewed distribution. For example, out of 132 sites, 58 are less than 1.2 ha and only cover 3.5% of the recorded area while the three largest sites extend to 130.8 ha or 10.9% of the whole registered area. As in Greater London, many of the smaller sites are owned by the local authorities (Table 8.4) and represent the residues of comprehensive re-development schemes, for which there is now no money to complete, or which have become surplus with a shift in policy from housing clearance to housing rehabilitation. Most of the big sites are held by nationalised industries and have become redundant with the decline in the national and regional economies. More-over, there is no reason to believe that even with an up-turn in the economy a large proportion of this land will be developed. Some of it is unsuited to re-development, being low-lying or contaminated, and the demand for land in the conurbation continues to fall (see Tyne and Wear County Council 1979). But if the land registers generally are to be adjudged a successful initiative, evidence will be required to show that registered land is being marketed, disposed of and developed.

REGISTERED LAND: ITS LIKELY DEVELOPMENT
Land is not placed on the registers because it is regarded as ripe for development but because it is surplus to the operational needs of its public owner. Some of it is quite unsuited to any form of development, although the evidence contained in the registers is inadequate to reach an informed view about the development potential of any particular site. There is no discussion of local market circum-stances for example. As a result, the government has sought to establish

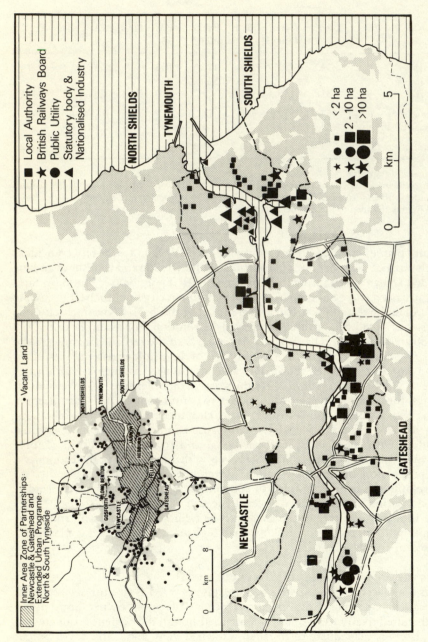

Figure 8.3 Registered land on Tyneside by type of owner, 1983. (*Source:* Land registers.)

Table 8.3   Urban fringe, in-fill and inner city sites on Tyneside.

	Number of sites	Area of land (ha)*	Mean size of site (ha)
inner city sites	132	465.1	3.5
in-fill sites inside the remaining urban area	67	143.1	2.1
urban fringe sites	81	591.9	7.3
Total	280	1200.1	4.3

Source: Land registers.
* All figures rounded to the first decimal place.

Table 8.4   Pattern of ownership of sites in the inner area of Tyneside, October 1983.

Owner	Number of sites	Total area* (ha)	Mean size of site (ha)
district authority	73	137.4	1.9
county council	15	36.1	2.4
British Railways Board	20	103.8	5.2
British Shipbuilders/ Port of Tyne Authority	18	125.6	7.0
public utilities	4	57.3	14.3
other	2	4.9	2.5
Total	132	465.1	3.5

Source: Land registers.
* All figures are rounded to the first decimal place.

whether individual sites have development potential by setting up small teams of valuers to examine each site in turn, backed up by architects who draw up schemes for particular sites in order to improve their marketability. The precise means by which judgements have been reached for particular sites have not been disclosed and neither have the results for individual sites. Aggregate data on the development potential of the land have, however, been published (see Howes 1984). Overall, nearly half the land inspected was thought to have moderate or high potential for development (Table 8.5). The data are recorded by standard region and they show considerable variations between regions. Most notably, there is a very low percentage in the moderate – high potential category for the North (7%) and a very high figure for the East Midlands (73%). Unfortunately, there is no breakdown specific to the inner cities.

As a separate study of development potential, but for only about one-sixth of the registers, has been conducted by the House Builders' Federation (HBF). The HBF examined the entries in 63 registers from all parts of the country in an attempt to establish what proportion of registered land could reasonably be expected to be developed for *private housing* (HBF 1982). The registers were

Table 8.5 The development potential of registered land.

Standard region	No potential (%)	Low potential (%)	Moderate/high potential (%)	Total
North	41	52	7	100
Yorkshire and Humberside	30	29	41	100
North West	14	24	62	100
East Midlands	13	14	73	100
West Midlands	15	26	59	100
East Anglia	7	45	48	100
South East*	18	36	46	100
(Greater London)	(16)	(49)	(35)	(100)
South–West	28	24	48	100
England	21	32	47	100

Source: Howes (1984, p. 29).
  * Figures for the South East contain those for Greater London. Figures may not add up to 100% due to rounding.

subjected to a desk study to eliminate sites that were quite hopeless for housing. The entries for the remaining sites were then sent to local builders who, having inspected the properties, approached the local authority to see whether the land they, the builders, considered suitable might be released for private housing. Only 11% of the land in the registers was suitable and of a type upon which the local authority would be likely to allow private residential development. Were such a percentage to apply to all registered land then the land identified would amount to less than 5000 ha. If this land were developed at 30 dwellings to the hectare, it would provide less than one year's supply of housing land (see Ch. 2, p. 26; Joint Land Requirements Committee 1983). Such a modest figure is hardly surprising given the poor local environments, the physical constraints that pertain to many sites and the wish of many local authorities to retain some of the best sites for employment–creating uses or for their own housing developments.

It is difficult at this early stage to assess the contribution which the registers will make to bringing land forward for development. The registers are only one of several policy initiatives aimed at resuscitating inner city areas, and there is no separate assessment of the potential of the sites located in the inner city. Moreover, a more detailed explanation of the wide regional variations in development potential noted in Table 8.5 is called for. About 7.8% of the total area entered on the registers has been removed and given the generally depressed state of the economy this could be regarded as satisfactory. But these sites are likely to be among the more attractive to developers, and an up–turn in the economy may be necessary to sustain this rate of disposal.

Two inner city case studies

NOTTINGHAM
The last part of this chapter discusses two investigations carried out by other researchers. The first was conducted in the city of Nottingham and in the

Broxtowe District to the west of the city (Nicholls *et al.* 1980). The main purpose of this study was to examine critically the widely held view that the inner city does not provide a satisfactory location for private residential development. No case study is ever fully representative and the findings must be treated accordingly, but Nottingham is a fairly typical medium-sized city with a population in 1981 of approximately 270 000. The City Council began a substantial slum clearance programme in the 1960s and the inner area contains a manufacturing sector which has experienced a noticeable decline in its economic fortunes during the current recession.

The authors begin by identifying sites *suitable* and *available* for private residential development, and then evaluate the roles played by the landowner, developer and those financing the house-building industry in the development process. Using schedules of vacant land and residential land availability supplied by the local planning authorities, a total of 481 possible housing sites were identified. For various reasons these were reduced to a final sample of 379 sites of which 79.9% were owned by the councils of Nottingham and Broxtowe. Within the inner city, defined as the land included in the Inner Area Programme for Nottingham, 209 sites were identified of which 84.6% were owned by the city council. Among the other 36 sites in the inner city, 20 were held by private companies and six by other public bodies.

The *suitability* of each site for private residential development was assessed, noting its physical, access and legal constraints, and whether the local authority would treat a planning application sympathetically. In the inner city about 60% of the sites were deemed suitable, 20% being rejected on planning grounds. These sites were similar to those for the rest of the study area indicating that, in the case of Nottingham at least, development was not inherently more problematic in the inner city than in the urban fringe. The figure of 60% conceals an important difference by type of owner. Of land in the city council's ownership, 77.5% could be developed without undue difficulty. For other owners, the proportion was only 26.3%.

When it came to assessing the *availability* of land suitable for residential development, over 75% was deemed to be unavailable, at least in the short term, because public and private owners alike stated a wish to retain their interest in a majority of their sites. Nottingham City Council wished to retain an interest in nearly 80% of their sites as it was the general policy of the Labour-controlled administration to retain most of its land for its own use. The council knew what it wanted to do. On only 10 sites (out of 232) in the whole city had the council not made its intentions explicit, but the council had not acquired or sought planning permission of any kind for 95 sites even though residential development was regarded as *suitable* on 46 of these. The local authority had acquired land ahead of its re-development programme and with reductions in public expenditure now owned land it could not afford to develop but was reluctant to release. Among the other owners were statutory bodies holding large sites surplus to their requirements which were often difficult to re-develop for housing, and a group of private companies who were retaining land adjacent to their existing premises in the hope of extending their businesses. Little land was being held speculatively awaiting a rise in land prices.

Even if land is available, developers will only be interested in it if they can build houses on it at a profit. The study of 43 developers operating in the

Nottingham area shows that only 30% had neither built nor indicated any interest in building in the inner city. Those with no experience of building in the inner city claim that there was too little demand for private housing there. This complaint was not confirmed by those with experience of development in the inner city. Instead, they argued that land prices were too high. Two further points arose out of the survey. First, developers did not have widespread knowledge of the suitable sites in the inner city. Second, although there was general agreement over which sites were to be preferred for the development of private housing, developers expressed a wide variety of opinions on the quality of individual sites. Thus, given the range of housing markets which the developer seeks to satisfy and the different sizes of site that were attractive to them, largely a function of the scale of their building operations, most of the sites would have been developed by someone if offered for sale at a reasonable price.

Several matters of interest are raised by this case study. First, there is land *suitable* for development which is not being made *available* by its current owner for a number of reasons. These reasons range from the ideological (the city council), to physical constraints and to the wish of companies to retain land on which they might wish to expand their business premises. Land speculation was not an important reason for holding on to land. Second, experience of inner city development changes the outlook of developers, usually by making them more enthusiastic towards building there. Third, in the case of Nottingham at least, many inner city sites could be made attractive to private developers without undue public expenditure.

TOWER HAMLETS

The study in the London Borough of Tower Hamlets (Thames Television 1980) raises different issues to those noted in central Nottingham, partly because it began as an analysis of vacant land starting from a study conducted by the Borough in 1977 (Tower Hamlets 1978), partly because the problems of re-development are more extensive there than in Nottingham, and partly because the severity of these problems has resulted in a different institutional structure. Under the 1978 Inner Urban Areas Act, that part of Tower Hamlets that lay within London's docklands (about 40% of the borough) became a Partnership Area and available for the most preferential treatment. In 1980, the London docklands area, the subject of its own strategic plan (Docklands Joint Committee 1976), was placed under the responsibility of the London Docklands Development Corporation (LDDC) with its much extended powers; and in April 1982 the Isle of Dogs Enterprise Zone, to be run by the LDDC and lying very largely within Tower Hamlets, was declared.

These designations, with their current orientation towards private enterprise do not sit comfortably in a borough where the council has traditionally espoused civic intervention, slum clearance and public housing. The borough plan laments the restrictions which these designated areas place on the council's freedom of action and the undue attention that may be given to these areas at the expense of the remainder of the borough (Tower Hamlets 1983). These are perfectly legitimate concerns but the borough will need outside assistance. Without question the area of vacant land in Tower Hamlets is considerable; the scale of economic change since the early 1960s has been enormous with the abandonment of London's upstream docks; and the decline in resident population has been dramatic (by almost one-third since 1961).

In the study, the causes of vacant land are linked to the re-development process and the attitudes of the major holders of vacant land. In 1977, 193 ha of vacant land on 506 sites covering 11% of the borough were identified (Tower Hamlets 1978), giving figures very much in line with those reported for other inner city areas (see, for example, Markowski 1978). In particular, public bodies were shown to own 75% of the sites and 87% of the area, with local authorities holding 72% of the sites and 65% of the area. The Thames Television report examined vacant land owned by nationalised industries, the private sector and the local authorities (GLC and LBTH) in turn. The report concludes that the nationalised industries have dragged their feet and are more ready to justify their inaction rather than to look for ways of disposing of surplus assets. These owners said it was difficult to be absolutely sure that some sites would not be needed again (see also Markowski 1978), that some of their land was contaminated and that many properties would be expensive to rehabilitate. They also noted that they were expected by the Treasury to sell their land at the highest possible price and, therefore, there was no reason why they should act in concert with the local authority, with which they had weak links anyway, in order to meet the authority's social or environmental goals.

Much of what the local authorities owned was the result, as in Nottingham, of unfinished re-development schemes. There was little incentive to do anything about the remaining vacant sites:

> Holding costs were cheap and central government grants insulated the potential user against interest charges. Moreover, sites not wanted for several years have seldom been disposed of to encourage early development. Local authorities were unwilling to sell land and compromise the realisation of the plans. In any case, there has been little financial incentive gained from disposal; proceeds of the sale would normally have been less than acquisition costs, and if any profit had arisen it would merely be set off against a loss-making account (Thames Television 1980, pp. 67–9).

That housing development for owner-occupation can and will take place in London's docklands if sufficient financial incentive is given to the private developer is shown by the progress reported by the LDDC. The LDDC proposes to build nearly 9 000 low-cost houses on its own land between 1981 and 1985 and claims considerable demand for the first of its houses (LDDC 1982). Whether the demand for these houses will be maintained, thus creating satisfactory profits for the developer, only time will tell, but the level of demand may well depend on public investment in the Borough's infrastructure in roads, schools and hospitals.

Vacant land in private ownership was widely distributed in small parcels throughout the borough. There were many vacant plots and derelict houses in areas of low demand for residential development where no profit could be made from re-building. These sites contrast sharply with those alongside the River Thames at Wapping where up-market residential development is being promoted by the LDDC within walking distance of the City. There were also vacant industrial premises, some of which may now be less attractive than the subsidised premises being offered by the LDDC, especially in the enterprise zone, although this was not a consideration when the report was written in 1980. Other premises remained empty whilst their owners sought planning permission for office development, especially in the west of the borough close to the City of London. Office development commands a much higher rent and permission for a change of use will substantially raise the value of the site. The authors of the report go so far as to suggest that if such properties were in active industrial use, 'there would be almost no chance of obtaining permission for office development. Vacancy can be used as a lever against the planning authority' (Thames Television 1980, p. 49). The general antipathy of the local authority towards both office development and private house-building means that sites with such permissions are few. Shortage has tended to raise land values in those *particular* locations in the borough where such development is most demanded (edge of the City; along the River Thames). Average land values for the borough as a whole are largely meaningless, there being many sites with a negative market value for development and few with a very high positive value.

The circumstances described in the report relate to those prevailing in 1980, since when both attitudes among owners and institutional structures have changed. Nevertheless, the report highlights a number of continuing concerns. These include:

(a)   The different prospects for re-development *within* a single inner city authority – the importance of site location
(b)   The dangers that public subsidy in any form – for public housing in Whitechapel as much as private industry in the Isle of Dogs – can create 'artificial' land values that may produce new vendors but at the same time price some purchasers out of the market
(c)   The lack of incentive to release land where holding costs are low and the proceeds do not immediately benefit the vendor.

Conclusion

It was suggested in Chapter 5 that owners of urban sites who wished to maximise their return from the re-development of their land should behave in a given way. In particular, attention was drawn to the importance of the general level of land values and how these might change, rather than to the need to obtain planning permission. Unlike the urban fringe, or even on the edge of the CBD, permission to re-develop is often encouraged by the local authority whilst a successful application would not necessarily lead to a significant increase in the value of the land. It was also argued that owners should always be aware of the market value of their property, be prepared to sell their land, and should not make improvements to it unless these would enhance its re-development value.

The actual behaviour of owners only meets these assumptions in part. A significant proportion of property in the inner city is held in public ownership and public owners have to meet a range of social, environmental and statutory obligations as well as being concerned with the economically optimal use of public assets. Some public owners have been slow to market land surplus to their current needs, often having to be cajoled into doing so by government action, whilst others are fully cognisant of the market value of their land but have no incentive to sell it. The disinclination to sell may also reflect a reluctance to accept the changed economic circumstances of the inner city in the 1980s or to accept a continued reduction in levels of public spending. It is difficult to see how the economy of the inner city can be revived to its former importance or how, in the short term, some of the inner city re-development plans of the 1970s can be completed. However, hope springs eternal – the economy may pick up and governments do not last forever – and where holding costs are low (in terms of cash payments), some owners are prepared to take a long-term view. This makes them most unwilling to sell off any properties that may prove to be of value to them in the future and, in the housing field in particular, these sites may also be those most attractive to the private sector developer.

Over much, but not all, of the inner city the key problem is one of market failure. The study of Tower Hamlets shows that in places, on the edge of the City of London, for example, land values are sufficient to encourage commercial and residential re-development without government subsidy. The same cannot be said for most of the borough. This is not to say that demand is non-existent, or that land values are always negative, but the costs of site rehabilitation and the perceived risk surrounding residential re-development make the development of greenfield sites a safer commercial venture. In short, government attempts to raise the value of the land, either by giving fiscal incentives to new land users or by reducing the cost of re-development through derelict land and urban development grants, are essential to the re-development of the inner city. The danger, however, with the present market-oriented policy is that too much attention will become focused on sites within preferred areas (such as enterprise zones), which will simply shift the location of re-development rather than create additional economic activity, and that re-development will be seen largely as a short-term commercial matter and not as a means of making the inner city a more pleasant place for its local inhabitants to live and work.

The extent of vacant and derelict property has become much more visible recently as the inner city economy has faltered and as national attention has been focused on inner city areas following the riots of 1981. Nevertheless, there is evidence (see Markowski 1978) that land vacancy, for example, has long existed in the inner city. Vacancy has been tolerated during happier economic circumstances when many sites have been put to effective, if temporary (and often unsightly) uses; and with recession temporary uses may become permanent. The income raised from 'temporary' car parks, scrap-metal yards and open storage has, on occasion, been sufficient to encourage the owner to take a 'wait and see' approach to the re-development of the land. On the other hand, the loss of these sources of income, especially if the occupiers are able to move to subsidised premises, will do nothing to encourage the re-development of these sites.

Notes

1   It is, of course, also possible to find vacant urban fringe sites for which there are no buyers. These
    include sites adjacent to unsuccessful public housing schemes around conurbations with a

depressed local economy. See, for example, entries in the land register for Knowsley, Lancashire, on the eastern edge of Merseyside.

2   The first directions for disposal were issued by the SOS in November 1984 to the Borough Councils of Darlington, Oldham and Sunderland and to Nottingham City Council.

3   The registers are fully up-dated 6-monthly on 1 January and 1 July. In between times, delay in up-dating makes the registers inaccurate to a small degree.

9 Review and policy implications

Introduction

While we would not argue that the landowner is the most important actor in the development process, a claim that could be more readily substantiated for the developer or planner, we believe that the part the owner plays is too readily dismissed and, as a result, is poorly understood. Except under conditions of compulsory purchase, or the threat to use these powers, *all* actors in the development process, including the owner, have to be in favour of the development of a particular site if development is to occur; and it is primarily for this reason that we have examined the role of the landowner in the development of land in Britain today.

Our analysis has included all kinds of owner who hold land with development or re-development potential, even if that potential cannot be realised immediately because of either adverse planning policies or a current lack of demand for the land. The activities of land dealers, or those who purchase the land with the intention of re-selling it for a short-term capital gain, have not been considered as a specific group. Such owners are comparatively few in number in Britain, unlike the numerous land dealers that operate in the fringes of North American cities, because of the comparative certainty of the development process brought about by the statutory planning system. Most owners hold their land for reasons of either use and occupation or as an investment, although these motives may be combined together. Control as a motive of ownership is less common but is important, particularly for public sector owners. Landowners in Britain are generally pre-development landowners, they rarely carry out development themselves and, even then, it is usually for their own use. The only exceptions to this rule are 'professional landowners' who are often developers any way (see Ch. 6).

Every kind of owner, whether private individual or company, charity, institution, or nationalised industry holds some land with development potential and their behaviour has been analysed in the context of three separate but related decision-making areas. First, and foremost, we assessed the owner's financial strategy and, in particular, the reasons that influenced the *timing* of the decision to sell the land for development. Second, we analysed the owner's operational strategy, or what contribution the owner makes to the development process. Finally, we discussed the owners' management decisions as they affect the maintenance of their property while development is awaited. In Chapter 5 these issues were brought together and a model of behaviour was outlined on the assumption that the owner wished to maximise the return to his investment in land. In practice, few owners meet in full the requirements laid down in the model but at least the model provides a vantage point from which to observe what owners do.

The model is set in the context of broader matters that influence the owner's decisions. In particular, there is the policy setting which consists of a wide range of planning, taxation and land policies, and the effects arising from the operation of various development land markets. Evidence from three case studies – an expanding city (Leicester), an area of severe restraint (the Metropolitan Green Belt) and a zone of intermittent demand for re-development (the inner city) – was then related to the assumptions on which the model was based.

This final chapter consists of two main parts. In the first, the findings of the book are re-examined and conclusions are drawn. In the second, we discuss certain policy implications that derive from our findings, paying particular attention to the need to draw together aspects of the planning system and elements of taxation policy, both of which are major influences on landowners' behaviour, so that the development process may be made to work more effectively than at present.

The owner and the development process

There are three main reasons why the landowner has not attracted more attention in previous analyses of the development process in Britain. First, economists have traditionally but erroneously assumed that the supply of development land is purely a function of the kind and level of demand; second, detailed information on the pattern of land ownership is extremely restricted for England and Wales; and third, the owner's role has been relegated to a minor place by comparison with the planner and developer. Empirical analyses of the development process suggest the need for reappraisal.

Past research has tended to allocate to different actors carefully prescribed roles and, by so doing to imply that each actor operates semi-independently. Indeed, each group often assumes that the others have too much power over the development of land and they too little. The diffusion of power means that land passes through the development process by a variety of routes and therefore the process is better viewed in terms of *key events* rather than key actors (see Ch. 4). Two events in particular, the *identification* of development land and the *initiation* of development upon it, are of critical importance. It is how the various actors interact with each other with regard to these events that is of particular significance.

Furthermore, the roles that each actor plays differ according to the general circumstances surrounding the development site in question. Broadly speaking, where the financial incentive to develop is considerable but the outcome is uncertain, as on white land at the urban edge, the landowner is likely to play a passive role, often not even being involved in the acquisition of planning permission, and the owner's actions may have but a slight effect on the timing of development. In the case of relatively small infill sites within the urban area, the owner may prove to be the most important actor (see Ch. 6) being primarily responsible for both identifying land and initiating development upon it. Developers also vary in their approach to seeking out development land, depending largely upon their scale of operations and the size of site they prefer to develop. The volume house-builders, for instance, are able to support teams of staff who are constantly searching for development sites and, as large-scale businesses, they are usually more prepared than small builders to acquire land without planning permission for development, or to take out options and conditional contracts – in other words, to share more fully in the financial risks of bringing land forward (see Ch. 3).

Similarly, it would be incorrect to assume that the roles of the principal actors have always been the same. Traditionally, financial intermediaries oiled the financial wheels of development without becoming directly involved. Today, in the area of commercial and industrial development, pension funds and insurance companies not only fund developments but are major consumers of the finished product as well as developers in their own right. Planners' roles have also changed. For example, they have become more determined in recent years to insert social and environmental conditions into development control decisions as bargaining between them, owners and developers has become a more established feature of the development process.

This book also provides evidence of the wide range of attitudes held by landowners towards the development of their land and the large differences in level of understanding that they have of the complex policy environment within which development occurs. Many owners have little direct experience of development, although plenty of professional advice is available at a price; and although most landowners on the urban edge are aware they can realise a large capital gain from acquiring planning permission for residential development, that does not mean to say that they hold realistic opinions as to the value of their land, of the chance they have of getting planning permission or of the net of tax sale proceeds they will receive. Land prices have risen significantly in real terms during most of the post-war period and owners might, therefore, be inclined to hold an inflated view of what their land is worth in monetary terms. Moreover, many owners have inherited their properties and attach use and non-pecuniary occupancy values to their land which may influence the timing of the land's development. This is particularly so for residential owner-occupiers. Owners may argue that if land values are rising, why can the sale of their land not wait until their retirement? Different considerations apply to public owners. Much of their land has an existing statutory use, but where it is no longer required and where it is located in areas of low demand for other uses, the site's value may not warrant the costs of re-habilitation, especially if holding costs are low and any profits made from the sale of the land cannot be retained by the 'owner' but go to the Treasury (see Ch. 8).

The amount of the sale proceeds after tax is significantly affected by the changing policy context. Confronting the landowner is an amalgam of planning, taxation and compulsory purchase and compensation policies that are complicated, change rapidly and do not act in concert. Arguably, some of these policies, especially in the field of taxation (e.g. CTT), have not been introduced with the development process specifically in mind or with any idea of what impact they might have on the supply of development land, and a number of points arising from our review of current policies in Chapter 2 are worth re-emphasising.

As far as *planning* policy is concerned, two issues are of particular significance to the landowner. First, as a result of the slowness with which plans are prepared and the number of unanticipated developments that occur during the life of a plan, many development plans date rapidly. During the life of a plan, the development prospects of some parcels of land change significantly and landowners are able to submit planning applications with a reasonable chance of success for areas not identified for development in the plan. Second, plans often contain vague or unrealisable policies increasing the scope for negotiations between the owner and the planning authority over particular proposals. In the field of *taxation* landowners often believe that the impact of taxes on the sale proceeds of development land will be greater than it need be. This is partly because the media coverage of tax changes emphasises the new level of liabilities while paying insufficient attention to how the tax burden might be mitigated. As a result increases in tax liability reduce the supply of development land quite significantly in the short run, if only because a change from a Labour to a Conservative government has normally led to a lower rate of tax, or even to its abolition, encouraging owners to wait and see. Private landowners also harbour exaggerated fears as to the effects of *compulsory purchase and compensation* policies that permit direct intervention in the land market by public authorities. Owners distrust the terms of the compensation code and dislike the loss of freedom to act independently that is entailed in the use of compulsory purchase orders, even though the latter are used relatively infrequently and as a measure of last resort. In conclusion, the non-professional landowner often believes that the policy context is unduly weighted against him and, as a result of imperfect knowledge, under-estimates his ability to influence events and to increase his level of profit. In the hands of the experienced landowner and his advisers, the same policy constraints can be quite flexible.

A lack of knowledge and understanding of the land market can also influence the owner's willingness to sell. Three general issues underlying the creation of land values were discussed in Chapter 3. The first concerned the pattern of land values in and around the city in Great Britain and the effect of planning policies on that pattern. Given the inherent tendency of the planning system to under-supply development land on the urban edge, the acquisition of planning permission increases the value of land by, on average, 20 times and in particular locations, such as in the MGB, by between 50 and 100 times. Such enormous increases in the value of land encourage speculation, but, because of the uncertainty over obtaining planning permission, land prices fall very rapidly to agricultural values only a small distance from the urban edge. This is not to say that there is no 'intermediate' market in urban fringe land with hope value, but it does not normally take the conventional form with buyers and sellers. Instead owners are much more likely to grant options or conditional contracts. Within the urban area, land values decline rapidly away from the peak of the CBD, reaching a low point in the inner city area before rising again slightly in suburbia.

The widely held view that land values will continue to rise in real terms, as they have done for most of the post-war period, was also examined. We prefer the position that land values will rise and fall in line with the rate of economic growth and urban expansion. Development land prices will not rise in real terms come what may unless the supply of development land is continuously and increasingly squeezed by public policies below the amount demanded by society. We also conclude that landowners have a supply price below which they will not sell, and this price will vary in real terms over time. But only rarely are landowners, either individually or in combination, in a position to drive the price of land upwards. Owners infrequently act together and the land held by one owner can usually be substituted for land held by another. Since the early 1970s the proportion of housing stock on sale at any one time consisting of new houses has fallen from 25% to 10% and in most residential areas, we would argue, the price of second-hand houses largely determines the price of new houses. This means that, unless the price of second-hand houses rises, permitting the price of new houses to rise, developers will not be able to offer owners higher prices for their land.

In an attempt to bring together all these matters we present a model in Chapter 5 that describes the kinds of decisions an owner should take. The model is based on the assumptions that the owner is familiar with both the development prospects of his land and the policy context, and is holding his land primarily as an investment. In the case of greenfield sites it was argued that the landowner should sell the land immediately upon obtaining outline planning permission unless the owner could reasonably anticipate a further, major rise in land values or a significant fall in the rate of tax on development land. The study of owners in Leicester showed that although comparatively few owners had purchased land for speculative reasons, financial reasons were important in determining the timing of the decision to sell for all but residential owner-occupiers. Most owners of greenfield sites recognised the importance of planning permission and the rate of tax was found to be an important reason for the postponement of the sale decision, especially among the owners of large sites in the urban fringe. In the case of sites in the inner city, the model indicated that the timing of the decision to sell should be determined by changes in land values and not by the receipt of planning permission, and the examples reported in Chapter 8 showed that where holding costs were low and demand uncertain both public and private owners were reluctant to sell. They preferred to wait and see if their own prospects would improve, in the hope of completing development schemes they had planned years earlier, before being prepared to market their land.

It was also argued in Chapter 5 that if the owner is to obtain the best return on his investment he should actively seek planning permission himself and be prepared to market the land, not just accept the first offer. By so doing he would avoid sharing some of the development value with the developer. In Leicester, 65% of owners sold after getting planning consent and 42% were prepared to take the matter to appeal if necessary. In the MGB, the small chance of obtaining planning permission, even after an appeal, meant that while owners regularly applied for permission (unsuccessfully) many were prepared to incorporate the developer's skills through joint applications, options and conditional contracts. It is the government's view that many public owners of surplus land, especially those with such land in the inner city, show much less initiative and do not actively market their land. In support of this view, in Tower Hamlets at least, the nationalised industries were regarded as cautious at best and obstructive at worst in assessing the re-development potential of their land (Thames Television 1980). They were simply not geared up, mentally or practically, to take positive decisions, although it does seem that attitudes have changed markedly since this particular study was undertaken early in 1980.

In the analysis of land management decisions, it was asserted in Chapter 5 that prior to the sale of their land, owners of urban sites should minimise any outgoings that would not add to the re-development value of the site, whilst seeking to take advantage of any temporary earnings. Entries in the registers of public sector vacant land include a listing of any short-term leases granted on the properties. In the case of the 132 sites in the inner area of Tyneside (see Ch. 8), only 18 could be said to be earning any temporary rental income. Eight sites were used as car parks, six as temporary storage areas and four as construction sites for development on adjacent land. Farmland on the urban edge, it was argued, should neither be let on secure leases nor attract investment in improvements that were of no value to a developer. Evidence from the MGB indicated that land next to urban development was poorly maintained, but it was impossible to prove on the basis of the information collected that this low standard of maintenance was the direct result of attempts to acquire planning permission rather than the effects of urban intrusion on farming practice. Nevertheless, a disproportionate amount of farmland right on the urban edge was let short term and was often very badly maintained.

Summary

In conclusion to this review we wish to re-emphasise two matters. First, our evidence demonstrates that the owner's role in the development process should not be ignored, and it is likely to become more important in the future for two reasons. First, the present government continues to increase the scope and influence of the private sector (owner, developer, financial institution) into aspects of the development process that, traditionally, planners effectively controlled. The increased extent to which planners have to consult representatives of the construction industry over the supply of land for residential development is but one example (see Ch. 2). Another is the attempt to restrict the planner's say on the design of buildings, although in this case development interests will not get all they want. The circular on planning gain (DOE 1983a) does not restrict the planner's scope as much as the Property Advisory Group had wished (see Ch. 2). Nevertheless, in recent years, the balance of power has shifted away from the local planner in favour of private initiative. In addition, the development potential of urban areas will be looked at more closely in the future as it becomes increasingly necessary to develop these in order to meet both the demands for land of the construction industry and the preservationist instincts towards greenfield sites of outer-suburban residents. This potential will include not only the large areas of vacant land, mainly in public sector ownership, but also the re-development of infill sites in suburban areas – exactly the type of site where the landowner often plays the leading role in identifying and initiating development.

Second, the evidence also draws attention to the different types of owner and the range of attitudes they have towards the development of their land. The great majority of owners are not professional landowners and it is only the latter who behave in a manner that closely corresponds with the model presented in Chapter 5. Although financial incentive is an important consideration for the great majority of owners in the development of their land, the motive of financial gain is regularly combined with other motives, especially those relating to use and occupancy; but in the case of residential owner-occupiers financial gain is often of little importance. For farmers, agricultural landlords, commercial undertakings and nationalised industries holding surplus land, the level of net gains following disposal is a major consideration in the *timing* of their decision to sell. Most *have* to be able to realise a significant gain, as reflected in new business premises or a larger farm, if they are going to be prepared to sell, and the more problems – financial and non-financial – that the loss of their existing land will bring, the more they will be inclined to put off the sale.

Some policy considerations

The complexity of the policy context is such that we cannot consider all those aspects of relevance to the landowner. We have to take some basic features as given and to treat others all too briefly. Given our concern with the landowner we shall focus our attention on the relations between the planning system, the taxation of betterment and fiscal incentives.

It is important to point out at the outset that we remain committed to a publicly accountable land-use planning system. This is not the place to assess the strengths and weaknesses of the current system but if it is seen to act in the public interest (diffuse and imprecise though this notion may be) as a result of public discussion of planning policies and through the decisions of elected members, it remains the best means of determining which land should be developed and for what purpose. In principle it is right that the planner rather than any other actor in the development process should largely determine, albeit in discussion with other participants, the amount, location and timing of development because, a few cases aside, the planner and the elected member are the only actors without a direct financial interest in the outcome. Nevertheless, the development process needs to be made to work in a more positive way than it does at present, encouraging development where it is wanted and inhibiting it where it is not wanted. Planners and policy makers should learn to manipulate the market in land to assist in the achievement of planning ends (see Moor 1983).

Broadly speaking, there are two ways of going about this. *First*, there could be an increase in the scope of direct control powers over the development land market operated through the public sector. The Community Land Scheme represents the most recent attempt to introduce such an approach (DOE 1974). The scheme sought to get the land market to operate more in accord with planners' wishes by placing a duty on local planning authorities to acquire a sufficient stock of potential development land in order to meet the needs of their areas and to allow authorities to purchase the land, compulsorily if necessary, at its existing use value. It is fair to say that the Community Land Scheme was neither properly financed because of cuts in public expenditure nor in operation long enough for its effectiveness to be properly assessed (for an analysis see Barrett and Whitting 1980, 1981). Nevertheless, at the level of principle, we are not persuaded that the responsibility for identifying development land should be left *solely* to the public sector. Given the time it takes to approve and modify development plans, the system needs landowners and developers to identify additional sites if only to provide the flexibility required to respond quickly to unforeseen circumstances. Indeed, if such a scheme was operated locally, as under the Community Land Scheme, for local political reasons it would almost certainly lead to an under-supply of land where pressures for development are greatest. Most local authorities in the urban fringe are inherently conservative and parochial in outlook and the forces opposing development are very powerful, as the recent furore over the draft circular on green belt has shown (see Ch. 7).

Where a national body is set up to identify development land, as in the case of the Land Commission (see Ch. 2), conflicts are often not resolved in those areas with the greatest shortages of development land. Not unreasonably, locally elected planning committees dislike losing their powers to what they characterise as a distant, undemocratic, cumbersome and inflexible body. Equally, planning committees dislike the imposition of other local public bodies if these promote development on the basis of a different ideology to their own. A good example of this is the tension that exists between the London Borough of Tower Hamlets and the London Docklands Development Corporation (see Ch. 8). In between these alternatives are regional bodies such as the Land Authority for Wales (LAW). Within its remit (see Howell 1979), LAW had undoubtedly had much success in promoting development, being able to combine a common regional identity and a similar ideological perspective on how best to initiate development as held by most local authorities in Wales. A comparable level of success might not be achieved in other parts of Britain, especially in the context of residential development in 'comfortable' Britain, where different local political circumstances prevail and the social imperative to create jobs is often not given the same priority as environmental protection.

Second, there is the approach that accepts the continued existence of a private market in development land, the right of landowners and developers to identify land not identified by the planners and the opportunity for landowners and developers to try to persuade the planning authority of their way of thinking. *Provided* that the question of betterment is effectively and equitably handled and the actions of owners and developers are not allowed to undermine the general intent of planning policies, especially those designed to protect and promote the poorer sections of the community, then this approach best fits the nature of society in contemporary Britain. Moreover, with increasing home ownership this approach will, we believe, continue to be the one that is preferred by the majority of the electorate. The most effective way of making this kind of development process work more positively is to ensure that the taxation system, to which the landowner (see Ch. 6), developer and final consumer do respond, operate in support of planning policies. We therefore turn to possible ways in which the taxation system might be amended to assist in this process.

In the first instance we return to certain of the principles put forward more than 40 years ago by the Expert Committee on Compensation and Betterment in the Uthwatt Committee Report (1942). Among the principles expressed was the recommendation that, for taxation purposes, land outside urban areas should be treated differently from land within them. This recommendation was not adopted by the government of the day partly because of the practical difficulties involved in defining the urban edge for all settlements in the country (Cullingworth 1981). Nevertheless, the distinction has considerable merit and for the purposes of taxation, development land could be divided into three categories:

(a)   Land outside (or even inside) the urban area where development should, in principle, *never* take place, as for example, within much of the approved MGB
(b)   Other land outside urban areas (the great majority)
(c)   Land within urban areas.

The idea that the rate and nature of taxation should vary between areas, like planning policies, is neither revolutionary nor novel. Tax concessions and subsidies have long been a tool of regional policy, with companies locating in assisted areas benefitting from incentives unavailable elsewhere (for a description of current polices see Regional Studies Association 1983). The present government has endorsed the practicality of spatially-differentiated taxes through the establishment of enterprise zones and freeports, and through the notion that 'heritage land and property' can be identified which merits relief from capital transfer tax. As in all such situations, the drawing of boundaries and the decisions in individual cases will create what are seen as inequities; but this is nothing new. Tax might be levied on the three categories of development land noted above as follows:

Category A   DLT assessed at 100%
Category B   DLT assessed at 60%, i.e. no change (but see below)
Category C   DLT assessed at 60%, but with more generous reliefs so that the taxable amount can be reduced.

Only land within category A would have to be delineated precisely because the tax rate is the same for the other two categories and the greater reliefs available on an urban property can be granted by extending the present assumptions for 'material development' and current use value (see pp. 32–3 and p. 40).

The purpose of setting DLT at 100% for land that should never be developed is to help achieve that objective not to raise revenue. A tax at this level should substantially reduce speculative pressures on such land were there to be all-party agreement to this principle. Today, because of high land prices, a DLT rate of 60% is insufficient to discourage these pressures in areas of high development potential, even where the prospect of obtaining planning permission is very low. Owners still try to get their land released for development because the financial gain remains considerable; and every time there is the least suggestion that restraint policies might be relaxed, however slightly, speculative motives are re-fuelled (see Ch. 7). Speculative pressures can only be removed completely if this new level of tax is not varied and if the area of land to which it is applied is not changed. In practice and in detail, it is impossible to achieve the latter, but unless the general principle of permanence is stated and adhered to by central government (see Ch. 7), landowners will not accept that the planning and tax regimes are truly fixed.

Such a 'permanent' tax policy should minimise speculation, reduce the extent of poorly maintained land in the urban fringe and permit amenities to be enhanced (and compensated for) at existing rural land-use values. The point of permanence is extremely important as experience of farmland preservation programmes in North America shows (for a review see Furuseth & Pierce 1982, pp. 41–76). But even in these 'green' zones, the owner and developer would not be denied the right to submit planning applications as some limited change in the accommodation of those who already live and work there would have to be catered for. There would though be no financial gain in terms of the owner profiting from the increase in land values if planning permission was granted because the gain in value would be immediately taxed at 100% under the terms of DLT.

In other urban fringe areas, where there are no special restraint policies in operation but the presumption is still against development, we see no need for a major change to the present DLT regime, although there is scope for a higher marginal rate than 60% where the amount of realised development value is substantial. Increases in land values at the urban fringe when planning permission is granted can be massive and there is, therefore, merit in retaining a special form of taxation because the increase is mainly due to 'community' action. But DLT assessed at a basic rate of 60% still gives sufficient incentive for owners to draw planners' attention to their sites even though over half the proceeds go to the Treasury. As long as this rate of tax remains unchanged and the amount of development value that can be realised free of tax stays constant in real terms, the results from the Leicester survey – a survey conducted in a representative city but one that could usefully be repeated – suggest that a sensible compromise has been reached between public and private interests.

The development and re-development of land within urban areas is likely to be of increasing concern as the housing stock and other buildings age. During the last decade a large number of old dwellings have been successfully rehabilitated but there eventually comes a point when the continual repair of old structures becomes impracticable. In the slum clearance schemes of the past, many of the homes had been rented from private landlords but as the extent of owner-occupation continues to grow will it be possible, politically, for public bodies to acquire compulsorily areas of old suburban housing? Or is the land-ownership pattern effectively sterilised? The problem of what to do with old, and in some cases not so old, industrial properties is also with us and it has been suggested that grants should be given for the demolition of such buildings (King 1981). Bringing these sites back into use through the development process requires the removal of several barriers, real or perceived. As the studies of Leicester and the inner city show, the level of land values is a major barrier, but a lack of awareness of the effect that DLT will have on the net of tax proceeds also contributes to some owners' reluctance to sell. The complexities in calculating the current use value of an urban property (see Ch. 2) make it difficult for landowners to accept that there will not be a significant DLT liability even if this is rarely the case. It would help if the DLT office was given the task of publicising how rarely DLT 'bites' on the sale of an urban site.

There is no doubt in our minds that the level of DLT affects landowners' behaviour and we believe that our studies in Leicester and the MGB show this conclusively. DLT can be used to help the development process by increasing the tax burden where development is not desired and by reducing it where development is to be encouraged. It is not practical to vary DLT at a local level on a widespread scale because of the need to define precise boundaries which is time consuming and costly. But where there are real benefits from a differential rate, as in the case of the MGB around London, then the time spent should be worthwhile.

Small urban sites are likely to become of increasing importance to the development process. This is already recognised in those areas under the greatest development pressure where local political forces are opposed to too much development on greenfield sites. One such area is Essex where it is estimated that 6% of the development capacity will be contained on sites of less than four units (Essex County Council 1982). Furthermore, the report of the panel of inquiry into the Essex county structure plan accepted that over 7% of the new dwellings planned up to 1991 will arise from the 'intensification' of use on urban sites not identified by the planning authority. In the south-east, outside Greater London, it is estimated that 18% of the five years supply of residential building land is from small private sites (Standing Conference 1983c). These are precisely those sites where the landowner's role in the development process is most important (see Ch. 6). But if planners are to rely increasingly on shortfalls in land availability being met from small sites, this role must be recognised and, if the supply needs to be increased, ways must be found to encourage owners to sell earlier. This may prove difficult because the owners of small sites are often residential owner-occupiers and, as we have shown, they are least susceptible to financial inducement. No doubt both planners and developers will respond to find new means of ensuring an adequate supply of small sites, but it is likely that landowners will retain a significant role in relation to identifying and initiating development on this type of site.

In the inner city different issues arise. The value of the land in a new use is often insufficient to warrant the costs of rehabilitating and redeveloping the site; and even where a small profit might be realised (albeit at a risk) and where holding costs are low, the owner may be prepared to adopt a long-term 'wait and see' policy. Two issues arise from this conclusion. One concerns the feasibility of forcing some of this land on to the market, not only by insisting that owners 'market' their land (as represented by the introduction of the land registers) but also through financial penalties of various kinds, such as site value rating (see below). The other is the effectiveness of tax incentives, or grants of various kinds, in aiding the rehabilitation of sites and in permitting the owner to retain a larger proportion of the sale proceeds than is possible under current DLT arrangements.

Publicly at least, central government does not seriously question the need to bring vacant and derelict land back into an acceptable use in the inner city, if necessary at some public expense. However, the case for rehabilitating inner city land is often taken for granted – the external diseconomies arising from derelict land; the need for a fuller use of past investment in the social infrastructure; the need to create jobs in areas of high unemployment, and so on – but the opportunity costs of investing in the inner city as opposed to other geographical locations are rarely detailed or critically evaluated. It may be impossible to assess such costs and the degree of government commitment to inner city regeneration may have to remain at the level of political judgement. Nevertheless, the social, environmental and economic objectives of inner city policy *imply* a *vast* injection of money and while attempts to attract private and institutional capital into the inner city should not be derided they are likely to prove hopelessly inadequate on their own without government direction. Furthermore, when the *objectives* of private and institutional capital are put alongside the primarily social objectives of inner city policy, it is evident that these sources of capital will do no more than contribute at the margin to the needs of those who live and work there in the absence of a much greater commitment of public money than is being made available at present.

It is within this wider context that current government initiatives which favour private investment have to be seen. This is not to suggest that the existing derelict land grants and urban development grants should not be retained and further publicised as they provide both the developer with some financial incentive to undertake an otherwise unprofitable scheme, and the landowner with the opportunity to dispose of an asset which would otherwise be unsaleable. The first evidence that UDGs are having some impact is now available (June 1984). A total investment of over £300 million had been made by the autumn of 1983 since the inception of UDGs at the commencement of that year, £239 million of which had been provided by the private sector (Mallinson & Gilbert 1983). DLGs have to date had less impact, but where the development costs of a site are abnormally high and they are the only barrier to development, DLGs are most appropriate. DLT does not normally prevent the development of inner city land, provided that the owner is well informed, because the level of land values is low. However, there is one circumstance where DLT is a problem and this is almost entirely confined to vacant land held by the nationalised industries. It is therefore doubly ironic that a transfer payment within the public sector should have 'real' consequences. Even where British Rail's redundant marshalling yards have development potential, virtually the whole of the sale proceeds are liable to DLT because the current use value for railway purposes is negligible. If this type of property could be regarded as open storage land for valuation purposes, the problem would be resolved and the DLT office would still collect some tax if the property was sold for commercial development.

The alternative to providing incentives to encourage the development of inner city sites is the imposition of penalties while the land remains vacant, i.e. site value rating. The theory is that, to mitigate the liability, the owner will either develop the land to make it income producing or sell the land to someone who is prepared to develop it. The assumption is that the land *can* be profitably developed and the only person preventing this is the owner. In the inner city this situation is the exception not the rule. The problem with most sites is that they cannot be developed profitably because of lack of demand. The most likely effect of site value rating would be the transfer of land from its existing owner to a person or body prepared to pay the charge and speculate on the land's future worth. It is possible that more temporary use would be made of vacant sites and some would be developed, but it is clear that site value rating is not a panacea for bringing about the development of vacant inner city land. In our view there is no alternative to providing incentives to achieve this, either by direct public sector investment or by subsidising the private sector.

Final comment

In this book we have collected and analysed the evidence that is available about landowners in Britain, including our own sources. The evidence is not as comprehensive as we should like, emanating as it does from studies in a few locations. It is, however, all that is available and this book is the first to concentrate on landowners and the roles they play in the development process. Research on landowners in England and Wales is difficult, so it is not surprising that the number of research studies is comparatively few. One of the reasons for this is the unnecessary lengths to which government goes to protect the confidentiality of owners and property transactions (see for example the presentation of land values data in *Inland Revenue statistics*). In the age of information technology this is little short of a national scandal and the sooner the HM Land Registry computerises title records and makes the information available to the public the better. We are pleased to see that the Law Commission has recently decided to canvass public opinion on this issue and we await the results of their survey with considerable interest (Law Commission 1984).

The research that has been conducted on landowners is very largely cross-sectional, in that owners have been investigated at one moment in time, and yet the development process is dynamic. There is very little empirical evidence in Britain of how the development process operates right from the crucial stage when land is *first* identified as development land on a plan. There is a need for the detailed monitoring of specific areas over perhaps a ten year period starting with early indications that development might take place, say in the first draft plan, through to the precise boundaries of development being delineated in a district plan. There has been no research either on how long it takes for land to pass through the first stage in the cycle – from allocation to the grant of planning permission. Research on these matters is long over-due and without them policies may be seriously flawed. Is, for example, the identification of five years supply of residential building land sufficient or even too great for planning purposes? This is the type of question such studies could attempt to answer.

Lastly, there is a growing awareness within the planning profession that planners do not operate in a 'command' economy and that the future prospect of doing so seems remote, except perhaps in particularly depressed industrial areas. If they are to achieve their objectives planners will have to do so through manipulating market forces and not by imposing heavy handed controls or spending many millions of pounds of public sector capital. This book is a contribution to the growing literature that seeks to explain how the market operates and, in particular, the role played by landowners in the development process.

References

ACAH (Advisory Council for Agriculture and Horticulture in England and Wales) 1978. *Agriculture and the Countryside* (Strutt report). Chesham: Robendene.

Agriculture EDC (Economic Development Council) 1977. *The ownership of land by agricultural landlords in England and Wales*. London: NEDO.

Alonso, W. 1964. *Location and land use*. Cambridge, Mass.: Harvard University Press.

Ambrose, P. and B. Colenutt 1975. *The property machine*. Harmondsworth: Penguin.

Anderson, R., M. Bulos and S. Walker 1983. Sow's ear into silk purse? *Estates Gazette* **267**, 822–6.

Bahl, R. W. 1968. A land speculation model: the role of the property tax as a constraint to urban sprawl. *J. Reg. Sci.* **8**, 199–208.

Ball, M. 1983. *Housing policy and economic power: the political economy of owner occupation*. London: Methuen.

Barlowe, R. 1958. *Land resource economics: the political economy of rural and urban land resource use*. Englewood Cliffs, N.J.: Prentice-Hall.

Barras, R. 1979. The first ten years of English structure planning: current progress and future directions. *Planning Outlook* **22**, 19–23.

Barrett, S. and C. Fudge (eds) 1981. *Policy and action: essays on the implementation of public policy*. London: Methuen.

Barrett, S. and G. Whitting 1980. *Local authorities and the supply of development land to the private sector*. Working Paper No. 19, School of Advanced Urban Studies, University of Bristol.

Barrett, S., M. Stewart and J. Underwood 1978. *The land market and development process*. Occasional Paper No. 2, School for Advanced Urban Studies, University of Bristol.

Barrett, S., M. Boddy and M. Stewart 1979. *The implementation of the community land scheme: interim report*. Occasional Paper No. 3, School of Advanced Urban Studies, University of Bristol.

Bassett, K. A. and J. R. Short 1980. *Housing and residential structure: alternative approaches*. London: Routledge and Kegan Paul.

Bather, N. J. 1976. *The speculative residential developer and urban growth*. Geographical Paper No. 47, Department of Geography, University of Reading.

Bell, M. 1979. Agricultural compensation: the way forward. *J. Plann. Environ. Law*, September, 577–96.

Bell, M., A. Hearne and D. van Rest 1978. Agricultural land take for new roads. *Town and Country Planning* **46**, 164–7.

Berkman, H. G. 1956. Decentralization and blighted vacant land. *Land Econ.* **32**, 270–80.

Berry, D. 1978. Effects of urbanization on agricultural activities. *Growth and Change* **9**, 2–8.

Berry, D. 1979. The sensitivity of dairying to urbanization: a study of north–eastern Illinois. *Prof. Geog.* **31**, 170–6.

BIPC (Birmingham Inner City Partnership) 1981. *Vacant land in the core area: March 1981*. Birmingham: BICP.

Blacksell, M. and A. Gilg 1981. *The Countryside: planning and change*. London: George Allen and Unwin.

Blair, A. M. 1980. Compulsory purchase: a neglected factor in the agricultural land loss debate. *Area* **12**, 183–9.

Blowers, A. 1980. *The limits of power: the politics of local planning policy*. Urban and Regional Planning Series, Vol. 22. Oxford: Pergamon.

Boal, F. W. 1970. Urban growth and land value patterns. *Prof. Geog.* **22**, 79–82.

Boddy, M. J. (ed.) 1979. *Land, property and finance*. Working Paper No. 2, School for Advanced Urban Studies, University of Bristol.

Boddy, M. J. 1980. *The building societies*. London: Macmillan.

Bourne, L. S. 1967. *Private re-development of the central city*. Geography Research Paper No. 112: University of Chicago.

Boynton, J. K. 1979. Planning Policy – its formation and implementation. In *Development control – thirty years on*. Occasional Paper, *J. Plann. Environ. Law*, 2–9.

Bridges, L. and C. Vielba 1976. *Structure plan examinations in public: a descriptive analysis*. Birmingham: Institute of Judicial Administration, University of Birmingham.

Brocklebank, J., N. Kaldor, J. Maynard, R. Nield and O. Stutchbury 1978. *The case for nationalising land*. London: Campaign for Nationalising Land.

Brown, H. J., R. S. Phillips and N. A. Roberts 1981. Land markets at the urban fringe, *J. Am. Plann. Ass.* **47**, 131–44.

Brown, H. J., R. S. Phillips and N. A. Roberts 1982. Landownership and market dynamics at the urban periphery: implications for land policy design and implementation. In *World Congress on Land Policy, 1980*. Cullen, M. and S. Woolery. Lexington, Mass.: Heath.

Bruton, M. J. 1983. Local plans, local planning and development schemes in England, 1974–1982. *Town Plann. Rev.* **54**, 4–23.

Bruton, M. J. and A. Gore 1980. *Vacant urban land in Cardiff*. Department of Town Planning. Cardiff: UWIST.

Bryant, C. R. 1974. The anticipation of urban development. Part I: Some implications for agricultural land use practices and land use zoning. *Geog. Polonica* **28**, 93–102.

Bryant, C. R. 1981. Agriculture in an urbanizing environment: a case study from the Paris region, 1968–1976. *Can. Geor.* **25**, 27–45.

Bryant, C. R. 1982. *The rural real estate market*. Publications Series No. 18. Department of Geography, University of Waterloo.

Bryant, C. R. and S. M. Greaves 1978. The importance of regional variation in the analysis of urbanisation – agriculture interactions. *Cahiers de Géographie du Quebec* **22**, 329–48.

Burrows, J. 1977. How much vacant land? *Architects' Journal* **165**, 923–6.

Cadman, D. 1979. Private capital and the inner city. *Estates Gazette* **249**, 1257–60.

Cadman, D. 1984. Property finance in the UK in the post-war period. *Land Development Studies* **1**, 61–82.

Cadman, D. and L. Austin-Crowe 1983. *Property development*, 2nd edn. London: E. and F. N. Spon.

Caddy, C. 1978. Development control 3. *J. R. Town Plann. Inst.* **64**, 64–8.

Carman, H. F. 1977. California landowners' adoption of a use-value assessment program. *Land Econ.* **53**, 275–87.

Chapin, F. S. and S. F. Weiss (eds) 1962. *Urban growth dynamics*. New York: Wiley.

Cheshire, P. and A. Evans 1983. The banks and the housing market: here to stay? *Estates Gazette* **266**, 503–5.

City of Leicester 1956. *City development plan: written statement*. Leicester: City Corporation.

Civic Trust 1977. *Urban wasteland*. London: Civic Trust.

Clark, G. L. 1982. Rights, property and the community. *Econ. Geog.* **58**, 120–38.

Clawson, M. 1971. *Suburban land conversion in the United States: an economic and governmental process*. Baltimore: Johns Hopkins University Press.

Clawson, M. and P. Hall 1973. *Planning and urban growth: an Anglo-American comparison*. Baltimore: Johns Hopkins University Press.

Clemenson, H. A. 1982. *English country houses and landed estates*. London: Croom Helm.

Clonts, H. A. 1970. Influence of urbanisation on land values at the urban periphery. *Land Econ.* **46**, 489–97.

Coleman, A. 1976. Is planning necessary? *Geog. J.* **142**, 411–30.

Coleman, A. 1977. Land use planning – success or failure? *Architects' Journal* **165**, 95–134.

Corfield, F. and R. J. Carnwath 1978. *Compulsory acquisition and compensation*. London: Butterworths.

Countryside Commission 1981. *Countryside management in the urban fringe*, CCP 136. Cheltenham: Countryside Commission.

Cox, A. W. 1980. The limits of central government intervention in the land and the development market: the case of the Land Commission. *Policy and Politics* **8**, 267–84.

Craven, E. A. 1969. Private residential expansion in Kent 1956–1964: a study of pattern and process in urban growth. *Urban Studies* **16**, 1–16.

Craven, E. A. and R. E. Pahl 1967. Residential expansion: a preliminary assessment of the role of the private developer in the South East. *J. Town Plann. Inst.* **53**, 137–43.

Cullingworth, J. B. 1981. *Peacetime history: environment planning 1939–69*, Vol. IV, *Land values, compensation and betterment*. London: HMSO.

Cullingworth, J. B. 1982. *Town and country planning in Britain*, 8th edn. London: George Allen and Unwin.

Curry, N. R. 1978. Public planning in land use: an economic perspective. In *Land, planning and the market*, B. J. Pearce (ed.), 49–78. Occasional Paper No. 9, Department of Land Economy, University of Cambridge.

Darin-Drabkin, H. 1965. *Seminar on the supply, development and allocation of land for housing and related purposes*. United Nations: Paris.

Darin-Drabkin, H. 1977. *Land policy and urban growth*. Urban and Regional Planning Series No. 16. Oxford: Pergamon Press.

Davies, H. W. E. 1980. Policy forum: the relevance of development control. *Town Plann. Rev.* **51**, 7–17.

Davies, R. L. and D. J. Bennison 1977. Preliminary effects of the Eldon Square shopping centre. *Estates Gazette* **244**, 709–13.

Dear, M. and A. J. Scott (eds) 1981. *Urbanization and urban planning in a capitalist society*. London: Methuen.

Denman, D. R. 1978. *The place of property*. Berkhamsted: Geographical Publications.

Denman, D. R. and S. Prodano 1972. *Land use: an introduction to proprietary land use analysis*. London: George Allen and Unwin.

Denyer-Green, B. 1984. Human rights and leasehold tenure. *Chartered Surveyor Weekly* **8**, 632–3.

Docklands Joint Committeee 1976. *London docklands strategic plan*. London: Docklands Joint Committee.

DOE (Department of the Environment) 1970. *Land availability for housing*, Circular 10/70 London: HMSO.

DOE 1972a. *Land availability for housing*, Circular 102/72. London: HMSO.

DOE 1972b. *The Sheaf Report: report of the working party on local authority/private enterprise partnership schemes*. London: HMSO.

DOE 1973a. *Greater London Development Plan: report of the panel of enquiry* (Layfield Report). London: HMSO.

DOE 1973b. *Land availability for housing*, Circular 122/73. London: HMSO.

DOE 1973c. *Widening the choice: the next steps in housing*, White Paper, Cmnd 5280. London: HMSO.

DOE 1974. *Land*, White Paper, Cmnd 5730. London: HMSO

DOE 1975a. *Statistics of land with outstanding planning permission*, Circular 32/75. London: HMSO.

DOE 1975b. *Housing land availability in the south-east: a consultant's study*. London: HMSO.

DOE 1976. *Development involving agricultural land*, Circular 75/76. London: HMSO.

DOE 1977a. *Memorandum on structure and local plans*, Circular 55/77. London: HMSO.

DOE 1977b. *Local government and the industrial strategy*, Circular 71/77. London: HMSO.

DOE 1977c. *Policy for the inner cities*, White Paper, Cmnd 6845. London: HMSO.

DOE 1977d. *Guidance note on the Land Act (GNLA)* 12. London: DOE.

DOE 1977e. *Inner area studies: Liverpool, Birmingham and Lambeth: summaries of consultants' final reports*. London: HMSO.

DOE 1978a. *Private sector land: requirements and supply*, Circular 44/78. London: HMSO.

DOE 1978b. *Developed areas 1969: a survey of England and Wales from air photography*. London: DOE.

DOE 1978c. *Land availability: a study of land with residential planning permission*. London: Economist Intelligence Unit.

DOE 1979a. *Development control and agricultural land*, Press Notice 131, 21 March 1979. London: DOE.

DOE 1979b. *Hertfordshire county structure plan – statement related to the Secretary of State's proposed modifications*. London: DOE.

DOE 1980a. *Local Government, Planning and Land Act*. London: HMSO.

DOE 1980b. *Development control – policy and practice*, Circular 22/80. London: HMSO.

DOE 1980c. *Land for private housebuilding*, Circular 9/80. London: HMSO.

DOE 1981a. *Local Government, Planning and Land Act 1980 (Town and Country Planning: development control functions)*, Circular 2/81. London: HMSO.

DOE 1981b. *Planning gain – report by the Property Advisory Group*. London: HMSO.

DOE 1981c. Better use of public land. Press release no. 466, 24th November. London: DOE.

DOE 1981d. *Local Government, Planning and Land Act (Town and Country Planning: development plans)*, Circular 23/81. London: HMSO.

DOE 1983a. *Town and Country Planning Act 1971: planning gain*, Circular 22/83. London: HMSO.

DOE 1983b. *Memorandum on structure and local plans and green belt*, draft circular. London: DOE.

DOE 1983c. *Land for housing*, draft circular X/83. London: DOE.

DOE 1984a. *Land for housing*, Circular 15/84. London: DOE.

DOE 1984b. *Green belts*, Circular 14/84. London: DOE.

DOE 1984c. *Memorandum on structure and local plans*, Circular 22/84. London: DOE.

DOE/HBF (House Builders' Federation) 1979. *Study of the availability of private housebuilding land in Greater Manchester*. London: DOE.

Drewett, J. R. 1973. The developers' decision process. Land values and the suburban land market. In *The containment of urban England*, P. Hall *et al.* (eds), Vol. II, Chs 6 and 7, 163–245. London: George Allen and Unwin.

Dwyer, R. G. 1976. Central buildings, Southwark. *Chart. Surveyor Urban Quarterly* **3**, 5–7.

Elson, M. J. 1983. Containment in Hertfordshire: changing attitudes to land release for new employment-generating development. Unpublished paper presented at a conference on Land Policy – Problems and Alternatives, Oxford Polytechnic.

Ely, R. T. and G. S. Wehrwein 1940. *Land economics*. Madison, Wisc.: University of Wisconsin Press.

Esseks, J. D. 1978. The politics of farmland preservation. In *The new politics of food*, D. F. Hadwiger and W. P. Browne (eds), 199–216. Lexington, Mass.: Lexington Books.

Essex County Council 1982. *Essex structure plan: approved written statement*. Chelmsford: Essex County Council.

Evans, A. W. 1983. The determination of the price of land. *Urban Studies* **20**, 119–29.

Fagg, J. J. 1973. Spatial changes in manufacturing employment in Greater Leicester 1947–1970. *East Midlands Georgrapher* **5**, 400–15.

Federation of Master Builders 1981. *Future of house building: a national survey on land availability, production, planning and other restrictions.* London: Federation of Master Builders.

Ferguson, M. J. and R. J. C. Munton 1979. Informal recreation sites in London's Green Belt. *Area* **11**, 196–205.

Field, B. G. 1983. Local plans and local planning in Greater London: a review. *Town Plann. Rev.* **54**, 24–40.

Financial Times 1978. Property market indicators: investment market cools. *Financial Times* 14 July 1978.

Fothergill, S. and G. Gudgin 1982. *Unequal growth. Urban and regional employment change in the UK.* London: Heinemann.

Fothergill, S., M. Kitson and S. Monk 1983. The supply of land for industrial development. Unpublished paper presented at a conference on Land Policy – Problems and Alternatives, Oxford Polytechnic.

Furuseth, D. J. and J. T. Pierce 1982. *Agricultural land in an urban society.* Washington, DC.: Association of American Geographers.

Gasson, R. 1983. *Gainful occupations of farm families.* School of Rural Economics, Wye College.

Gault, I. 1981. *Green belt policies in development plans.* Working Paper No. 41. Department of Town Planning, Oxford Polytechnic.

Gayler, H. J. 1970. Land speculation and urban development: contrasts in south-east Essex. *Urban Studies* **7**, 21–36.

Gibbons, A. A. 1977. *Valuation and inner city areas.* Paper presented to the Royal Institution of Chartered Surveyors, 20 May 1977.

Gilg, A. W. 1975. Development control and agricultural land quality. *Town and Country Planning* **43**, 387–9.

Goodall, B. 1972. *The economics of urban areas.* Oxford: Pergamon Press.

Goodchild, R. N. 1978a. The operation of the private land market. In *Land, planning and the market*, B. J. Pearce (ed), 11–48. Occasional Paper No. 9. Department of Land Economy, University of Cambridge.

Goodchild, R. N. 1978b. *The supply of development land: the role of the landowner.* D Phil thesis, University of Cambridge.

Green, P. 1982. Local plans in use: Central Leicester district plan. *J. R. Town Plann. Inst.* **68**, 149.

Hall, P. G. 1981a. *Great planning disasters*, 2nd edn. London: Penguin.

Hall, P. G. (ed.) 1981b. *The inner city in context*, the final report of the Social Science Research Council Inner Cities Working Party. London: Heinemann.

Hall, P. G. 1983. Housing, planning, land and local finance: the British experience. *Urban Law and Policy* **6**, 75–86.

Hall, P. G., H. Gracey, R. Drewett and R. Thomas 1973. *The containment of urban England*, 2 vols. London: George Allen and Unwin.

Hallett, G. 1977. *Housing and land policies in West Germany and Britain.* London: Macmillan.

Hallett, G. 1979. *Urban land economics: principles and policy.* Oxford: Blackwell

Harloe, M., R. Issacharoff and R. Minns 1974. *The organization of housing: public and private enterprise in London.* London: Heinemann.

Harrison, A. 1975. *Farmers and farm businesses in England.* Miscellaneous Studies No. 62, Department of Agricultural Economics and Management, University of Reading.

Harrison, A., R. B. Tranter and R. S. Gibbs 1977. *Landownership by public and semi-public institutions in the UK.* Paper No. 3, Centre for Agricultural Strategy, University of Reading.

Harrison, A. J. 1977. *Economics and land use planning*. London: Croom Helm.

Harrison M. L. 1972. Development control: the influence of political, legal and ideological factors. *Town Plann. Rev.* **43**, 254–74.

Hart, J. F. 1968. Loss and abandonment of cleared farmland in the eastern United States. *Ann. Ass. Am. Geogr.* **58**, 417–40.

HBF (House Builders' Federation) 1982. Report on initial land register inspections. London: House Builders' Federation.

Healey, P., S. Evans and S. Terry 1980. *The implementation of selective restraint policy: approaches to land release for local needs in the South East*. Working Paper No. 45. Department of Town Planning, Oxford Polytechnic.

Heap, D. and A. J. Ward 1980. Planning bargaining – the pros and cons: or, how much can the system stand? *J. Plann. Environ. Law*, October, 631–7.

Hearne, A., M. Bell and D. van Rest 1977. The physical and economic impact of motorways on agriculture. *Int. J. Environ. Stud.* **11**, 29–33.

Herington, J. 1982. Circular 22/80 – the demise of settlement planning? *Area* **14**, 157–66.

Herington, J. 1984. *The outer city*. London: Harper and Row.

Hooper, A. 1983. Estimating land availability for private house-building: some methodological issues. Paper presented at a conference on Land Policy – Problems and Alternatives, Oxford Polytechnic.

House of Commons 1977. *Planning procedures*. Eighth report from the Expenditure Committee. Paper 564. London: HMSO.

House of Commons 1984. *Green belt and land for housing*. First report from the Environment Committee, session 1983–4. Paper 215–I. London: HMSO.

Howe, E. 1980. Role choices of urban planners. *J. Am. Plann. Ass.* **46**, 398–409.

Howe, E. and J. Kaufman 1979. The ethics of contemporary American planners. *J. Am. Plann. Ass.* **45**, 243–55.

Howell, E. W. G. C. 1979. Thoughts on the need for government sponsored land-dealing organisations. *Estates Gazette* **249**, 729–30.

Howes, C. K. 1983. Central government re-development initiatives in the United Kingdom. *Urban Law and Policy* **6**, 151–68.

Howes, C. K. 1984. The ownership of vacant land by public agencies. *Land Development Studies* **1**, 23–33.

Howick, C. and T. Key 1978. *The local economy of Tower Hamlets: an inner city profile*, Research Series No. 26. London: Centre for Environmental Studies.

Hurd, R. M. 1970. *Principles of city land values*, 1924 edn, reprinted in 1970. New York: Arno Press.

Hushak, L. J. 1975. The urban demand for urban–rural fringe land. *Land Econ.* **51**, 112–23.

Jenkins, S. 1975. *Landlords to London*. London: Constable

Jowell, J. 1977. Bargaining in development control. *J. Plann. Environ. Law*, July, 414–33.

Jowell, J. and M. Grant 1983. Guideline for planning gain? *J. Plann. Environ. Law*, July, 427–31.

Jowell, J. and D. Millichap 1983. The enforcement of planning control in London. *J. Plann. Environ. Law*, October, 644–54.

Jowell, J. and D. Noble 1981. Structure plans as instruments of social and economic policy. *J. Plann. Environ. Law*, July, 466–80.

Joint Land Requirements Committee 1982. *Is there sufficient housing land for the 1980s?* Paper 1. *How many houses should we plan for?* London: Housing Research Foundation.

Joint Land Requirements Committee 1983. *Is there sufficient housing land for the 1980s?* Paper 2. *How many houses have we planned for? Is there a problem?* London: Housing Research Foundation.

JURUE (Joint Unit for Research on the Urban Environment) 1974. *Land availability and the residential land conversion process*. Birmingham: University of Aston.

JURUE 1977. *Planning and land availability*. Birmingham: University of Aston.

Kaiser, E. J., R. W. Massie, S. F. Weiss and J. E. Smith 1968. Predicting the behaviour of pre-development landowners on the urban fringe. *J. Am. Inst. Plann.* **34**, 328–33.

Kaiser, E. J. and S. F. Weiss 1970. Public policy and the residential development process. *J. Am. Inst. Plann.* **36**, 30–7.

Kenny, K. B. 1965. *Pre-development land ownership factors and their influence on residential development*. Center for Urban and Regional Studies, University of North Carolina, Chapel Hill.

King, D. 1981. Letter to the *Financial Times*, 4 September 1981.

King & Co. 1981. *Industrial floorspace survey*. London: King & Co.

Knox, P. and J. Cullen 1981. Planners as urban managers: an exploration of the attitudes and self-image of senior British planners. *Environ. Plann.* A **13**, 855–98.

Labour Party 1983. *New hope for Britain*. London: Labour Party.

Law Commission 1984. *Who owns that house? A question about titles to land*. London: HMSO.

Lawless, P. 1981. *Britain's inner cities: problems and policies*. London: Harper and Row.

Lawrence, D. M. and V. Moore 1972. *Compensation and compulsory purchase*, 5th edn. London: *Estates Gazette*.

LDDC (London Docklands Development Corporation) 1982. *Annual report and accounts 1981/82*. London: LDDC.

Leach, S. and N. Moore 1979. County/district relations in shire and metropolitan counties in the field of town and country planning: a comparison. *Policy and Politics* **7**, 165–79.

Leicestershire County Council 1959. *Leicestershire development plan: analysis of survey*. Leicester: Leicestershire County Council.

Leicestershire County Council 1976. *Leicestershire structure plan: written statement*. Leicester: Leicestershire County Council.

Leung, H. L. 1979. *Redistribution of land values: a re-examination of the 1947 Scheme*. Occasional Paper No. 11, Department of Land Economy, University of Cambridge.

Lichfield, N. 1956. *Economics of planned development*. London: Estates Gazette.

Lichfield, N. and H. Darin-Drabkin 1980. *Land policy in planning*. London: Allen and Unwin.

Lindeman, B. 1976. Anatomy of land speculation. *J. Am. Inst. Plann.* **42**, 142–52.

Lipsey, R. G. 1983. *An introduction to positive economics*, 6th edn. London: Weidenfeld and Nicolson.

Loughlin, M. 1978. Bargaining as a tool of development control: a case of all gain and no loss. *J. Plann. Environ. Law*, May, 290–5.

Lund, P. J. and J. M. Slater 1979. Agricultural land: its ownership, price and rent – a guide to statistical sources of information. *Econ. Trends* **314**, 97–110.

McAuslan, P. 1975. *Land, law and planning*. London: Weidenfeld and Nicolson.

McAuslan, P. 1980. *The ideologies of planning law*. Urban and Regional Planning Series Vol. 22. Oxford: Pergamon.

McAuslan, P. 1981. Local government and resource allocation in England: changing ideology, unchanging law. *Urban Law and Policy* **4**, 215–68.

McEwen, J. 1981. *Who owns Scotland? A study in land ownership*, 2nd edn. Edinburgh: Polygon Books.

MacKay, D. M. and A. W. Cox 1979. *The politics of urban change*. London: Croom Helm.

McNamara, P. F. 1983. Towards a classification of land developers. *Urban Law and Policy* **6**, 87–94.

McNamara, P. F. 1984. The role of local estate agents in the residential development process. *Land Development Studies* **1**, 101–12.

MAFF (Ministry of Agriculture, Fisheries and Food) 1973. *Agriculture in the urban fringe: Slough/Hillingdon area*, ADAS Technical Report No. 30. London: HMSO.

MAFF 1976. *Agriculture in the urban fringe: Metropolitan County of Tyne and Wear.* ADAS Technical Report No. 30/1. London: HMSO.

MAFF 1978. *Ownership and occupation in the Wyre Forest District of Hereford and Worcester.* London: MAFF.

MAFF 1982. *Farm lotting project (final report)*, Report No. RD/LMC/02. London: ADAS, Land and Water Service.

Mallinson, H. and M. Gilbert 1983. The urban development grant scheme. *Estates Gazette* **268**, 970–4.

Markowski, S. 1978. *Study of vacant land in urban areas.* London: Centre for Environmental Studies.

Markusen, J. R. and D. T. Scheffman 1977. Ownership concentration in the urban land market: analytic foundations and empirical evidence. In *Public property: the habitat debate continued* (L. M. Smith and M. Walker) (eds), 147–76. Vancouver: The Fraser Institute.

Massey, D. and A. Catalano 1978. *Capital and land: landownership by capital in Great Britain.* London: Edward Arnold.

Massey, D. and R. Meegan 1982. *The anatomy of job loss: the how, why and where of employment decline.* London: Methuen.

Massey, D. W. 1969. *Landownership and development.* D Phil thesis. University of Cambridge.

Mattingly A. 1972. Intensity of agricultural land use near cities. *Prof. Geog.* **24**, 7–10.

Mellows, A. R. 1982. *Taxation of land transactions*, 3rd edn. London: Butterworth.

Merrett, S. 1982. *Owner occupation in Britain* (with F. Gray). London: Routledge and Kegan Paul.

MHLG (Ministry of Housing and Local Government) 1955. *Green belts*, Circular 42/55. London: HMSO.

MHLG 1957. *Green belts*, Circular 50/57. London: HMSO.

MHLG 1963. *London – employment: housing: land*, White Paper, Cmnd 1952. London: HMSO.

Milgram, G. 1967. *The city expands: a study of the conversion of land from rural to urban use, Philadelphia, 1945–62.* Institute of Environmental Studies, University of Philadelphia.

Mill, J. S. 1871. *Principles of political economy*, as edited by D. Winch. London: Penguin, 1970.

Mills, D. E. 1969. Urban residential development timing. *Reg. Sci. Urban Econ.* **11**, 239–54.

Moor, N. 1976. Who takes the risk? *Built Environment* **2**, 276–8.

Moor, N. 1983. *The planner and the market: an examination of the role of the planner in the development market.* Harlow: Longmans.

Moran, W. 1979. Spatial patterns of agriculture on the periphery: the Auckland case. *Tijdschr. Econ. Soc. Geog.* **70**, 164–76.

Mortimore, M. J. 1969. Landownership and urban growth in Bradford and its environs in the West Riding conurbation. *Trans. Inst. Br. Geogr.* **46**, 99–113.

Moss, G. 1981. *Britain's wasting acres: land use in a changing society.* London: Architectural Press.

Munton, R. J. C. 1975. The state of the agricultural land market 1971–1973: a survey of auctioneers' property transactions. *Oxford Agrarian Studies* **4** (New Series), 111–30.

Munton, R. J. C. 1976. An analysis of price trends in the agricultural land market of England and Wales. *Tijdschr. Econ. Soc. Geog.* **67**, 202–12.

Munton, R. J. C. 1983. *London's Green Belt: containment in practice.* London: George Allen and Unwin.

Munton, R. J. C. 1984. Land speculation and the under-use of farmland in the Metropolitan Green Belt. In *Planning in the remoter rural and peri-urban areas*, G. Clark (ed.). Norwich: Geo Books.

Muth, R. F. 1961. Economic change and rural–urban land conversions. *Econometrica* **29**, 1–23.

Nabarro, R. 1980. Inner city partnerships. An assessment of the first programmes. *Town Plann. Rev.* **51**, 25–38.

Neuburger, H. L. T. and B. M. Nicol 1976. *The recent course of land and property prices and the factors underlying it*, DOE Research Report No. 4. London: HMSO.

Neutze, G. M. 1973. *The price of land and land use planning: policy instruments in the urban land market*. Paris: OECD.

Newby, H. 1979. *Green and pleasant land*? Harmondsworth: Penguin.

Newby, H., C. Bell, D. Rose and P. Saunders 1978. *Property, paternalism and power: class and control in rural England*. London: Hutchinson.

NHBC (National House Building Council) 1983. *Private house-building statistics*. Amersham: NHBC.

Nicholls, D. C., D. M. Turner, R. Kirby-Smith and J. D. Cullen 1980. *The private sector housing development process in inner city areas*. Department of Land Economy, University of Cambridge.

Nicholson, D. J. 1984. The public ownership of vacant urban land. *The Planner* **70**, 18–20.

Northfield Committee Report 1979. *Committee of inquiry into the acquisition and occupancy of agricultural land*. Cmnd 7599. London: HMSO.

Nottinghamshire County Council 1980. *Nottinghamshire structure plan*. Nottingham: Nottinghamshire County Council.

Oadby and Wigston District Council 1979. *Wigston district plan*. Leicester: Oadby and Wigston District Council.

OECD (Organisation for Economic Co-operation and Development) 1979. *Agriculture in the planning and management of peri-urban areas*. Vol. I: *Synthesis*. Paris: OECD.

Olsen, M. J. 1973. House upon house: estate development in London and Sheffield. In *Victorian city: images and reality*. H. J. Dyos and M. Wolff (eds) Vol. 1, 333–57. London: Routledge and Kegan Paul.

PAG (Planning Advisory Group) 1975. *Commercial property development: first report of the advisory group on commercial property development*. London: HMSO.

PAG 1980. *Structure and activity of the development industry*. London: HMSO.

Pahl, R. E. 1975. *Whose city*? Harmondsworth: Penguin.

Parker, H. R. 1954. The financial aspects of the town and country planning legislation. *Econ. J.* **64**, 72–86.

Pearce, B. J. 1980. Instruments for land policy: a classification. *Urban Law and Policy* **3**, 115–56.

Pearce, B. J. 1981. Property rights versus development control: a preliminary evaluation of alternative policy instruments. *Town Plann. Rev.* **52**, 47–60.

Pennance, F. G. 1969. *Housing market analysis and policy*. Hobart Paper No. 48. London: Institute of Economic Affairs.

Plender, J. 1982. *Thats the way the money goes: the financial institutions and your savings*. London: André Deutsche.

Pountney, M. T. and P. W. Kingsbury, 1983. Aspects of development control. Part I: The relationship with local plans. *Town Plann. Rev.* **54**, 139–54.

Purdue, M. 1977. The scope of planning authorities' discretion – or what's material? *J. Plann. Environ. Law* July, 490–97.

Raiffa, H. 1968. *Decision analysis: introductory lectures on choice under uncertainty*. Reading, Mass.: Addison-Wesley.

Ratcliff, R. U. 1949. *Urban land economics*. New York: McGraw Hill.

Ratcliffe, J. 1976. *Land policy: an exploration of the nature of land in society*. London: Hutchinson.

Ratcliffe, J. 1984. Preletting. *Estates Gazette* **269**, 20–4.

Rayner, M. 1979. *National and local taxation*. London: Macmillan.

Regional Studies Association 1983. *Report of an inquiry into regional problems in the United Kingdom*. Norwich: Geo Books.

Richardson, H. W. 1978. *Regional and urban economics*. Harmondsworth: Penguin Books.

Robson, B. T. 1975. *Urban social areas*. Oxford: Oxford University Press.

Rossi, H. 1977. Property policies: the Tory approach. *Estates Gazette* **244**, 619.

RTPI (Royal Town Planning Institute) 1976. *Planning and the future*. London: RTPI

Rydin, Y. 1983. State involvement in the residential development process through the operation of development control: the local impact of Circulars 9/80 and 22/80. Paper presented at a conference on Land Policy: Problems and Alternatives, Oxford Polytechnic.

Schofield, W. H. 1957. Prevailing land market forces. *J. Farm Econ.* **39**, 1500–10.

Scott, A. 1982. Industrial activity in the modern metropolis. *Urban Studies* **19**, 111–42.

SEJPT (South East Joint Planning Team) 1970. *Strategic plan for the south east: report*. London: HMSO.

SEJPT 1976. *Strategy for the south east: 1976 review*. London: HMSO.

Shankland Cox Partnership 1972. *Land availability for residential development*. London: Shankland Cox Partnership.

Simmie, J. M. 1974. *Citizens in conflict: the sociology of town planning*. London: Hutchinson.

Simmie, J. M. 1981. *Power, property and corporation: the political sociology of planning*. London: Macmillan.

Sinclair, R. 1967. Von Thunen and urban sprawl. *Ann. Ass. Am. Geogr.* **57**, 72–87.

Smith, H. 1982. *Land banking, land availability and planning for private house building*. Working Paper No. 23, School for Advanced Urban Studies, University of Bristol.

Smith, J. E. 1967. *Towards a theory of landowner behaviour on the urban periphery*. Center for Urban and Regional Studies, University of North Carolina.

Smith, K. 1983. Planning decisions: the application of green belt policy. *J. Plann. Environ. Law*, December, 777–85.

Standing Conference (Standing Conference on London and South East Regional Planning – SCLSERP) 1976. *The improvement of London's Green Belt*, SC 620. London: Standing Conference.

Standing Conference 1983a. *South East regional monitor 1982/83*, SC 1859. London: Standing Conference.

Standing Conference 1983b. *South East regional monitor 1982/83: the Metropolitan Green Belt*, SC 1816. London: Standing Conference.

Standing Conference 1983c. *Housing land supply in the South East (outside London)*, SC 1891. London: Standing Conference.

Standing Conference/HBF 1981. *Housing land in South East England*, SC 1600. London: Standing Conference.

Strachan, A. J. 1977. New office development in Leicester. *Town and Country Planning* **45**, 31–5.

Strong, A. L. 1975. *Private property and the public interest: the Brandywine experience*. Baltimore: Johns Hopkins University Press.

Stungo, A. 1980. The local authority viewpoint. Paper delivered to the RTPI and RICS, 4 November 1980.

Stungo, A. 1984. Public sector land. *Estates Gazette* **269**, 291–5.

Tarmac 1982. *Annual report*. Wolverhampton: Tarmac.

Thames Television 1980. *Wasteland*. London: Thames Television.

Thomas, D. 1970. *London's Green Belt*. London: Faber and Faber.

Thomas, K. 1977. The impact of renewal on small firms. *J. R. Town Plann. Inst.* **63**, 48–9.

Thompson F. M. L. 1971. *English landed society in the nineteenth century*. London: Routledge and Kegan Paul.

Thompson, M. J. and D. A. Edmondson 1984. Whither derelict land grant? *J. R. Town Plann. Inst.* **70**, 16–18.

Thomson, K. J. 1981. *Farming in the fringe*, CCP 142. Cheltenham: Countryside Commission.

Tower Hamlets 1978. *Vacant land in Tower Hamlets*. London: Tower Hamlets Borough Council.

Tower Hamlets 1983. *Borough Plan*. London: Tower Hamlets Borough Council.

Traill, W. B. 1980. An empirical model of the UK land market and the impact of price policy on land values and rents. *Eur. Rev. Agric. Econ* **6**, 209–32.

Traill, W. B. 1982. The effect of price support policies on agricultural investment, employment, farm incomes and land values in the UK. *J. Agric. Econ.* **33**, 369–86.

Turner, D. M. 1977. *An approach to land values*. Berkhamsted: Geographical Publications.

Turner, D. M. and T. J. Forse 1976. Landlords, their wealth and capital taxation. In *Farming the land and changing taxation*. A Harrison (ed.), Department of Agricultural Economics and Management, University of Reading.

Tym, Roger & Partners 1983. *Monitoring enterprise zones: year two report*. London: HMSO.

Tyne and Wear County Council 1979. *Structure plan*. Newcastle: Tyne and Wear County Council.

Underwood, J. 1981. Development control: a case study of discretion in action. In *Policy and action*, S. Barrett and C. Fudge (eds), 143–62. London: Methuen.

Uthwatt Committee Report 1942. *Expert committee on compensation and betterment: final report*, Cmd 8386. London: HMSO.

Vallis, E. A. 1972. Urban land and building prices. *Estates Gazette* **222**, 1015–9, 1209–13, 1406–7, 1604–5.

Vasu, M. L. 1979. *Politics and planning: a national study of American planners*. Chapel Hill: University of North Carolina Press.

Ward, D. 1962. The pre-urban cadaster and the urban pattern of Leeds. *Ann. Assoc. Am. Geogr.* **52**, 150–60.

Weinburg, M. 1976. Property investment: an individual viewpoint. *Estates Gazette* **238**, 703–9.

Weiss, S. F., J. E. Smith, E. J. Kaiser and K. B. Kenny 1966. *Residential developer decisions*. Center for Urban and Regional Studies, University of North Carolina.

West Sussex County Council 1980. *West Sussex county structure plan: written statement*. Chichester: West Sussex County Council

Williams, H. M. 1979. *The management of publicly-owned land in the Hertfordshire/Barnet experiment area*, Working Paper No. 17. Cheltenham: Countryside Commission.

Willis, K. 1982. Planning agreements and planning gain. *Planning Outlook* **25**, 55–62.

Wilson Committee Report 1980. *Committee to review the functioning of the financial institutions*, Cmnd 7937. London: HMSO.

Wilson, H. and L. Wormsley 1977. *Change or decay: final report of the Liverpool inner area study*. London: DOE.

Wood, M. 1982. *High Wycombe – the implementation of strategic planning policy in a restraint area in the south-east*. Working Paper No. 67, Department of Town Planning, Oxford Polytechnic.

List of cases

Steeple v. Derbyshire County Council 1981. *Journal of Planning Law and Environment*, 582–91.

Horn v. Sunderland Corporation 1941. *All England Law Reports*, 480–512.

Appelby and Ireland v. Hampshire County Council 1978. *Estates Gazette* **247**, 1 183–6; **248**, 54–6, 143–8, 235–7, 326–30.

Wilkinson, Gale and Hall v. Middlesbrough Borough Council 1979. *Property and Compensation Reports* **39**, 212–22 (Lands Tribunal); 1982. **45**, 142–55 (Court of Appeal).

Index

Italic numbers (e.g. *5.1*) refer to text illustrations.

Addendum: 1985 budget and abolition of DLT

Throughout this book we maintain that the private sector has been given, by the present government, an increasingly favourable policy environment in which to operate when bringing land forward for development. A further significant and unexpected concession in favour of the private landowner was made by the Chancellor of the Exchequer in his Budget speech of 19 March 1985 when he announced the abolition of Development Land Tax, with immediate effect, and cancellation of all deferred charges. He is also to amend the way in which indexation relief for capital gains tax is calculated so that, where an asset which has been held for some time is sold, the indexation relief will be based on the gain between March 1982 and the date of sale, not just applied to the acquisition cost or 1965 value. These changes return the tax regime on development land to a position even more favourable than the one subsisting between July 1970 and December 1973, because most owners will be liable only to Capital Gains Tax – which can be 'rolled-over' (see pp. 27–34).

The Chancellor justified his decision to abolish DLT on the following grounds:

(a)   it is a particularly complex tax;
(b)   it was introduced in response to the problem of soaring land values at a time of high inflation;
(c)   its chief practical effect is to discourage the bringing forward of land for development and that this disincentive will increase as the disparity widens between a tax rate of 60% for DLT and a rate of 35% for Corporation Tax; *and*
(d)   it raised little revenue but was expensive to collect.

We agree that DLT is a complex tax and that it raises comparatively little revenue (see pp. 31–3). However, we do not regard the Chancellor's other arguments as sound.

Although there was an inflation rate of 16.5% in 1976, when DLT was introduced, land prices were comparatively stable (see Figs. 3.2 & 5.8). The Chancellor may, in fact, be confusing the introduction of DLT with the introduction of Development Gains Tax in December 1973 when land values were certainly 'soaring'. DLT was introduced to discourage speculation and it has certainly had this effect. Our study of landowners in the Leicester area demonstrates that they respond both to changes in the tax regime and anticipate future changes in taxation. In our view, few owners expected DLT to be abolished and so few were holding out for this event. Most were prepared to pay DLT at a rate of 60% because they believed what the government said (through the then Chancellor) in 1979 (see p. 32). It is possible that there will be a short-term increase in development activity as developers and landowners take advantage of the unexpected situation before it changes, but the main effect is likely to be a substantial increase in the number of planning applications submitted, and in the appeals lodged on sites in the Green Belt and other open land in an attempt to obtain planning permission and the development value attaching to it. Between 1970 and 1973, when the tax regime was last this favourable, there was a significant increase in the number of applications and appeals (see Tables 2.1 & 2.3) and a similar outcome can be expected following DLT's abolition.

The main beneficiaries of the change are landowners, rather than developers and the construction industry. It is true that there is a potential liability to DLT every time a project of material development commences but, in practice, comparatively few projects result in a significant liability. The DLT that has been paid comes from landowners and, particularly, sellers of green field sites. To illustrate their benefit from the Chancellor's

Table A.1 Relative property valuations: agricultural land and building land, MGB, 1969–85 (no adjustment for inflation).

	1969	1973	1977	1984	1985
agricultural land (£/ha)	703	2 169	2 256	6 427	5 560
building land (£/ha)	56 700	171 240	115 570	642 750	741 300
absolute difference (gross) between agricultural and building land prices (£/ha)	55 997	169 071	113 314	636 323	735 740
difference net of tax (£/ha)	33 626	118 530	36 843	282 216	530 209

Sources: Table 7.5 and House of Commons (1984) p. 564.
The 1985 figures are based on our own informed estimates. (See p. 150 above for further details.)

decision, we have up-dated Table 7.5 with data for 1984 and 1985 and this is set out in Table A.1. This indicates that the net of tax profit from converting agricultural land into development land has almost doubled as a result of the Chancellor's decision.

In Chapter 9 (pp. 183–8) we press the case not only for the retention of DLT but also its reorganisation to help encourage the private sector to produce development that is more likely to implement development plans. DLT should be used primarily as a means of helping the planning system achieve its goals and not, as the Chancellor sees it, as an inefficient means of raising revenue. DLT is needed to ensure both an acceptable level of equity between owners and non-owners of development land, and to reduce the amount of speculation in trying to get planning permission where it is clearly contrary to planning policy. That is why we advocate a DLT rate of 100% on those parts of the Metropolitan Green Belt where development should never take place, and a reduction in DLT on urban sites where market failure prevents development. The *blanket* abolition of DLT is likely to have little impact on the development of inner-city sites, because attention will be diverted to green-field sites by the prospect of large net of tax profits. Unless the change in tax leads not only to a flood of planning applications but also to the *release* of much more land for development – and that seems highly unlikely given the strength of the conservation lobby (see pp. 142–3) – then neither the construction industry nor the consumer is likely to benefit through lower land values.

Lastly, the abolition of DLT means the removal of another major element of the Community Land System; only the Land Authority for Wales now remains. It also means the end of a tax regime which appeared to offer a reasonable consensus between the major political parties and so allow the market to operate within known parameters. These have now been removed and the pendulum has swung back to the position it occupied in 1970. History suggests that it will swing back and, at some time, landowners will be faced with yet another new tax. The Chancellor's action has, therefore, ensured both that the betterment question will remain an important political issue and that, when the new tax regime is introduced, landowners will have even more justification for ignoring it.

London
31 March 1985